FROM SHARPEVILLE TO RIVONIA
1959 to 1964

FROM SHARPEVILLE TO RIVONIA
1959 to 1964

A personal view of resistance in
South Africa from the letters of
Clare & James Currey

MERLIN PRESS

Published in 2021 by
The Merlin Press Limited
Central Books Building
50 Freshwater Road
Dagenham
RM8 1RX

www.merlinpress.co.uk

ISBN. 9780850367584

© James Currey, 2021

Part 3 was first published by The Merlin Press in 2014 as part of *The New African. A History 1962-69, with Cape Escape 1964*

The author's moral rights have been asserted.

CIP data is available from the British Library.

Printed in the UK by Imprint Digital, Exeter

CONTENTS

Background Notes vi

Liberal Journalists, Authors & Publishers vi
Families & South Africa vi
Dates of Independence of Colonies in Eastern, Central
 & Southern Africa viii
British High Commission Territories viii
Union of South Africa 1910-1996 ix

Introduction 1

PART ONE

Letters from South Africa
James Currey July 1959 to July 1962 9

PART TWO

Letters from South Africa
Clare & James Currey January 1963 to July 1964 117

PART THREE

Cape Escape 1964
James Currey
With contributions by Jean Ridge, Gillian Vigne,
Clare Currey, Norman Bromberger & Randolph Vigne 155

Index 192

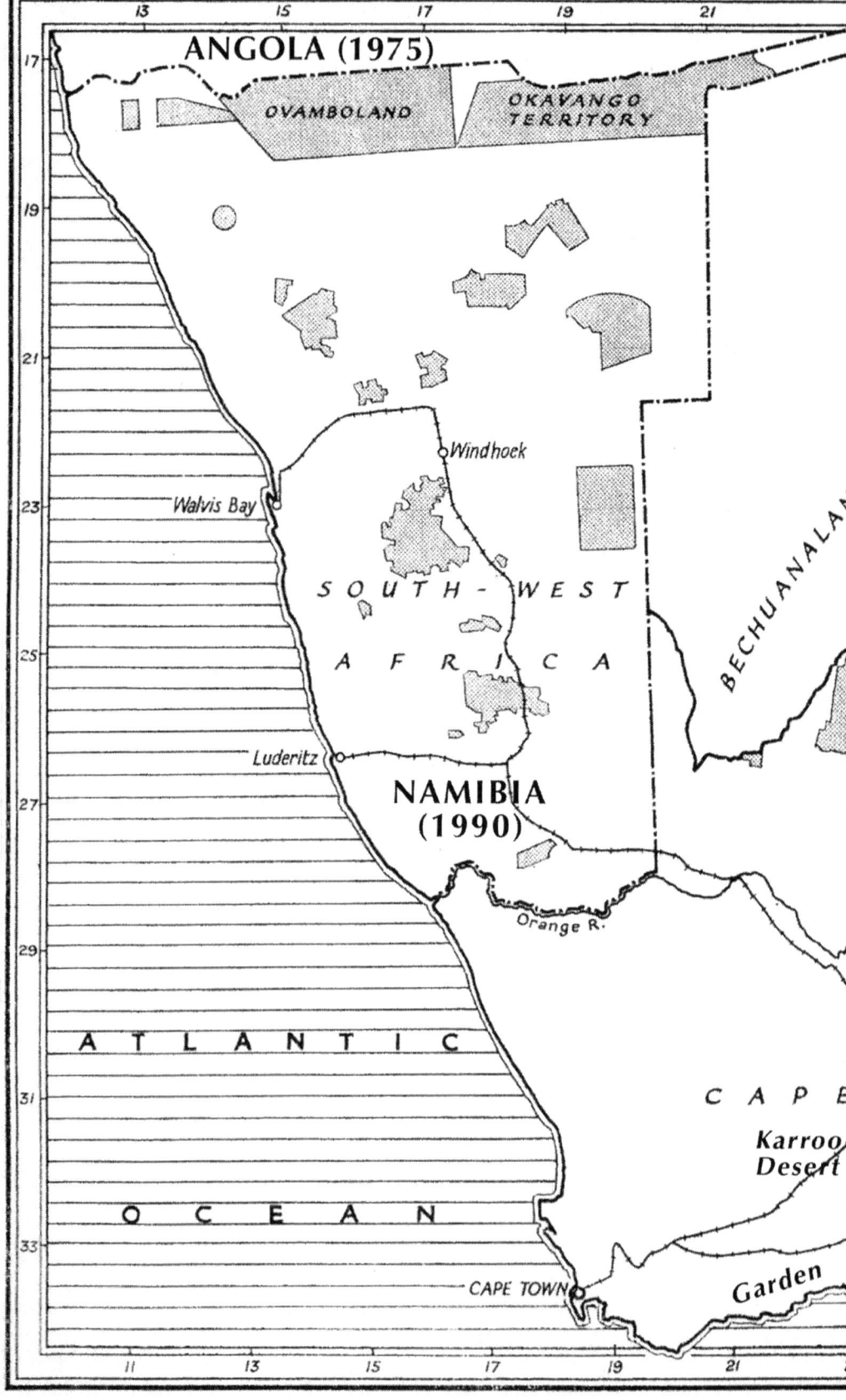

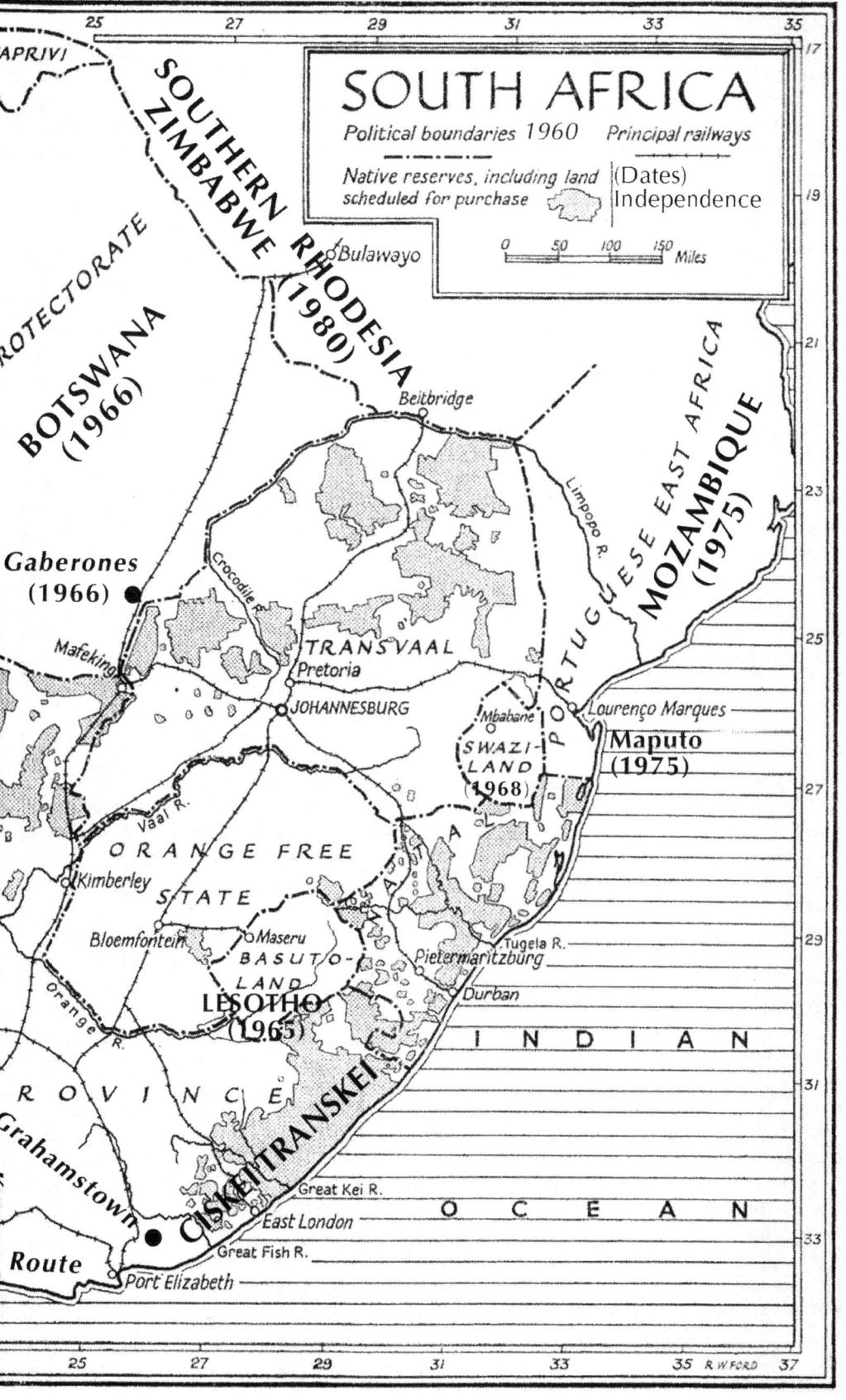

BACKGROUND NOTES

Liberal Journalists, Authors & Publishers

Patrick Duncan had in 1958 founded the illustrated Liberal fortnightly *Contact* bringing cheering news of countries in Africa as they became independent and the news about South Africa that the established press dare not print.

Randolph Vigne, Literary Editor of *Contact,* was in 1962 the founder of the radical monthly *The New African.* The Co-founders were **James Currey, Tim Holmes** Editor of *Contact* and **Neville Rubin**, University of Cape Town, whose legal ingenuity enabled the journal to survive attacks by the state and its Special Branch police.

Leo Marquard, Editorial Manager at Oxford University Press, was a founder of the National Union of Students in 1923 and, after a Rhodes Scholarship, in 1932 of the South African Liberal Party with the novelist Alan Paton. In 1946 he was sent by South Africa to San Francisco as a delegate at the founding of UNESCO.

David Philip worked in the Oxford University Press in Cape Town during the fifties and in 1959 opened the branch in Rhodesia, which was also for Zambia and Malawi as they built up to independence in 1963. He was Editorial Manager in Cape Town from 1962. In 1971 he and Marie Philip started David Philip Publishers in Cape Town and in 1985 Clare and James Currey started James Currey Publishers in Islington. The two publishers were to co-publish much work on changing the regime and ending apartheid in South Africa.

James Currey worked from 1959 to 1964 during the day at the Oxford University Press in Cape Town. After hours he drew bold maps for *Contact* with Letraset in the style of the London *Observer*. The *Contact Freedom Calendar* became blacker and blacker as each year independent countries ate into the white redoubt in the south of Africa. The typesetting and design of *The New African* went on all the month with much help from Clare. A weekend at home would be devoted to laying out designing and illustrating a monthly the same size and length as *The New Statesman* .

Families & South Africa

Both of **James Currey**'s grandfathers, Rev. John Currey and Rev. J.P. Martin, were sent to South Africa as missionaries by the Wesleyan Methodist Church soon after the Boer War (1899-1902). The Relief of Mafeking in 1900 was one of the most famous British victories. Mafeking was strategically placed on the great railway south from Rhodesia at the junction to Johannesburg with its gold before going on to Kimberley with its diamonds and on to the Cape with its international port. In September 1906 both grandfathers were sent as Ministers to the two Methodist circuits in Mafeking.

Rev. John Currey had arrived in South Africa in 1902 and married **Edith Vinnicombe** in 1906, whose Devonshire family had emigrated to Natal in 1849. **Ralph Currey** was born in December 1907 in Mafeking. John Currey ran the Wesleyan mission in the 'location' on the edge of the town where Tswana lived. Great-Aunt **Iris** (**Vinnicombe**) **Linder** married Iver. The **Phipson/Colborne** and **Vinnicombe** families are still centred on Natal. **Freda Wood** (née Phipson) was married to Lieutenant-Colonel Wood, former mayor of Pietermaritzburg.

Stella Martin's father **Rev. J.P. Martin** was engaged to Nancy Mann when he went out in 1904 to run the Methodist Church in Pilgrim's Rest. He was only allowed to marry in 1906 and **Helen Estella Martin** was born in Roodepoort, Transvaal in July 1907. In September 1907 J.P. and Nancy Martin took over Mafeking Wesleyan chapel built as a Memorial for the Relief of the Mafeking in 1900. It being South Africa, the chapel was restricted for whites, whether of the English or Afrikander 'races', or for 'coloureds' who had some European blood.

Edith and John Currey's children were Ralph, Ian and Joan, and Nancy and J.P. Martin's were Stella, Grace, John and Hal. These seven children became lifelong friends and stayed with one another's families in England.

Ralph Currey left South Africa at the age of 14 to go to John Wesley's Kingswood School, Bath and Wadham College, Oxford; he became established as a writer in England and was acclaimed as an outstanding South African poet. **Stella Martin** left South Africa at the age of four and by 1960, when they returned on a speaking tour, she had published seven novels, was a short story writer and an active playwright for theatre and television. *One Woman's Year* was issued in 2019 in a new edition by Persephone.

In 1964 **Andrew Currey** married **Elspeth Meyer**, whose Dutch father had South African connections. Their daughter is **Kate**.

James Currey was born in 1936 in Colchester and, like his father, went to Kingswood School, Bath and Wadham College, Oxford. He typed air-letters most weeks to his parents (1959-62 /1963-4).

Catherine Clare Wilson married **James Martin Currey** on 21 December 1962 at Jesus Lane Quaker Meeting House, Cambridge. They arrived in Cape Town on 2 January 1963.

Clare Currey (b. 1936) wrote air-letters (most weeks 1963-4) to her parents in Cambridge.

Dr Henry Wilson had retired as a Clinical Psychologist at the London Hospital and in Harley Street. **Ruth Wilson** was a founder of Marriage Guidance in 1937. They were both active members of The Society of Friends in Cambridge.

Clare and James, after their escape from South Africa on 11 July 1964, were to live in Clare's house Paddocks Wells, Cottered, Buntingford, Hertfordshire. **Hal Stephenson Currey** (27 April 1965) and **Tamsin Sarah Currey** (6 September 1967) were born at Mount Pleasant, Cambridge. Some of the letters quoted are to Clare's brothers and their wives **Lyn** and **Jeanetta** and **Chris** and **Jane Wilson**.

Dates of Independence of Colonies in Eastern, Central & Southern Africa

Tanganyika	renamed Tanzania	9 December 1961
Capital	Dar es Salaam	
Uganda	stays Uganda	9 October 1962
Capital	Kampala	
Kenya	stays Kenya	12 December 1963
Capital	Nairobi	
Nyasaland	renamed Malawi	6 July 1964
Capital	Blantyre moves to Lilongwe	
Northern Rhodesia (NR)	renamed Zambia	24 October 1964
Capital	Lusaka	
Southern Rhodesia (SR) Unilateral Declaration of Independence (UDI) 11 November 1965		
	renamed Zimbabwe	18 April 1980
Capital	Salisbury becomes Harare	

British High Commission Territories
ruled from the Cape Town Embassy

Bechuanaland	renamed Botswana	30 September 1966
Capital	Mafeking (Cape) becomes Gaberones	
Basutoland	renamed Lesotho	4 October 1966
Capital	Maseru	
Swaziland	stays Swaziland	6 September 1968
Capital	Mbabane	

Mozambique
Capital	stays Mozambique
Lourenco Marques
becomes Maputo	25 June 1975
Angola
Capital	stays Angola
Luanda	1 November 1975
South-West Africa
Capital	renamed Namibia
Windhoek	21 March 1990

Details of Union of South Africa 1910-1996

Four Provinces

Cape, Transvaal, Orange Free State (OFS), Natal

Three Capitals

Cape Town	Capital	Parliament
Bloemfontein	Capital	High Court
Pretoria	Capital	Civil Service

Abbreviations

SB	South African Police Security Branch or Special Branch
SABC	South African Broadcasting Corporation (Radio South Africa, no TV)
UNESCO	United Nations Educational, Scientific and Cultural Organization

Electoral Parties

HNP	National Party won National Election 1948 – to establish Apartheid ('apartness' in Afrikaans which was institutionalised racialism appropriately pronounced APART HATE).
UP	United Party predominately English-speaking in white parliament
Progressive Party	split from UP 1959 white liberal Party – working for Progressive Franchise
LP /LPSA	South African Liberal Party 1953-67 – working for Non-Racial Franchise

Political Organisations

ANC	African National Congress 1912
MK	uMkhonto we Sizwe – Armed Wing of the ANC 1961
COD	Congress of Democrats/ Congress Alliance 1952
PAC	Pan Africanist Congress 1959
Poqo	Armed Wing of the Pan Africanist Congress 1961
SWAPO	South-West Africa People's Organisation 1960
FNLA	National Liberation Front of Angola 1954

Religious Organizations

C of E	Church of England
DRC	Dutch Reformed Church
Friends	Society of Friends – Quakers
LMS	London Missionary Society
RC	Roman Catholic Church

Universities

UCT	University of Cape Town
Wits	Witwatersrand University, Johannesburg
Free State	University of the Orange Free State. Bloemfontein
Natal, PMB	University of Natal, Pietermaritzburg
Natal, Durban	University of Natal, Durban

Afrikaans (Dutch African) words which are much used in English

baaskaap	keeping *nie blankes* in their place
blankes	*blankes* whites *nie blankes* non-whites
dassies	rock-rabbits
dorp, dorpie	small upcountry town
drifts	fords, often dry
munt	(insulting for African) singular of prefix Bantu (Bantustan)
pondokkies	dwellings, tin shacks
rondavel	small, round African dwelling
skollies	street riff-raff
stoep	verandah, roofed portico on in front or on edge of house

INTRODUCTION

From mid-1959 to mid-1964 were five years in South Africa when a series of crises gave repeated hopes of change. These letters show the day-to-day responses of Randolph Vigne and Patrick Duncan of the liberal left and indeed of friendly members of the PAC and the Congress alliance. My father, out of loyalty to his South African mother's family, thought that as a visitor to the country I should not become involved in their political affairs. Randolph Vigne cured me of that, and Patrick Duncan swept me into conspiracy as the National Party brought in apartheid law after apartheid law. These letters capture the excitement as political dramas evolved. The events of daily life are brought back by the vividness of captured conversations.

In February 1960 the British Prime Minister Macmillan in the 'Winds of Change' speech told the whites only parliament that they would have to change. Macmillan was wrong. White supremacy was to survive for another thirty years. The state in South Africa would resort to any means, however violent, to survive.

Since the Defiance Campaign in 1952 extra-parliamentary opposition had used non-violent means of protest. On 21 March 1960 at Sharpeville in the Transvaal the police shot in the back at least 69 peaceful protesters. It was a turning point in South African history. On 29 March 1960 some 35,000 Africans marched on Cape Town led by the student Kgosana; they responded to his chanted request for 'ab-sol-ute non-viol-ence' and dispersed. The police responded with savagery in the townships and on the streets of central Cape Town.

Patrick Duncan was editor and owner of the news magazine *Contact* which, though independent, supported the Liberal Party. The fortnightly brought us cheering news of Africa as countries to the north became independent. It reported the news from South Africa that the journalists on the established papers dare not print. Tim Holmes was Assistant Editor. Randolph Vigne, a publisher at Maskew Miller, was the Literary Editor and had far more copy submitted than there was space to publish in *Contact*.

He saw the need for a political and cultural monthly in the style of *The New Statesman*.

In 1961 Randolph Vigne, Neville Rubin, Tim Holmes and I founded *The New African* as a radical review of politics and the arts. It was published in Cape Town from 1962 to 1964 and in exile in London from 1965 to 1969. It was packed with political coverage of decolonising Africa in general and of apartheid South Africa in particular. It took delight in the outburst of cultural activity both inside and outside the country. This journal was to give publication in South Africa – often for the first time – to writers such as Bessie Head, Chinua Achebe, Dennis Brutus, Wole Soyinka, Ngugi, and Lewis Nkosi. They were to be among the writers I was to publish with Chinua Achebe from 1967 in the African Writers' Series.

The South African government could have stopped *The New African* at any time but, as they maintained they had a free press, they wanted to avoid outright censorship that would have been attacked in the South African and international press. The liberal journalists could report in *Contact* and *The New African* what the big papers dare not print. This was what was happening at the same time in London in the newly established *Private Eye*.

The authorities expected that they could make *The New African* give up and shut up. In 1964 they used the Special Branch to censor by harassment – police raids, confiscation of equipment, destruction of copies of the magazine, intimidation of printers, and a verdict of obscenity which was turned down on appeal.

In Part Two, Clare Currey's letters from 1963 to 1964 show how she had married into *The New African* – and also into close friendship with Gillian and Randolph Vigne. Soon after Clare arrived in New Year 1963, Randolph went into hiding to delay being banned. *The New African* was put together monthly in the Currey flat with Randolph Vigne – even after he was banned. Clare reported on the last phase of the Rivonia Trial in Pretoria for *The New African*. The Sunday after the Rivonia verdict on 12 June 1964 the Johannesburg *Sunday Times* had a headline across the front quoting the police chief saying all resistance in the country was at an end. That night pylons were felled near Cape Town and Johannesburg. From where did this resistance come? The police did not know. In fury on 4 July 1964 they launched raids against the whole range of the left-wing opposition across the country.

Academic research has identified that in the year following Sharpeville and Langa at least 22 underground opposition groups were formed in desperation at the failure of non-violent methods in face of the relentless violence of the state. Randolph Vigne was a founder in 1960 of the National Committee of Liberation (NCL) which became the African Resistance Movement (ARM). He hid sabotage plans under layers and layers of legal activity in which I was continually involved. He contributed to Patrick Duncan's newspaper *Contact*. Randolph Vigne even stood as Liberal Party candidate for the whites-only parliament to advance the message of non-racialism. The Liberal Party was at its most radical in the Cape. Randolph Vigne made continuous visits to work with the opposition in the Transkei who won a popular election success and revealed the way the South African state kept control through the chiefs of the first Bantustan. The South African Special Branch, despite its close attention to *The New African*, did not discover that all the time that Vigne and Rubin were editing the magazine that they were members of the African Resistance Movement (ARM). The intense comings and goings of producing a small magazine, *The New African*, had served as effective cover for planning sabotage in the Cape.

On 9 July 1964 Randolph Vigne appealed to Clare and me to enable him escape. Clare had no hesitation; she stated 'Randolph and Gillian are our friends.' Randolph did not tell us why he was desperate to get out. I could use my British passport, which meant that I did not need a visa for Canada, to buy a ticket on a Norwegian freighter so that Vigne could travel under my name to Montreal. I had to jump off the ship, *The Thorstream*, to prevent my going to Canada as well. On Saturday 11 July 1964 Clare and I flew out of Johannesburg – I signed myself out of South Africa twice in forty-eight hours. These five years of letters give the build-up to *The Cape Escape*, which has been reprinted in Part 3 of this book.

Oxford University Press, London and Cape Town 1958-64
It had taken five interviews for me to be offered a job at the Oxford University Press. The second interview was to be with 'The Secretary'. Despite the modest title Colin Roberts, as 'Secretary to the Delegates of the University of Oxford', was the chief executive of the worldwide Oxford University Press in its college-like headquarters in Walton Street.

In OUP London it was exciting to be asked at the age of 22, 'Where would you like to go?' My answer to Eric Parnwell, the Deputy Publisher, was 'India, South Africa, America. Anywhere but Australia and New Zealand'. He asked: 'Why South Africa? Nobody has ever asked to go to South Africa.' South Africa, with ten years of apartheid, was already infamous. I replied: 'I have a South African grandmother and I'm curious to find out.' Parnwell had a hidden agenda in that it was planned to send David Philip, the assistant editor in Cape Town, to open a Sales Office in Salisbury in Southern Rhodesia and they needed somebody to take over his job in Cape Town while he was away for three years.

Conservatives in Britain were horrified when Macmillan, with his Colonial Secretary Macleod, had decided that after the emergencies in Kenya and Malaya, it would be cheaper to give colonies their independence. Ghana had become independent in 1957 and education was a priority. Six more African colonies followed. The Oxford University Press realised that, wherever they had sales offices in Africa or Asia, they must set up editorial offices to produce textbooks for the new national syllabuses. They had decided in 1956 to recruit three graduates a year who, after eight months training in London, would be sent out to pass on their newly-won knowledge to the trainee editors in the independent countries. The British Empire was ending but the OUP Empire would continue because the press had the English language to sell.

In 1959 Oxford University Press in Amen House, in the shadow of St Pauls, was like a college of publishing with self-confident young Oxford graduates just back from or just about to go out to spread Oxford English across the dissolving British Empire. Rex Collings, who had been at Penguin, looked after us and told us about his struggles to publish new writers from India and Africa in the pioneering Three Crowns series; one of his authors, the playwright and poet Wole Soyinka, was to be the first African to win the Nobel Prize for Literature. With him we established 'The Rules Committee' which looked worthy on internal memos but was the group who met for dinner at Rules Restaurant in Maiden Lane. We trainees were based in the Overseas Education Department and attached for some weeks at a time to the different editorial, production, sales and administrative departments. At my own initiative and cost, I spent evenings in the Central College of Art and Design learning typographical design; I had planned that if I did not get a job I might take a year's course at the London College of Printing. A particularly valuable experience was to be sent round all the jobs in the OUP warehouse at Neasden. It is easy to publish books. It is hard to sell and distribute them. We editors needed the packers, the lookers out, and the invoicers to get books out across the country and across the world. The new mainframe computer was in an air-conditioned hanger with its needs being attended to by the new IT master race in white overalls; by the time Clare and I were to set up our publishing imprint in 1985 the personal computer on one's desk could equal the power of that large machine.

There was great excitement in the Currey family that I was to go to South Africa. Mafeking was famous in British tribal history because it was where

Baden-Powell, founder of the Boy Scouts, commanded the garrison that had held out in the siege against the Boer sharpshooters. John and Edith Currey ran the Wesleyan Methodist circuit in the African location; my father, R.N. Currey, was born there in December 1907. J.P. and Nancy Martin had arrived in Mafeking in September 1907 with their daughter Stella who had been born in July 1907; J.P. Martin was in charge of the new chapel built in the town centre as a memorial to the siege. As a child in Colchester in England I had loved the visits of Edith Currey's Vinnicombe and Phipson relations whose forbears had reached Natal in 1849. Thomas Phipson was to become Sheriff of Natal. Some, like Cecil from a sugar plantation in Natal, had just been released from a German prisoner of war camp and delighted a twelve-year-old boy with exciting stories about the dangers of crocodiles. Then, having accepted the OUP job in South Africa, I panicked. I began to realise how reactionary my relations were, although perhaps they were not quite as racist as most Afrikaners. And here I was, going half-way round the world to be with people like that. Fortunately, in the autumn of 1959 Faber published James Morris's *South African Winter* and I read it with relief one weekend. He revealed what a fascinatingly varied place South Africa was with its interacting tribes: black, white and brown. There were even some liberal Afrikaners; he described a civilised dinner in Stellenbosch, the centre of Afrikanerdom, with a liberal historian and his university wife; I was to find out later that the couple were Nell and Leo Marquard – he who was to be my boss at the Oxford University Press.

I avoided spending a fortnight on a Union Castle liner playing deck quoits with people like my relations. It took 24 hours to fly to Johannesburg in a BOAC turboprop Britannia reading *The Warden*. After another three or four hours down to Cape Town I was met by David Philip, who had booked me into the Cecil Hotel (like Cecil John Rhodes) near the Newlands Rugby and Cricket stadium. The Plumstead Badminton Club was having its annual dinner dance. I thought, I have come half-way round the world for this!

Next day, David Philip introduced me to OUP's Editorial Manager, the liberal historian Leo Marquard – Afrikaner, austere and moderately formidable. The Sales Manager was Freddie Cannon – British, cheerful and reactionary. David Philip, who was reluctantly going to open a sales office in Salisbury, handed over to my care the liberal list built up by Marquard. Our academic authors were taking apartheid apart in their books. Cannon lived in continual fear that they would be censored and, even worse, might offend his bookseller friends. Marquard calmly took on books such as Ndabaningi Sithole's *African Nationalism,* Monica Wilson and Archie Mafeje's *Langa:*

Social groups in an African township and Alan Paton's *Hofmeyr*. The school textbooks he took on in English, Zulu and Xhosa provided opportunities for typographical design.

Leo Marquard had been, with Alan Paton, a founder of the Liberal Party in 1953. When he was about to become an Oxford Rhodes Scholar for the Orange Free State he founded the National Union of South African Students (NUSAS) and in 1929 helped found the South African Institute of Race Relations. He quietly used his OUP office to advance Liberal causes across the whole country and left me to get the books designed and printed and publicised; I had an unbelievable freedom to experiment which I could never have had at the age of 23 in London. I spent long times out at printers with the quaint names of Rustica and Gothic being told by the craftsmen what they could and could not do with lead type, and challenging them with the great freedoms being brought in by litho. Clare said, rather critically, that my letters from Cape Town were always full of the what books I was designing 'Yes you certainly did go on about *The Wreck of the Grosvenor, East Indiaman*'; anyhow that book was shortlisted for a book design prize in Johannesburg.

The most elegant books in the great Van Krimpen Dutch tradition were produced by A.A. Balkema who had come out to South Africa after printing secret books of elegance literally under the feet of Nazi soldiers in Amsterdam. I took my design roughs round to him and, rather glumly over his sandwiches, he taught me all the details such as letter spacing capitals on a title page. Julian Rollnick set out at Gothic to build elegance into their production. He, David Philip and I were later to share the delights and problems of typography over lunch each Wednesday. The OUP gave me the chance to organise my own apprenticeship in publishing and design. I asked question after question and people were responsive.

I looked, with some gloom, at various places to live in the southern suburbs. Then, practically on its own, there was a very long advertisement in *The Cape Times* for a flat 'suitable for a young male professional'. It was in Oranjezicht, which is up under Table Mountain above the Gardens but near to the centre of Cape Town. It was in a generous 1840 house with a dramatic *stoep* looking out across the city and bay. Joy and Anthony Millar showed me a two room flat and bathroom which they had converted from the servants' quarters at the back of their house; wooden blinds and a little white courtyard were elegantly right. It was the beginning of a friendship and they were kindly to keep the flat vacant for me when in 1963 I was to go on home leave to England for five months. When I came back from England married, they welcomed Clare as family.

Contact was in Parliament Chambers opposite the Houses of Parliament. It had most of the offices on the top floor up under the sloping rooves. They were substantial but not too grand. At the centre was the *Contact* board room which provided a meeting space for liberals and sympathisers. The single room Liberal Party office was down a floor. With marvellous incongruity wives of National Party MPs swept out in garden party hats from the milliners next door to *Contact* on the top floor. The South African MPs across the road ran their pure white democracy with all the tribal rights of Westminster.

Peter Hjul was chairman of the Liberals in the Cape and he, Randolph and Pat came up with imaginative initiatives which were not always approved by the Liberal Party national headquarters in Natal. Peter Brown in Natal was the charming and reliable chairman. The President, also in Natal, was the internationally renowned novelist Alan Paton – he had a tendency to growl. His novel *Cry, the beloved country* came out in 1948, the year of the National Party victory. From that date the novel was important in rousing the liberal conscience about South Africa across the world.

The National Party was elected to government in 1948 to bring in apartheid: total segregation. They pushed out the United Party which, with the Afrikaner Smuts as its leader and its policy of segregation by colour bar, had largely been supported by the English-speaking South Africans.

Five years later in 1953 the Liberal Party had been formed in order to try and get members into Parliament to campaign for a qualified franchise for non-whites. It was hoped that they would be joined by some of the liberal MPs splitting off from the United Party, but they, in 1959, formed the Progressive Party with a qualified franchise. The Liberals were non-racial and set out to recruit people of any colour. They could not get their candidates elected into the whites-only parliament. The two Liberal senators Leslie Rubin and Margaret Ballinger were the token Native Representatives and even that position was soon abolished.

Anybody in the liberal network across South Africa knew that if they visited Cape Town they would meet up with other liberals in Parliament Buildings. The most provocative opposition in the country was from NUSAS, the National Union of South African Students and the young Presidents, almost always members of the South African Liberal Party, would be encountered in the rickety lift grinding up to the top floors of Parliament Chambers. A year after Randolph Vigne, Tim Holmes, Neville Rubin and I founded *The New African*, we opened an office in the Chambers.

PART ONE

Letters from South Africa
James Currey July 1959 to July 1962

Selections from letters from James Currey to R.N. Currey and Stella Martin Currey in Colchester, England. They were mostly typed on standard airletter forms and posted from Cape Town.

Up until the sixties the rhythm of the Cape Town week centred on the arrival of the Union Castle liner from Southampton on a Thursday and its departure for its voyage back on Friday. Sailing on a floating hotel for thirteen nights still cost far less than air. My 30 hour flight from London to Cape Town cost OUP more than they paid me for a whole year. The navigational pilot, having sailed the liner out into Table Bay, would transfer to the vessel below to come back to port.

Surprisingly the Director of the Flemish National Theatre over from Belgium gave me a minor part as a soldier in his production of The Caucasian Chalk Circle *at the university Gardens Theatre. I thought it would be a chance to learn about Brecht and to meet young South Africans. I had to rehearse in the evenings for six weeks and the production went on for twenty performances. It was an effective way of avoiding feeling lonely. 'Rare theatrical treat' said* The Cape Times.

The Millars lived in a delightful nineteenth century house on the classic English Cape pattern; single floor with a dramatic stoep (Dutch for balcony.) It was up in Oranjezicht in the bowl of hills underneath Table Mountain with views of Cape Town below. Joy Millar, an artist with a taste for dramatic dresses, is full of extravagant welcome. Anthony Millar is head of advertising at BP. Apparently their

advertisement in the Argus *had 31 replies and they did not want to let their elegant servant's quarters to any of them. So Anthony and one of his advertising colleagues in his department at BP set out to write an advertisement for the more upmarket* Cape Times *to describe the tenant they wanted. I was the only 'young professional gentleman' to reply. I was to be there for three years. It was on that stoep that I had a long talk with Randolph Vigne at one of the Millar parties.*

A.A. Balkema started as one of Holland's classic printers. When the Netherlands were invaded he was licensed by the Germans to print official forms and papers and he got permission to use two assistants who worked on the ground floor. Hidden in the cellar he ran what he and his wife called the 'Bicycle Press'. Mrs Balkema, who was inclined to put on weight, used to have a static exercise bike in the front room. When the Germans came to the press they found her pedalling away for exercise. She was actually generating electric power for the secret press in the cellar. There he secretly typeset works like Stanley Morrison's lectures on typography and the selected poems of John Donne in English. He then printed tiny editions on the very best paper of which he had secret stores hidden from before the war. He said that it was done purely for the sake of morale.

THE WORK OF
JAN VAN KRIMPEN

A RECORD IN HONOUR OF HIS
SIXTIETH BIRTHDAY · BY
JOHN DREYFUS

WITH A FOREWORD BY
STANLEY MORISON

ILLUSTRATED BY
REPRODUCTIONS OF DRAWINGS
SPECIMENS OF TYPES
LETTERING AND
BOOKWORK

A.A. BALKEMA · CAPE TOWN
MDCCCCLII

JOHN DONNE
POEMS

SELECTED FROM HIS
SONGS AND SONETS
ELEGIES
EPITHALAMIONS
VERSE LETTERS
DIVINE POEMS

AMSTERDAM
A.A. BALKEMA
1946

Sally Morgan and James Currey looking down on Hanover Street from the balcony of the photographer Joe Louw, whose work appeared regularly in the renowned Drum Magazine *and in* The Golden City Post. *Later his photograph was to become historic with the wall of hands on the first floor balcony in the Memphis motel in the United States pointing at the assassin of Martin Luther King.*

Hanover Street, in District Six, was the liveliest part of Cape Town. People of all races could meet, eat and dance there, though still they were still in danger of imprisonment under apartheid laws such as the Immorality Act. Every Sunday evening jazz would be played by Dollar Brand (later to become known internationally as Abdullah Ibrahim).

Patrick Duncan at work as editor of the photographic news fortnightly Contact *in the offices just opposite the Houses of Parliament. He always generously made these rooms available to meetings for the liberals. Anybody arriving in Cape Town could be sure to meet up with other activists and get involved in the next action.*

Harold Macmillan in his 'Winds of Change Speech' on 2 February 1960 told the whites only House of Assembly that they would have to change. No change! The National Party maintained apartheid for another thirty years. The British High Commission invited Patrick Duncan to talk with Macmillan at their garden party, just after his historic speech.

Colin Legum, Africa and Commonwealth Correspondent for the Observer, whose editor David Astor supported Patrick Duncan and Contact. Although the Liberal Party was small, the close association with international correspondents like Colin Legum and Stanley Uys meant that the international press gave outstanding coverage of the battle against the apartheid state. Colin Legum (right) is talking with Professor Austin at a UN congress on apartheid in Brasilia.

February 1960 Camps Bay Beach (Left to right): Mary Kirwood, James Currey and Joe Louw. Recumbent in the sand is Albie Sachs, on whose back Mary has drawn a

skeleton in sand. One of the times he was released from Roeland Street prison in central Cape Town he ran six miles to Clifton to this very beach and plunged fully clothed into the Atlantic. One of his arms was to be blown off in Maputo by the South African Special Branch. As a campaigning lawyer he was to draft the new South African constitution of 1996 and to keep President Zuma under pressure.

The coverage by Patrick Duncan's Contact *of the PAC March of the 35,000 into Cape Town. The Pan African Congress (PAC) had broken from the African National Congress (ANC) in 1959 and was led by Sobukwe (top left). The Sharpeville massacre of 69 people in the Transvaal on 21 March 1960 was the police response to the peaceful PAC anti-pass protest. Nine days later the PAC student Philip Kgosana in his shorts led 35,000 peaceful marchers without passes to surrender at the Police Station in Caledon Square in central Cape Town. Kgosana and the leadership were promised a meeting with Erasmus the Minister of Justice if they got the 35,000 to return peacefully to Langa and Nyanga. They did. That night Kgosana and the leadership were arrested. For several days the police brutally attacked Africans not only in the townships but even in the centre of Cape Town. The government showed that they would always resort with violence to peaceful protest. Apartheid was to stay.*

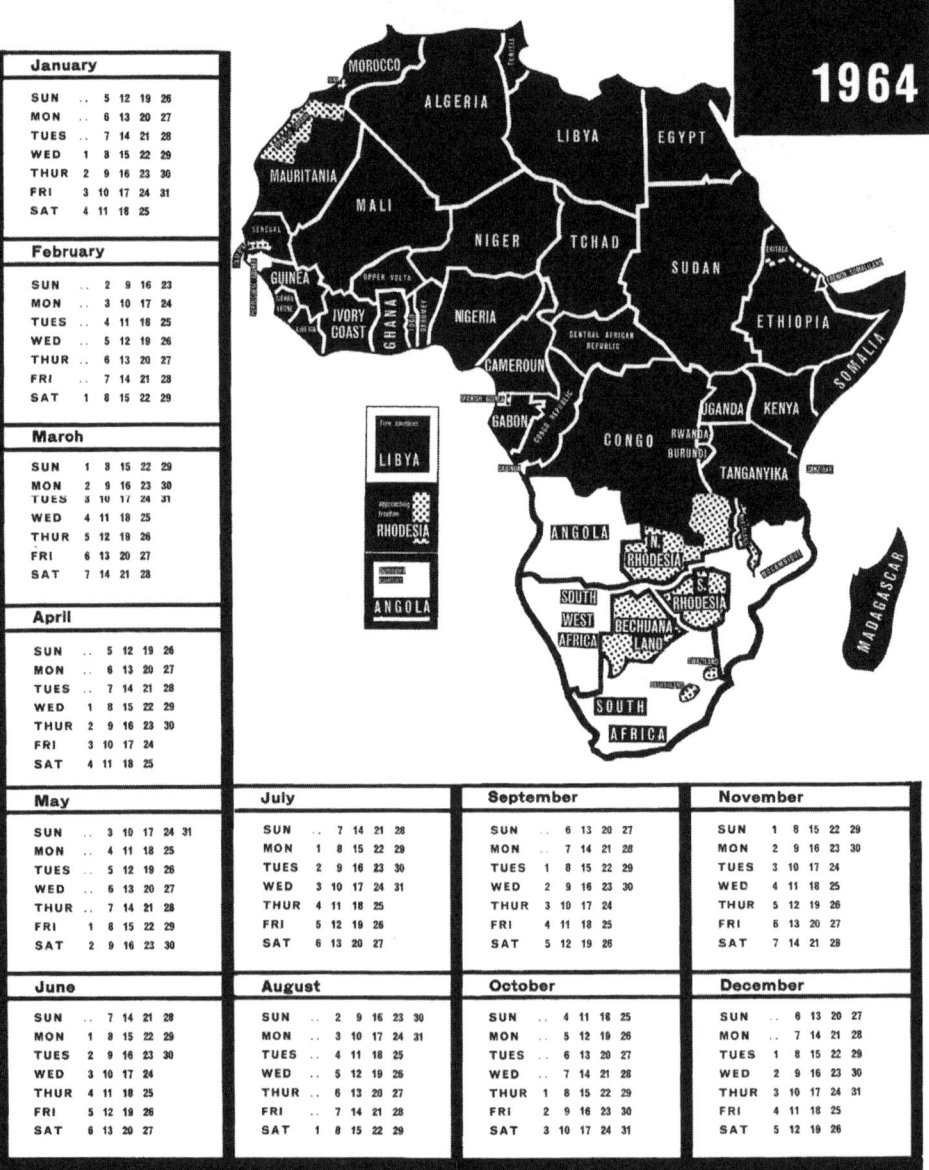

Two successful Oxford University Press, Cape Town books with James Currey covers: Ndabaningi Sithole African Nationalism *and Leo Marquard* The Peoples and Policies of South Africa.

July 1961 Mr Tabata on his way by donkey to the Liberal Party Congress in Durban. Cape Town cars and combis have a cheerful break in the middle of the Transkei.

The little boy (below) is back in charge of his commandeered donkey. In the centre is the redoubtable Liberal Party lawyer Barney Zackon who appears at several places in this book bailing out and representing Liberal Party members in court.
After this we were to encounter police road blocks as we descended towards Natal; the police had been tipped off that I was carrying the brother of Chief Sabata Dalindyebo who was the leader of the party which won the popular vote in the first Transkei election. This was then cancelled by the Pretoria government who bought the votes of the majority of the chiefs.

The New African

THE RADICAL REVIEW
VOLUME ONE   NUMBER NINE
15c/1s. 6d.   September 1962

J. T. NGUGI
Kenya—the Two Rifts ... 2

Ambitions
1. PETER MOTSOANE
   Jobs and Living ... 4
2. CARL MAFOKO
   Religion ... 5
3. S. N. NDLUMBINI
   Earnings ... 6
4. SY MOYA
   Schooling ... 10

BESSIE HEAD
Let me tell a story now... 8

E. L. NTLOEDIBE
Race and Nationhood ... 11

PETER MACKAY
Malawi's Symposium ... 12

Words, Words, Words ... 14

Reviews by
JOHN LAREDO ... 15
A. K. BROOKS ... 16

SUBSCRIPTION
12 months R2.00/£1/$2.80
6 months R1.00/10s./$1.40

THE NEW AFRICAN P.O. BOX 2068 CAPE TOWN

The New African

THE RADICAL REVIEW
VOLUME TWO   NUMBER SEVEN
15c/1s. 6d.   17 August 1963

Reviews and Pictures
Kozonguizi: First on S.W.A.
R. Kunene: Benson on the A.N.C.
Nagenda: Ekwensi's new novel
Donald Stuart:
Language in Africa

Zac de Beer   Anthony Delius
Peter Clarke

In this issue:
126 SOCIALISM IS UNNECESSARY: Z. J. de Beer
127 GHANA'S BENEVOLENT DICTATORSHIP: Harry Jaguar
130 THE MISSING LINK: Anthony Delius
132 IN A FAR COUNTRY: Peter Clarke
133 VIOLENCE COUNTER-VIOLENCE: Mary Benson
135-140 SPECIAL REVIEW SECTION: Reviews by Donald Stuart, Jariretundu Kozonguizi, John Nagenda, Sally Holmes, M. G. Field, Raymond Kunene, Reuben Hasson, Rosland Oliver.
140 THE REPUBLIC—A SATIRE: H. B. Kimmel
143 DEFENDING THE INDEFENSIBLE III: Peter Warren
145 THREE SCHOOLS FOR THE ELITE
125 Leader, 129 Comment, 141 Africana, 142 Words, Words, Words.

The ninth issue of The New African *shows that, with contributions by Ngugi and Bessie Head, it is beginning to live up to its plan to cover 'Africa in general and South Africa in particular'. Neville Rubin had flown in June/July to the renowned Mbari African Writers Conference at Makerere University College in Uganda. He got Wole Soyinka, on his way to the first Nobel Prize for an African writer, to allow* The New African *to publish for the very first time his famously funny poem 'Telephone conversation'. Carl Mafoko was the pseudonym for Jacob Mokholo to whom Clare and James Currey were in May 1964 to make a visit in a beautiful village of Vendaland.*

The Radical Review is now well into its second year and is well established. There is 'a New African Week-end' once a month when James and Clare's flat is taken over by galley proofs, cow gum and the paste up is put together for the printers to make up into pages and illustrations to be inserted. The magazine was designed by James Currey and proofed by Randolph Vigne with help from Clare Currey

The New African

CAN THEMBA STORY

&

ISLAM IN AFRICA

THE RADICAL REVIEW
VOLUME THREE NUMBER THREE
15c/1s. 6d.   28 March 1964

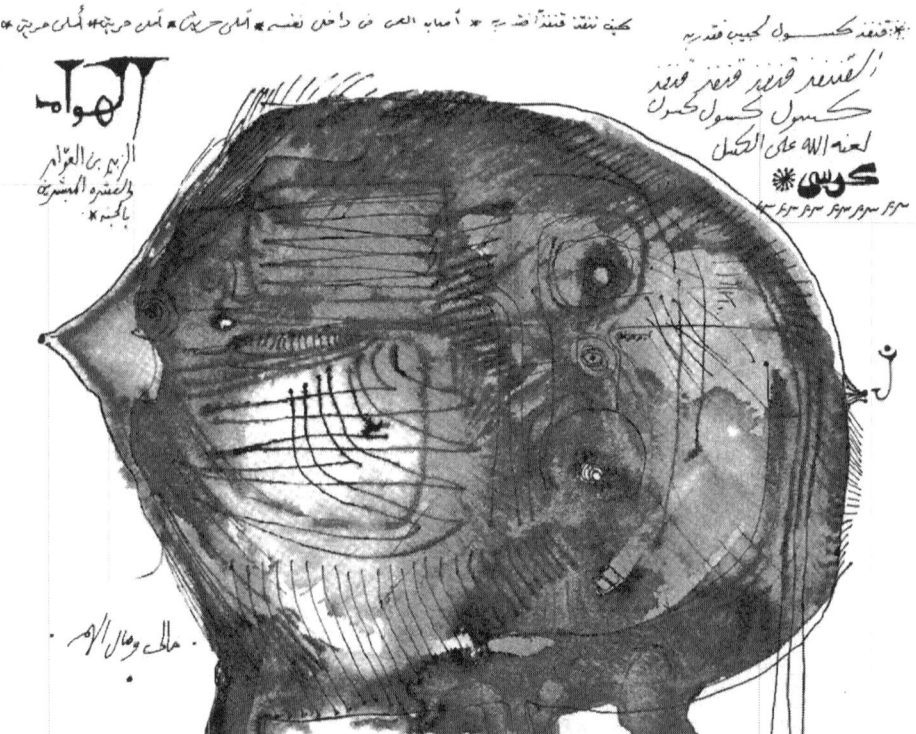

The New African

THE RADICAL REVIEW
VOLUME FOUR NUMBER SEVEN
2s   September 1965

Commonwealth Arts Festival Supplement

- Nadine Gordimer
- LEWIS NKOSI
- ALEX LA GUMA
- GERALD MOORE on Soyinka
- DENNIS DUERDEN on Art
- EZEKIEL Mphahlele
- Dan Jacobson
- BARRY RECKORD on plays
- BREYTEN BREYTENBACH
- ARTHUR MAIMANE on films 
- PEGGY HARPER on the new African dance

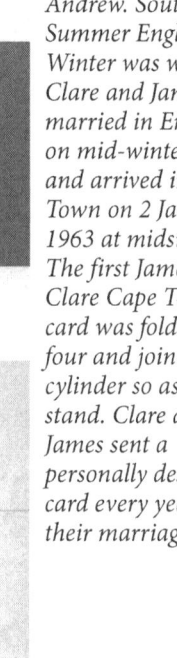

James designed this top card for his first Christmas in South Africa with a poem written by his brother Andrew. South Africa Summer England Winter was when Clare and James married in England on mid-winter's day, and arrived in Cape Town on 2 January 1963 at midsummer. The first James and Clare Cape Town card was folded in four and joined in a cylinder so as to stand. Clare and James sent a personally designed card every year of their marriage.

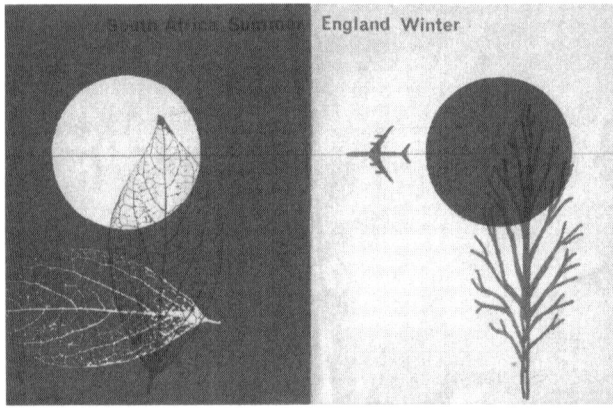

1959

An intoxication of books
(London Easter 1959) The OUP warehouse at Neasden is becoming intoxicating. The smell of all those books is quite heady. I am now 'looking out' which is collecting books according to orders. It is restful to be doing a physical job and one feels a little less tired than after sitting down with proofs all day.

Everybody knows Everybody
(Arrival Cape Town 17 July 1959/First letter 24 July 1959) Lesson 1. Everybody knows everybody. David Philip [editor at the Oxford University Press] within five minutes of arrival at the airport said he had rung Mrs Linder. I could not think who Mrs Linder was! Well [she was my] Great-Aunt Iris who knew somebody who knew somebody who knew Cannon the Trade Manager at OUP. (2 August 1959) First time at Hermanus. Aunt Iris and Uncle Iver as truly delightful as I remember them in England in1952. [Uncle Iver Linder manager in Standard Bank and then retirement job as bursar of Fort Hare, South Africa's one university college for Africans]

Searching for Quarters
Answered some *Cape Argus* advertisements with help of David and then Marie Philip. Today Saturday saw quite nice room in Rondebosch, English widow, well placed, but wishy-washy pastel. Decided I would take if other advertisement in *Cape Times* flopped.

Rang up house in Oranjezicht in the bowl of hills underneath Table Mountain.

Very English granny answered saying that daughter and son in law were very fussy, but that my being one week out from England was a GOOD THING. Went this evening at 6 o'clock. Delightful nineteenth century house on classic English Cape pattern; single floor with a dramatic stoep (Dutch for balcony) with views of Cape Town below.

[Anthony Millar, English reserve, is head of advertising at BP. Joy Millar, artist, dramatic dresses, full of extravagant welcome. Apparently their advertisement in the *Argus* had 31 replies and they did not want to let their elegant property to any of them. So Anthony and one of his advertising colleagues in his department at BP set out to write an advertisement for the more upmarket *Cape Times* to describe the tenant they wanted. I was the only 'young professional gentleman' to reply. I was to be there for three years.]

Flat at back corner of the house painted in white and (guess what? pale blue). Separate entrance. Whole bathroom and lavatory [electric ring to heat food up on the floor]. Sitting room and bedroom. £10.00 per month: Bed made. Dusting. Electricity. Hot water. Nearby is small hotel run by wife of Swiss Manager of Mount Nelson Hotel and it provides breakfast and dinner for £7 a week.

David Philip and typography
Truly delightful. I shall be very sad when he goes to Rhodesia. He adored Oxford. He could hardly believe his luck in joining OUP. As thrilled by typography as I am myself. His wife Marie; sister of renowned van Ryneveld brothers who played rugby for Oxford and one of them even for England. (One brother came in today in the blazer of an Oxford Blue with two golden infants.) Marie is as easy as anything to get on with. They swear that their house is open to me and it is. Built by David Philip's grandfather (descendants of famous missionary Philip founder of school which became Cape Town University). She came especially to have a look at this flat I was thinking of taking. Plus delightfully pretty, unspoilt four and half year old daughter.

The Arrival of the Mail Boat
(2 August 1959) It seems ages since leaving England and arriving here but on Wednesday the Union Castle boat arrived which left Southampton the Thursday I left Heathrow 24 hour flight by turboprop Britannia. It was late because of engine trouble so that I walked down after work to see it come in at sunset. Crowds of people made it an occasion. In fact one feels that CT is closer in its heart to England than it is to SA. The papers are full of who arrives and departs and the midday gun sounds from the castle.

(7 August 1959) Winter has come back at last. Snow on Table Mountain on Friday though melted immediately. But I have not used my overcoat and have only just started wearing waistcoat or pullovers.

Drama for the Currey family
(2 August 1959) Glad to hear play went well. Frightfully sorry not to have been there with everybody. Hope not too much rewriting. [Stella Martin Currey's latest play *French Polish* had been backed by a Director to go on in London's West End when a suitable theatre became available. I was to go to the opening night of the trial run in Birmingham but it got postponed and I had to leave for Cape Town. OUP had already co-operatively put off my departure.]

Got back from Hermanus to find letter about the death of Grandad aged 88 – how terribly sad for you and a relief that it did not last too long. The resilience of his body had really outlasted his faculties. But how sad, especially for Ian and Jean who had had him living with them so much. [Less than a month before John Currey had been telling James in Colchester about his life as a Wesleyan Minister in the first decade of the twentieth century and of how he was paddled to his first job in an open canoe up the River Nkomati through crocodiles to a Methodist mission on the border of Mozambique, Swaziland and South Africa. My departure for South Africa had given him an excited lift in his last days. He had in February that year 1959 lost my grandmother Edith (née Vinnicombe), whose Phipson/Colborne family had gone out to Natal in 1849 – 110 years before my arrival in South Africa. So within one month Stella and Ralph Currey had had the death of Ralph's father, the launch of Stella's first potential West End play and the departure of their eldest son for three years.]

Terrific about Hal [Martin's] novel. And terrific that it is a really good publisher Faber; they have published one or two rather original books in the last year or so such as *Lord of the Flies* and Hal's is unusual and powerful. I hope they like the title *The Hammering*.

Taking on the publishing at OUP
Things are beginning to get into a routine at the OUP and there is a great deal of work on hand. In school books alone there are two final books of the Oxford English Course for SA: revision of the first two books of that course: – the first four books of the Oxford English Course for Bantu Schools almost ready for publishing together with 4 corresponding teachers books.

Then I am dealing with a book by Patrick Duncan called *Sotho Law and Custom* sponsored by the Basutoland colonial government. In reading about this pastoral mountain society I get the same feeling as I did in reading books about the commutation of labour services in Thirteenth Century England and the beginning of use of money for payment. Basutoland is set right in the middle of South Africa and is going to give a vote to every adult male and female in October. Of course the whole constitution is cunningly worked out so that the voters cannot control the administration but it is a beginning and shows good will. [The first time I met Patrick Duncan was when I went round to discuss proofs with him at the offices of his radical fortnightly newspaper *Contact*.]

When Sithole *African Nationalism* is published in England ask for it. It is already out here and much discussed: *Die Burger* published articles on it on two consecutive days.

Nie-Blankes & Blankes

Marquard is most thoughtful and, while telling you where you might improve something, will immediately give you credit for something you think of yourself and anything you do well ... He is in contact with everyone and everything. Yesterday he came and showed David Philip and me a piece in *Die Burger* about the segregation of beaches and the sea. He said that he had sent a note round to David Marais at the *Cape Times* who is their brilliant cartoonist. Today the Marais cartoon is of Moses commanding the seas to part into *Nie-Blankes and Blankes* [Non-White and White].

The whole situation is comic if it was not for the tragedy in human terms.

For the greater part of time one feels that everything is all right except that there are segregation notices up and then something reminds you. Miss Williams [who keeps the Editorial Department running] said that the other day at the station she was walking out through a gateway she had always used when she was stopped by a policeman and told to go and use a *Blankes* gateway. To carry out this surly command she had to pass a whole queue of Africans. She was not being protected from the black masses but actually thrust among them for the sake of racial purity.

(7 August 1959) ... when the Nats get down to putting their Bantustans into action that they will find that the average taxpayers will object to spending all their money in that way. But probably the damage will have been done because the leaders of the Africans who are now willing to be moderate will have been imprisoned and the extremists will be in control.

The National Party [NP] appear not only to be funked of the mass of Africans but also of the English. The whole position of English and things English grows weaker. When the mission schools were appropriated by the government (1953) in every case an Afrikaner principal was put in and the whole of the teaching profession is markedly Afrikaner. They are trying to build up a position of complete Afrikaner isolation and domination. They dislike the Dutch if anything more than the English (as the Hollanders are more liberal than the reactionary English.) An English engineer was telling me that he has to spend most of every discussion arbitrating between his Dutch and his Afrikaner foremen. My tendency to use 'Dutch' rather than 'Afrikaner' has had to be countered. In Afrikaans a longer Germanic word is *de rigueur*. Initially you had to hail a 'hirecarriage'. Now they have finally agreed that 'taxi' is an international word.

Black Blood may be your birthright

(14 August 1959) *Drum*, the campaigning illustrated weekly for Africans, is edited by Tom Hopkinson in Johannesburg. When editor of *Picture Post*

in London he was sacked by the owner Hulton for insisting on printing South Korean war atrocity pictures. Great amusement has been caused in English circles by the *Drum* article which points out how few of the old Dutch families can have escaped Non-White blood. There is a large round diagram which shows how in eight generations a person has 128 forbears and that, as there were so few Dutch women, a lot of the children of the *volk* are not all that 'pure'. The apartness attitude is so pathetic. Self-imposed guilt about natural historic mixing. Everybody is so Anti-Nat that I am beginning to look forward to the day when I meet a Nat. [I took the OUP offer and turned down the offer of a job on two Hulton Journals in Fleet Street called *The Studio* and *Art & Industry*.]

Joy and delight with the Millars
(7 August 1959) The more I learn of the Millars the luckier I seem to be. Anthony Millar was a journalist, first in Southampton and then freelance and is rather ashamed of being in 'big business' as Advertising Manager at BP (the joke is that it has been spread that 'BP' stands for 'Boere Petrolie' rather than 'British Petroleum').

He is extremely interested in South African History and is writing a biography of Lord Charles Somerset, the Slachters Nek governor, trying to clear his name a little from the Boer and radical besmirching. Pringle, 1820 Settlers, the *South African Advertiser*, Raglan and so on all very much his interest and he told me all about it the other evening. He keeps muttering that the book is secret and the Joy Millar says cheerfully that it did not seem to have been very secret [when they lived] at Stellenbosch where people would call across the street 'How's Lord Somerset?'

Joy Millar also writes. She paints and draws very ably. I have one or two of her pictures in my flat. On the stoep and the little courtyard there are pen and ink drawings (Dry enough to keep them outside). Some of the Arabs looked familiar. Marrakesh in 1938. She and another girl had hitchhiked through Maroc and Alger. Two boys 11 and 14. I have not had to ask for anything. No wastepaper basket but Anthony Millar brought one in. I like him enormously; quietly witty. I think that Marquard finds Joy a bit of a strain. They were neighbours in Stellenbosch. I told him about where I was going to live and he told me not to get into a position where I said that I would accept their books, which rather amused me.

I am entertained by being called 'Massah' by the coloured 'boy'... Apparently some of the coloureds use 'Sieur' (cf. Monsieur).

(22 September 1959) Joy Millar took me to lunch at this fabulous place [at Stellenbosch] opened this fortnight. New hotel in a wine farm called

Lanzerac being started by a young man with superb taste. I have never seen a place like it. All stables, brandy distilleries turned into individually designed bedrooms. Old furniture bought at sales and done up. 'Georgian' windows bought from pulled down Victorian rectory. Owner showed us round personally after excellent lunch. Joy Millar took a look at the menu and said 'Let's have everything!' So we did including two entrées and two main courses and five types of pud. Wine, liqueur.

Random shots from the Cannon
(14 August 1959) This week has been chiefly marked by the return of Cannon, the Trade Manager. The whole feeling in the office has changed. The editorial end is amused, the trade end have had to buckle to. He is a great yeller as befits a South African sergeant. Apparently he enlisted as a private and refused a commission. 'Go on, run' echoes down the office at 'the coloured boys'. David P. was in fits of laughter in his office while Cannon was telephoning him on the internal phone because Cannon's voice ordering a boy to get him tea was louder coming in through the door than over the telephone. He looks sadly unhealthy. Apparently atrociously ill while prisoner of war and walked with sticks for some years. He drops off to sleep while dictating and he has a terribly red face. He tends to look through narrowed eyes when he is making, with heavy emphasis, a remark of crashing conventionality. Still he is willing to be kindly to me.

The Progressives go in to bat in Parliament
(22 August 1959) A weekend of gales followed by a week of sun and warmth making everything pleasant and easy. News of riots and of over 1,200 arrests in faraway Natal seems no nearer than such news seemed in England. There is some hope that the United Party crisis which has come to a head this week will mean a bit of a thaw in the frozen politics of South Africa. It may mean that the Nationalists can gain seats; on the other hand it does mean that more people are swinging round a bit from the idea that the only hope is to sit on the Africans.

Clive van Ryneveld has so far resigned, realigned, and resigned. He got elected because of his cricket and sporting popularity and, although a barrister, is more often swung by other people's arguments. For the next fortnight he is helping Marquard rewrite his book on *The Peoples and Policies of South Africa* and his re-resignation came after he paid Marquard a visit on Wednesday to discuss the book.

Cartoon in *Cape Times* of the scoreboard of the United Party disuniting:

Latest Score: Nats 102
>   United Party 42 for 11
>   (i.e. no. people who have so far resigned)
Last batsman: v. Ryneveld; bowled v. Ryneveld; caught v. Ryneveld 0

(22 August 1959) The famous Miss Williams is very funny about the Liberals. Alan Paton, author of the renowned novel *Cry, the Beloved Country*, is writing a biography of *J.F. Hofmeyr* for the OUP. At one time he was staying in Cape Town and making use of the office facilities. Gideon ran several messages for him and one day had seven pence change to return. Out came Paton's purse and away went the seven pence and not so much as a thank you, let alone letting Gideon keep the change. David Philip said that Gideon is still only in the firm because of Miss Williams. Each year he breaks out at least once and comes back stupidly drunk. The time before last Marquard said that he would have to go if it happened again. Miss W, the only teetotaller in the office, insisted that that would probably be to cast him off so that he would fritter away all his savings which she puts away for him each week. (Apparently he pays a pound a month for a room).

Brecht's Caucasian Chalk Circle in rehearsal
(24 July 1959) Little Theatre. Engelen of Belgian National Theatre is producer. Public audition on Thursday. I wanted to see Bert Brecht coming to life. So went along. Am now apparently cast as a soldier. Thought I might meet interesting people (University of Cape Town Little Theatre is in central Cape Town at the end of the Company Gardens within walking distance from where I now live.)

(7 August 1959) I am very glad that almost on the spur of the moment that I decided to accept my minor part in *The Caucasian Chalk Circle* because the producer is so brilliant. He knows exactly what he wants and he works until he gets a beginning. Before we ever got on stage he made sure that we understood every line of our parts. Now we are on the stage he is making sure that we know every movement before we try to learn our parts. He produces from among us, doing the more difficult things in front of you. He knows how to keep everything moving and the whole production should be highly dynamic in spite of the fact that it is amateurs who are performing. And there is one hell of a lot of moving. Except for eight lines of song in the second act I have nothing to say at all and yet I am occupied up to my hilt acting as a foil to a Corporal who is engaged in a jokey monologue at my

expense. When in later acts I am speaking there is just as much moving. The Little Theatre, in the absence of anything but spasmodic outside professional theatre, seems very much involved in CT life. Everybody knows what is going on and who is who.

Taking over from David Philip
(14 August 1959) A busy week before I take over from David Philip ... I'm now beginning to forget exactly how long it is since I came out. I realise it is just about a month. Everybody seems to be staggered by the amount of things that I have got involved with immediately...at a party, three people who were involved in Cape plays said they hadn't dared to try for the Brecht at the Little Theatre. So that is what comes of being ignorant of local reputations. Anyhow it suits me to do lots of things to find my way around.

(22 August 1959) No bad crisis has arisen since David Philip went up to Rhodesia with ten of these English course books on the move at once there is constant coming and going and the printers are working until ten at night to get these pretty large orders of 85,000 books printed and away. With 200 illustrations concerned things are continually tricky but Miss Williams knows the set up and I learn by helping. Alec Wright, the author of the course for Bantu schools is her brother-in-law and was at Kingswood in Bath.

(30 August 1959) It really has rained in a full scale manner for the first time since I arrived. The last two days have seen torrents sweeping grey across the woods at the foot of Table Mountain, and coloured people are gnome-like under sacks.

Comparing Cape Town and London
(30 August 1959) *The Observer* and the weekly *Times* would be terrific. I give the daily *Times* on airmail paper to the Millars who give me the London *Sunday Times* and *The Spectator*. I read quite a lot when I am waiting to go on in the six weeks of rehearsals of *The Caucasian Chalk Circle*. There are some interesting Cape Town students and past students involved and a great deal of informative conversation goes on with few holds barred about such topics as to whether the culture of the Afrikaner is too 'dedicated'. It may be that Cape Town is totally removed from the rest of the country but I am amazed by the lack of the feeling of bursting youth and vitality one expects from a new country. It may be that England's prosperity is particularly remarkable at the present moment and that trade and industry are a bit cramped here but there is little of that virility as one would expect to find in Australia....

The buildings are so out of touch with the best in modern building. The most mediocre buildings in London are a joy in comparison and the worst are at least full-blooded in their offensiveness. Here they are for the most part boxes. And for the Union fifty-year celebration in 1960 they are setting up a fountain which looks as though it was left in the thirties.

(9 November 1959) Thank you very much for the *Times* weekly. It started today. It even keeps me up with the OUP in England; Helen Gardner being made first woman Delegate [i.e. Director] to the illustrious Oxford University Press (the fact that she is first at this late date is incredible).

'Rare theatrical treat'
(30 August 1959) On Friday we have had the first dress rehearsal of the *Caucasian Chalk Circle* and our first audience – a coloured group which puts on shows in Cape Town. They seemed to find it funny at any rate and the corporal and I were the first actors to be individually clapped. [I did not realise it as a newcomer but as 'coloureds' they would not legally have been able to attend public performances.]

(5 September 1959) *The Caucasian Chalk Circle* is the biggest success they have had for a long time at the Little Theatre. *Cape Times*: 'Brilliant Production of Brecht Play … rare theatrical treat'. *Cape Argus* 'It is difficult to stem a rush of superlatives….This production simply must be seen'. *Die Burger* said that the Corporal and Soldier, who had a clowning scene together were unintentionally funny, which amuses us because of all the hard work which we have put in. [The Flemish Director had knowingly cast a very Afrikaner Corporal bullying a very English soldier. When the girl escapes across the canyon the Corporal shouts at his soldier 'Somebody's going to have pay for this, blockhead!' At yesterday's matinee the Corporal forgot to come on, and I got my own back, to the delighted relief of the cast in the wings, by running both our parts together and shouting in my very English accent 'Somebody's going to have to pay for this, blockhead!' Anyhow the audiences … have laughed at us each night.]

(5 September 1959) The Millars were going last night with friends who are lecturers at Stellenbosch University. They invited me to drinks and dinner before which was very kind. …Have just been told by the Millars that the Stellenbosch friends were so impressed by the play that they stayed until 1.15 a.m. discussing the play.

(11 September 1959) End of *Caucasian Chalk Circle* at University's Little Theatre. Duminy, Principal of UCT, gave vote of thanks as it was longest run ever at the theatre with highest percentage of seats sold. Cast party in

open at Sea Point went cheerfully and I gave rendering of Andrew's Bertie Rogers leprechaun story which seemed to kill people by its length and lack of point.

Meeting Randolph Vigne
[I went round to meet Randolph Vigne in my first week as he had been in correspondence with R.N. Currey about the rights in his poems for an anthology of South African verse.]

(24 July 1959) Consultations with Randolph Vigne at Maskew Miller only last week about ganging up to get local printers to put in Albertus type. [A robust design often used on Faber jackets and binding which seems to us suitable for books with African themes.]

(5 September 1959) Having drinks at the Millars … was Randolph Vigne of Maskew Miller. I liked him very much. Did you know that he was at Wadham? Naturally we had great discussions of Bowra 'dear boy'. Vigne was one of Bamborough's first pupils. He has invited me to go round for dinner this evening..

English novels and Australian poets on the shelves
(30 August 1959) I seem already to have already managed to establish some slight reputation in the OUP office for knowing how to make OUP systems work and where to find books. I seem to be the only person except for Cannon who knows how to use the stock-keeper's strip list. Cannon has found that I know already where books are in the showroom. This could become a nuisance but helps to justify me in his eyes. Really this is purely as a result of being deeply interested in the books themselves. Cannon is interested in them as merchandise. As, when for instance, the invoice typist asks 'Do you know Wright's *Generations of Man*? Not in catalogue, not in stock-keepers' strip!' It strikes some bell. Australian women poet! Then I think recent *Sunday Times* review by Cyril Connolly. I had looked for it on the shelves in showroom a day or two before because it had set me thinking that I would be interested to know about contemporary Australian poets and how they handled a new country in comparison with the South Africans. An office copy had come in from OUP Australia hoping for an order. Also I have been tidying up the shelves in the showroom. We have the most interesting collection of serious work in contemporary English. We are agents for several leading American university presses as well as for Jonathan Cape, John Murray and Hamish Hamilton.

Belongings arrive on The City of Durban
(30 August 1959) I swore that I was never going to buy another second-hand gramophone. Then I came across a HiFi Philips which had belonged to the French Consul. He bought it only a year ago but decided he wanted a stereophonic job….It is in a wooden box which helps with the tone and it certainly sounds magnificent with Mozart. I have had my gramophone this week; it is so good and I think that this time I got a bargain that works.... The Cape Town Library has a very good selection of records [what are now called 'vinyls'] which are in very much better condition than those belonging to Colchester Public Library. Different procedure which I think helps. Everybody has to put down a ten shilling deposit for every record… dealers have to check/replace needles every three months.

(5 September 1959) My belongings arrived on the *City of Durban* at 2 p.m. on Thursday; I saw the boat come in. However I will not get them until next week as they have to be cleared. It was strange to look through the criss-cross of cranes and think that buried in that Dinky toy over there is my typewriter and John Graham's picture of the trees at the bottom of Beverley Road [still at the Mill].

(8 September 1959) Just back from week-end at Hermanus. I feel as though at last I have moved in for last week-end I unpacked my trunk and during the last week I settled in my stuff. A huge packing case from the OUP warehouse at Neasden contained both my tin trunk and the Capt. R.N. Currey leather suitcase from India, but it was too big to go in the cellar in front of the house beneath the stoep [The leather suitcase was to feature in *The Great Escape*]. So I have covered the packing case with the Marrakesh blanket and my new HiFi booms resonantly from on top. Every bit of crockery intact. John Graham picture frame is slightly jolted. Trouble to find wall space. Wonderful to have it with its glow of May and laburnum in England. Joy Millar likes it very much.

Chosen People
(11 September 1959) Got on very well with Randolph Vigne who had your book of poetry *Tiresias* on his shelves. Married to Gillian a highly individual army daughter. By the way *Tiresias* and *Formal Spring* are being suggested for an exhibition of Books South African to be held in 1960 at Pretoria during the Union celebrations … Marquard is back … very easy to get on with and seems willing to give credit where credit is decently due. When I suggested Denys Reitz's *Commando* for World's Classics his note to London went: 'James Currey has made the suggestion which I heartily endorse…'

I put the idea to him that somebody should do a collection of interesting chunks out of documents connected with South African history. He and his wife Nell have been reading 'Chosen People' in your 'Early Mythology' with great enjoyment. He says that history lessons are if anything worse now: '*Mrs van Rensburg, in her short square person, Relived the myths of her dour nation*' (R.N. Currey, , p. 12)

Baaskap in the Dry Cleaners
(3 October 1959) I went to see the film of *The Ten Commandments* for interest's sake. It was gloriously unimaginative. The platteland Afrikaners have been making great automobile treks to see it. I suppose they identify themselves and the Great Trek with the Milk and Honey seeking Israelites. Two things never seem to occur to them; that the Israelites were the forbears of the Jews of Jew-burg and that it is possible for the *nie blankes* to draw completely different conclusions.

Baaskap [boss-ship] in the dry cleaners this morning. Afrikaans woman, with English as thick as her forearm, tells black fellow to wait for white people to be dealt with because she has 'not got time to find his things'. She then finds time to find the things for two white people. She doses me with molasses and raises her voice at him.

The Post Office, a monument to pomposity, divides racially into two in the semi-darkness. However the public library is not segregated; you see the thick lips of an African move painfully round words and then he quickly glances at his watch to see how near to the end of his lunch hour it is; the rest of the people at the table are white. Another hunch-backed African hands back a book published by McGraw-Hill called *The Psychology of Power Politics*.

In Sophiatown Jo'burg, people came back not long ago to find their houses down and their belongings in the street. The Transvaal-dominated government do their best to wake up Cape Town from its laissez-faire attitude and to get them to bring in apartheid everywhere. [Group Areas are being imposed to clear pockets of blacks in areas desired by whites]. Now 200 people at the smart seaside suburb of Sea Point have been told they must go. One woman has lived there for eighty years. Some families have been there for three generations. But this being Cape Town there is some hope that a way will be found out of it or of postponing the move. Ironically Sea Point has many Jewish families.

Did you know that in 1957 there more murders every day in South Africa than there were for the whole year in New Zealand? Daily average 5 in SA, 4 proven for whole year in NZ.

SuperMac and the end of Empire

(11 October 1959) Naturally there is rejoicing in white South Africa at the British election result. What they are able to forget at such a moment however is that Macmillan, Macleod and the Conservatives will carry out the same policy in Africa as the Labour Party would have done. They will of course be somewhat more tactful but in the end there will be black independence. [Iain Macleod was appointed Secretary of State for the Colonies on 5 October 1959 and speeded up the independence of six African colonies.]

David Philip, James Currey & Typography

(3 October 1959) Work at the office is becoming more and more my own and not merely carrying out what had already been started by David Philip. He educated himself typographically to a great extent and started in Cape Town with much less knowledge of the job than I have now. On Friday some proofs of a revised edition a school book came back. Marquard said 'Have a look at them.' Two things apparently impressed him. Firstly, I had worked out every letter and space of the lay-out was so that the printer would know exactly what I want from my drawing of the title page; everything of the little I gained at the Central School of Art and Design at St Martin's in London was put into producing a layout that looked impressive as long as you are no expert. [OUP did not send me to night school and I had to pay my own fees – a good personal investment.] David's system seemed to be more that of giving an approximate specification to the printer and then adjusting the proof. Either system works but mine looks a bit more impressive. Also I managed to do it with great speed as it was one of those happy occasions when the algebraic problem fell apart in my head.

Housing people cheaply

(11 October 1959) An interesting week here in other ways. I have been looking at a fascinating ms by an architect at Durban ... on experiments at the University of Natal into that old friend, the ideal proportion. He wants to work out a system of housing people cheaply and not with flattening deadly boredom of identical units. He says that the building trade ought to get itself modernised and rationalised so that you can build houses out of the same basic units. He and his researchers have planned a triangular house.

Cape Town 'Day in the Life of ...'

(17 October 1959) You led me to believe you wanted to hear some time what is my typical sort of day:

7.55. Alarm goes. Turn over until 8.10 when I get up knowing that I had made a resolution to get up at 8.00. Rush through shaving to try and leave by 8.30. As I open up yesterday's razor cuts the accompaniment to strokes is: Vivaldi, Brahms or Albinoni, not to mention Bach and others. 8.40. Leave flat, am just about to plunge down hill past Houseboy Nelson 'Goomorning Massah' but talk too long to Joy Millar. 8.45. Breakfast at guest house run by Swiss wife of manager of Mount Nelson. Corn flakes crunching down as I hear coloured waitress ask through hatch for 'Ein brekfast; ein swart the' for me. Most people have eaten as most offices start at half-past eight. 8.50. Just catch trolley bus, having bought *Cape Times* for a tickey from storekeeper in a red fez who hands out change too slowly. I may have noticed that there is a mist over the bay, and that wisps of cloud mixed with the sunlight hooked on Table Mountain behind mean a NorthEaster or some other wind is likely. The conductor, a soft-faced thug of an Afrikaner, appears to satisfy himself that the passengers are a. born morons. b. wrong. As the bus goes to the depot too many people are still on board when it reaches the Foreshore and everybody is accused by the conductor of not being able to read the destination boards.

Approx. 9.00. The office is airy as Gideon Zulu has opened the windows and put down the Venetian blinds. I go in with 'Good Morning' to Miss Williams who is saying that something else has gone wrong with the latest English course book. Marquard arrives and I put my head round his door to exchange the good morning which is sunny. On the building opposite on the other side of the street the Africans are running dangerously around the bouncing scaffolding ten floors up with barrows of concrete. I go through the previous day's mail and files, then make a list of things to be done from the previous day's list. About 10.00 Marquard on the intercom says 'Will you come here, James?' We discuss things in progress, new jobs that have arrived by post. 10.15. Tea arrives brought by coloured boy William 17, Standard VIII elementary but hardly reads now except newspaper. Separate pot. No milk. On separate tray. Usually get down to biggest or most urgent job. Miss Williams worries about something and I make a soothing remark. Jock Barbour from Trade Department drops in with broad Scottish grin. Production jobs. Advertising jobs. Reading mss. Writing reports. Phoning printer or blockmaker. Talking to printer who has called in with latest batch of proofs. Choose colours for jackets with Miss Williams. Somebody arrives to see Marquard. 'Do I know him?' he says to Miss Williams suspiciously. Miss W. asks for more credentials. When the man enters M's office it is all Christian names.

12.00. Midday gun booms at the Observatory and the sirens on all the building sites wail for lunch break; the Africans with pipes in their mouths, the European workmen in their white overalls and the overseeing engineers in their shorts knock off. About 12.50 look to see if Jock the traveller is there, or drop in at Longmans, also on the top of Thibault House, to see if Godsen, Oxford graduate ex-German, is there. Off to lunch at one of about five places. Some remark to Benny the coloured liftman necessary and most people thank him. Cafeteria in same building ten floors down good for pickled fish. Curry great standby. Kabeljauw fish on Fridays. Inferior bobuti. Chicken Inn threepence more all round, but excellent oiled salads speckled with pepper. Harlequin; canneloni or pizza done quite well. Wonderful meringues (Afrikaans *spoekspoor* translates as 'ghost's footprint'.) Good coffee. Toreador cafe is up among all the car dealers. Slightly dowdy but cheap things that are usually expensive: Wiener Schnitzel for 3/6. Slight shopping afterwards. OK Bazaars for anything mass-produced; cross between Woolworths and M&S. Stuttafords with lots of escalators. Or changing books or records at the Library. Streets crowded with people but few cars as everything is compact. Nice furniture and glass shops. Lots of bookshops. Africans and coloureds here and there in all the big stores, even Stuttafords. Less often in smaller shops. Veiled muslim women in OK Bazaars but not many elsewhere in the centre.

Approx. 2.00 back to work and jacket off. Tea 3.10. Same as morning occupations. At about 4.30 take in letters I have written and Miss Williams has typed for Marquard to sign. 5.00 Official knocking off time. Typist Yvonne and Marquard depart. I go between 5.10 and 5.25 usually depending upon on the state of things I am doing. Miss Williams departs 5.45. Cannon at any time up to 7.00. Jock Barbour makes a point of working to 6.00.

A Car of Palest Blue
(22 September 1959) I will probably be the possessor of a car by the time week is out. Or at least OUP will buy it and I will buy back at £20 per month. Hillman Minx and it is, guess what colour? pale blue and fawn. Two years old.

(28 September 1959) I get my car tomorrow. Fixing up all the paperwork today for insurance, AA etc.. It really looks very blue and grand. I hope that it is the right buy. I started off by thinking of the smaller ones, Fiats, Morris Minors and so on but this being slightly bigger and faster and as easy on the petrol so I thought the extra would be worthwhile if I am going to use it on some long trips to relations. [Its six seats were to prove valuable for Liberal Party work and food deliveries to starving families on the Cape Flats. It was to survive the broken roads of Basutoland. Hillmans were still running as

the standard taxi in Khartoum in 1980.]

(3 October 1959) Something of an occasion this week; my car handed over on Tuesday. I have a car and still await a driving test. Since then I have put in much rolling around and stopping and starting on these toboggan-run roads at the foot of the mountain. One is suddenly overwhelmed at the number of things that can go wrong. Today I ran out of petrol; this merely turned out to be a useful warning as I was up at the Millar's house and though the nearest petrol pump is between half and three-quarters of a mile away it is all downhill so we free-wheeled there in amused silence.

Gaily spinning along at thirty
(14 August 1959) ... I have found my first three driving lessons extremely entertaining and enjoyed them no end. I was astonished how fast one set off for the first time and was gaily spinning along at thirty. And the teacher is very kindly, a great ego booster and says that I am taking to it quite naturally. On the second time out we went out along the coast and down a very winding coast road with a great wall of storm rolling from across the Atlantic.

(17 October 1959) Passed my driving test this week. Jock Barbour gave me my last lesson the evening before and he realised that I had never reversed into a parking between cars on the side of the street, even during paid lessons. Fortunately, I could slip in with ease and it was indeed tested the next day. People kept making remarks about how difficult they hear the test is nowadays in Cape Town. This usually means that they were tested up-country by the local policeman whose sole job seems to be to state 'You don't suffer from epilepsy, man!' Test was really rather slack and I should think that the accident rate is to a great degree tied up with it. The examiner had just come back from 6 weeks in London and Paris. 'There's lots of employment in London'. He insisted that I had to walk into City Hall because I could not drive on my own without a co-driver until I had paid for a Driver's License. I had driven there that morning on my own and parked the car. [I had, as the test got nearer, in fact done a lot of practice without a co-driver as that was allowed in England at the time.]

Henry Currey private secretary to Rhodes
(22 August 1959) I went to have dinner last night with the Curreys with whom the driving instructor put me in touch as Mrs Currey and I shared the same spelling of the Currey surname. Charles Currey is senior physics master at Bishops School in Rondesbosch (where David Philip went). His

grandfather Henry Currey was private secretary to Rhodes. His father Ronald Currey was renowned headmaster of St Andrew's Grahamstown (where Randolph Vigne went) and who, slightly annoyingly, gets credited with the poetry of R.N. Currey. Yes, we are no relations!

Currey Curries
[Tom Kime had been in R.N. Currey's English Department at Cochester Royal Grammar School.] Dinner with Tom Kime and wife and impeccably English Australian (Geelong G.S. and Trinity Coll. Oxon at same time as me.) Personal ADC to Archbishop Joost de Blank for eighteen months before going back to join father's stockbroking firm. Tom Kime's wife said 'I have learned all I know about currys from Stella Martin Currey's book *One Woman's Year*.' We did not see the pun at the time. The curry she made was, sadly, not of the best.

South Africa House in Trafalgar Square and the League of Nations
(24 October 1959) [Kitty Black, South African and translator of the leading French postwar playwrights, was Stella Martin Currey's play agent at Curtis Brown and she gave James a generous number of introductions, one of which was to Charles te Water who was SA High Commissioner in London from 1929 to 1939. Amazingly from 1933 to 1934 he was also President of the League of Nations in Geneva, that is the forerunner of the United Nations.]

I visited Kitty Black's friend Charles te Water. I went last Sunday morning which seems to be their time of open house and quite a lot of people breezed in and out. I found him absolutely charming and friendly. He seemed to be glad to take me round his collection of paintings by South African artists after I showed a particular interest in one by Pierneef of a Jeraboam tree on the veld. He said that the artist had painted it from memory when in a nostalgic mood and the painting has come out as a very powerful study of homesickness. I have never seen a painting quite like it. The paintings were of one style and one period but there are several extremely good ones. [In the thirties te Water had built South Africa House on Trafalgar Square in the prime position at right angles to the National Gallery and alongside St Martins in the Fields. He set out to represent the best South African artists of that period. There is even a room which has a fresco of Zulu life round all four walls. The building and collection is now protected by English Heritage as a classic of the period.)

His son is an architect and built their house which overlooks the sea at St James's ... It is stylised modern but with a strong touch of the South African about it which is pleasant to see. His daughter is a sculptor and is about to have an exhibition in Cape Town. One of the people there was his brother-in-law who is head of the Old Mutual Insurance which is the second biggest in the world. Aunt Iris says that te Water is 'a blooming old Nat' because in 1939 he resigned as High Commissioner in London 'so that he could come back to South Africa and get ready to side with the Germans'. Te Water made jokes to me at the expense of the '*Die wonder van Afrikaans*' year the government are running. It is a real chance to be able to meet these people. Apparently he collected quite a lot of prize wines and then got gout. I said to him 'Oh what a pity!' 'It's not a pity, it's a tragedy!' He says that on Sunday mornings I am just to breeze in as his friends do and that lots of people go swimming.

Patrick Duncan fights Sea Point
(24 October 1959) I am surprised to hear of the interest in England about the provincial elections which have generally proved pretty inconclusive. I went to a meeting held by Patrick Duncan who was contesting Sea Point for the Liberals against the United Party. He is renowned as the son of the Governor-General and a leader in the Defiance Campaign of 1953. He is undoubtedly a most sincere man… On the platform with him was the most able politician I have heard in action, Senator Rubin, a Liberal Native Representative in the Senate.

Rustica Press in a Wynberg back-garden
(3 November 1959) Among many things that have happened in a busy ten days, I went to visit our printers at Wynberg. They rejoice in the name of Rustica and they indeed are rather rustic. A Dutch Professor called Elfers was compiling an English-Afrikaans/High Dutch dictionary for the bookshop Jutas. His family set it up and printed it in the back garden and from this began Rustica Press. The original house is still almost in the works. Amid the tree-lined lanes of Wynberg they do some of the best printing in South Africa and have our prestige letterpress and most ticklish jobs. One can leave a lot of the proof checking to Rustica who, unusually for a printer, have an Editor. It is amazing how Rustica get along. They have imported as Managing Director a very capable charming Englishman with a double-barrelled name, Ralph Sancroft-Baker, who is something of a Rotarian. I was taken to lunch at Baker's home which they have built in the corner of a vineyard. This is only about five six or so on miles from centre of Cape Town. In his front hall he has a picture of a forbear who was Master of the Norfolk hunt about 1832.

Our other printers Standard Press are a complete contrast. They are useful for big jobs quickly. Stan Violett, the Managing Director, was an apprentice on the *Cape Times* and has worked himself up. He is very cheery and pretty crude and very likeable. It was started by Randolph Vigne's Maskew Miller. The original Maskew Miller took one look at his sons and decided that they could not run the business, so appointed other directors and left his sons on the editorial board to draw their pay, keep out of the way and fish for trout at Somerset West.

A bicycle-powered press, the Nazis & John Donne
(3 November 1959) A.A. Balkema is a Publisher but started as one of Holland's classic printers. His typographical style is impeccable. He worked for Joh. Enschede en Zonen in Holland who are one of the old established Dutch firms and then set up on his own. He was in contact with all the great Dutch typographers and uses to this day Van Dyke and Lutetia, which were cut by the renowned van Krimpen.

When the Netherlands were invaded he was licensed by the Germans to print official forms and papers and he got permission to use two assistants who worked on the ground floor. Hidden in the cellar he ran what he and his wife called the 'Bicycle Press'. Mrs Balkema, who was inclined to put on weight, used to have a static exercise bike in the front room. When the Germans came to the press they found her pedalling away for exercise. She was actually generating electric power for the secret press in the cellar. There he secretly typeset works like Stanley Morrison's lectures on typography and the selected poems of John Donne in English. He then printed tiny editions on the very best paper of which he had secret stores hidden from before the war. He said that it was done purely for the sake of morale. [After I had known him for a while I managed to persuade him reluctantly to sell me a copy of the John Donne. I consider it my most valuable book.]

He continues as a wonderfully impractical businessman. His books are mostly in English, printed in Holland, look superb and are cheerfully amateurishly edited. Baker says that they got him to place a book with Rustica and then regretted it. He would go out to the press and spend a whole afternoon getting pulls of all his ideas and then scrapping them or altering them. He worked on the typesetters stone even altering his letter spacing by inserting paper between the pieces of type. Meanwhile his business wanders along. It took OUP eight years to get payment for some books that Marquard gave him on credit to help him start up his showroom deep in a basement in Victoria Street by the Company Gardens. Marquard was responsible for managing to get the Union government to allow him and his considerable family to settle in South Africa. Marquard says I must simply wander in and say I am from OUP.

Balkema published Tony Delius's first book of poems and some books by Guy Butler. He has also published a translation of a children's story about a Huguenot family by Joy Millar/Collier. Do you know Miller and Sergeant's *Critical Survey of English South African Poetry*? It has four pages on your work and is greatly concerned with your exile themes. It compares your political disassociation with the often 'naive' political associations of Auden, Spender, Day Lewis. Have you got a copy? I cannot remember it but surely you must know about it as it mentions and quotes 'Between Two Worlds' as your most ambitious work.

(28 November 1959) ... met Balkema who (importance of importance) offered to help me with any styling and to criticize my work. This ought to be a great opportunity as his work is so good of its kind. He is a funny little man riddled with smiling. He said that would like to have the Millar's house more than practically any house in Cape Town. He asked me my impressions of Cape Town and I said that I thought it was a civilised place. He said nothing so I asked him if he thought not. He said 'Only once you have seen Pretoria and Port Elizabeth.'

Crayfish & confidences
(15 November 1959) Tour of inspection by David Neale, Head of OUP Overseas Education in London who is my London boss. He had started in Uganda, Tanganyika, Kenya, Rhodesias and is finishing in Cape Town. 'Day of reckoning' feeling among people in the office. He stays till Friday when he returns to London. He was originally expected to be only spending the two days but he decided that there was too much to deal with. He took me out to a very good lunch today (Crayfish curry) and we talked extensively about Africa. In some ways he seemed to find me something of an old pal for, at any rate, he knows me better than he does anybody else here; and I think that he is finding it touchy not treading on toes, both editorial and trade. I saw more of him in four days in Cape Town than in four months in London.

Try for White
(15 November 1959) I went to see a homegrown play last week called *Try for White* which is about what it says, a coloured person of mixed race who looks European enough to try to pass for white. She marries a white man during the war, has a son and is then left by him when he discovers that she is coloured by half. Then she becomes the mistress of a Cape Town bus

conductor who is in every way her inferior and for eleven years she passes for white. One of her girlhood friends, who has tried for white with less success, tells the bus conductor her secret. In public on the bus he screams at the 'kaffirs' that she is 'coloured' and he is outraged lest 'the boys', the Africans, should laugh at him for being taken in. It seems to be entirely accepted that a play should be in contemporary terms and that no details should be spared – it gives me a view of the absurdities of what goes on all around one.

Painful additions at Night School
(15 November 1959) I did my first evening class teaching at Randolph Vigne's night school in District 6. I was put in charge of the elementary, very elementary, arithmetic class which had two people that night. There was a coloured girl, rather Malay, who got everything right, which was more than I did in checking her work; she spoke very quietly and then rubbed out my rough workings in her margin. The other one was a twenty-year old African, well dressed, who made mistakes in three out of four addition sums and which I got him painfully to add up again. He seemed very grateful. The year is almost finished, and I am just looking around so that I can start next term. The Southeaster buffeted through the broken panes of the windows of the School, which is an Afrikaans-medium Coloured school by day. It was gloomy but not too badly equipped. Randolph took me on to Cape Town's only multi-racial coffee bar run by an Indian and called the 'Naaz'. R. says that he heard it rumoured that the boss's brother is friendly with the secret police and so that it is not closed down.

Cape Dutch Architecture
(21 November 1959) Went to interesting meeting last night in the Supreme Court (in itself one of the gems of architecture of Cape Town). This was the fourth talk in a 'symposium' on restoration of old buildings and town planning. This one was given by a Pretoria architect who had been in charge of the reconstruction of the town of Graaf Reinet in the Eastern Cape (where incidentally Charles te Water came from). This man is a perfectionist all right and his description of the absolute detail of construction fascinating. One would feel it all a bit ingrown if it was not for the fact that he is a more than competent modern architect. The occasion was fascinating for the fact that the whole Cape architectural fraternity was there looking tweedy and very handsome. The Professor of Architecture stood there with his cheeks full of wine and a cheroot stuck somewhere in the middle of his talking.

Meet, the beloved Paton

(28 November 1959) Thing that comes to mind first because it happened most recently was meeting Alan Paton author of *Cry, the beloved country*. He came to discuss his biography of Hofmeyr with Marquard and was brought in to me with his wife. It is interesting to meet someone who is so revered, so notorious, so scorned. So many people have said so many things. For some reason I had thought him younger than fifties. He looked like a schoolmaster edition of Bowra. I can well believe that he has a somewhat prophet-like opinion of himself. Schoolmastery glasses with a tendency to slip off the end of nose.

Drum Beat

(28 November 1959) Interesting evening arguing with various left-wingers – white, coloured, black – at Peter Rodda's flat. There was this rather sinister Africanist Mahomo who argued by attacking your arguments as generalisations then got round to terrible generalisations himself and muttering, from behind his thick horn-rimmed glasses and from within his smart cavalry twill suit, that bloodshed must come. The Pan-Africanists are a strictly African only racial organisation and they will admit no white men because so many African organisations have come under the 'compromising' dominance of a white man.

Also there was Joe Louw the photographer from *Golden City Post* and *Drum* who had got bundled into a police Saracen armoured car outside the Paarl Riot Enquiry. 'I had taken one picture only and they told me to open the camera. I said I didn't know how. "Break it open, man" said the policeman. I said that it was insured. "Better leave it!".' 'Did they beat you up?' 'No they wouldn't. They banged me across the head with a truncheon but that was all. I was just wanting them to get on with it for the news story. Then they searched me and found a telegram WANT PAARL FULL STORY DRUM BEAT. The policeman thought that he had found a "secret" organisation and told the Colonel what he had found. They eventually took my story that I was a journalist.'

Contact across South Africa

(11 December 1959) Another example of the closeness of South Africa. I go out to dinner with a girl called Mary Kirwood whose father had been, before he died, Professor of English at Stellenbosch. It then turns out that Marquard would have become her guardian if her mother had died. Not all of this is all that strange because she has come from Pietermaritzburg to work during the vacation on *Contact* the Liberal paper. Yesterday Thursday

was one of those wildly busy days. I went round to the *Contact* offices to talk about the layout and how to improve it. Patrick Duncan the editor kept barging in a skittish manner while Randolph, Sally Morgan (who works in advertising) and myself were trying to solve typographical problems in between cartons of lunch brought up from the café below. Pat wanted us try his canned Chinese bean goulash.

Exit, pursued by a Christmas Tree
(21 December 1959) A happy Christmas to all of you I am sure that it will be very happy as all Timberscombe christmases are. It is all too strange. There is a misplaced feeling that summer holidays and Christmas are all rolled into one in spite of the snow in the shop windows and Santa Claus and his team of reindeer are plunging down the shaft between the seven stories of Stuttafords store.

The Day of the Covenant on Wednesday (Dingaan's Day) was muggy and drizzymizzy. I went with Mary Kirwood to visit the misplaced grandeur of the Rhodes acropolis monument with its statue of Energy by Watts up on the mountainside surrounded by roving quaggas and zebras. I could hardly get over the fact that I had never realised before, namely, that Rhodes died at 49.

We then went to visit a Dutch friend who lives in a hut on the edge of the woods at the bottom of the mountain near Newlands. He would not believe that we were not on the scrounge for a Christmas tree and insisted that we depart with one. Exit man looking like a Christmas tree. As we went down to the car a stand-by gang, in their huts passing the time waiting for forest fires and fallen trees, woke up to the fact that there seemed to be a tree moving along the road and started shouting and jeering and everybody was much amused.

In the evening Mary took me to visit a charming artist called Cecil Higgs who is quite well known in South Africa. She is one of the world's most gentle creatures and like somebody out of *Orlando the Marmalade Cat*. She lives surrounded by the most exotic shells and great sea-eaten froths of whale bone. There were psychiatrists there in mohair suits describing awful case histories in matter of fact voices.

A whirring scurler for mincing Chistmas fingers
(27 December 1959) I am at Hermanus where Ingie and Co are staying with Aunt Iris and Uncle Iver. I could not help feeling a bit miserable at the bottom as it all seemed a shadow of Christmas as it has always been. This is not to say that I have not enjoyed the swimming and the strawberries and

the sun. There is a feeling of intoxication by gadgetry led by the wretched Wally, Canadian husband of Ingie, who is quite content to run two cars on his salary as a prep school master at St Andrew's Grahamstown, which he starts in the New Year. They gave Aunt Iris a mixer, grinder, whirring scurler for mincing fingers and for making milk shakes for running up ones froth intake. Anyhow everybody spends their time looking at the thing and switching the time switches on and off. There is a general feeling that it is most useful for occupying everybody.

1960

New Year rattle of banjos rising from the town
(3 January 1960) Went to enormous party at the house of a chap called Brian Bunting who, before the Suppression of Communism Act, was a declared communist. The Congress of Democrats, though communist dominated, is not completely communist. [It is the Whites only part of the racially divided Congress Alliance which includes the African National Congress, the Coloured People's Congress and the Indian Congress.] Left wing Cape Town was there in force and the New Year was welcomed in with a fierce determined singing of African left songs such as The Red Flag in Xhosa and Follow Luthuli (the banned moderate chief who is head of the African National Congress). There was something so imperative about the singing. The burden of the males was given an exotic sword edge by the voices of the African women. Our group of people – Randolph and Gillian Vigne, Alby Sachs, Sally Morgan, Mary Kirwood, Joe Louw – drank in the New Year with a bottle of champagne given to me by our printers Standard Press. Randolph and I were frightfully amused by what the Manager of Standard Press would have thought of the circumstances in which his present was drunk. He is this most un-flower-like man Violet, who started as an apprentice on the *Cape Times* and has worked himself up. He is always 'Handing it out' to his coloured compositors and saying how good they are in a 'Do you know, you won't believe they can manage it?' tone of voice which really covers his true and right wing United Party heart.

There was a man doing magnificent shambling Kwela outside the window. Have you ever heard Kwela? It is the Johannesburg African dance sequence played on penny whistles. It is high pitched and monotonously exciting and as individual as HiLife in West Africa or Calypso in the West Indies.

By the time Sally Morgan and I took Joe Louw back to District 6 the place was alive in the dark and Hanover Street was crowded with the beginning of the 'coons'. This was about three o'clock in the morning. The banjos were rattling away. When I got back to Kensington Crescent I kept meeting coloured people coming down the hill from the Mountain. Enormous and effusive New Year greetings were exchanged. I woke up at about 7.00 on a superb still summer morning with the whole still silence of a holiday lying under the trees, but one could just hear the noise of banjos rising from the town.

Tweede Nuwe Jaar
Spent the morning with Joe Louw who was taking pictures of the carnival for *Drum* and *Golden City Post*. [The assassination of Martin Luther King on 4 April 1968 was at a motel in Memphis, Tennessee. The iconic picture of the three men on the balcony with arms raised pointing at the assassin was to be taken by our South African friend Joseph Louw.]

Strange troupes moving around and up and down Hanover Street were spectacular in a gory sort of way. This phenomenon Tweede Nuwe Jaar is so strange for the coloured people, who are so snobby about the Africans, copy the American negro with a golliwog effect. They go in for much white clown painting of the mouth in juicy circles. They wear these garish satins. Some of the troupes are large; two hundred or more. Others are a couple of dozen. Some of them dress as Red Indians and one subtle touch was the troupe led by devils, red from toe to their policeman's helmets with horns on. There was an effusive gaiety which was rather exciting. The trolley buses were loaded with people as they slipped along and people fell off. There were lots of children involved in these enormous feats of endurance. Whenever Joe tried to take pictures of the small ones adult coons would drone in determined to get into the photograph. Joe was continually begged to take photos. Each year they make completely new costumes. I tried hard not to feel nauseated but sadly I did in spite of enjoying a lot of it. The worst thing was the show in the Stadium was phoney, especially when an MP started talking about how 'the coloured people had got all this together by themselves.' with remarks about 'the coming of white civilisation to South Africa.' The amateurishness of the whole event, which is its saving grace, looked very shabby in the stadium.

Radio but no TV
(18 January 1960) The English and Afrikaans [radio] services maintain BBC standards. Springbok, which is the commercial service, is a glorified round of quizzes and pops. [They are all run by the South African Broadcasting Corporation (SABC)] There is quite a deal of recorded music from Vivaldi

through Beethoven to the Moderns. There is a good Alastair Cooke type weekly talk by Le Roux Smith Le Roux who was one of the keepers at the V &A in London. There is a lot of BBC recorded variety and everybody knows about Ron and Eth and makes Goon noises ... SABC is very BBC conscious and the BBC is idolised as are so many British things from this pink-tinted distance.

Marquard took me to lunch today in [the Netherlands Club] with Human and Rousseau who have been publishing for about a year under their own imprint. They are both my side of thirty and have published among other things Anthony Delius's long satire called *The Great Division*. Human writes articles about the great difficulty of publishing books in Afrikaans which the Afrikaners will not buy.

South Africa is a colonial power
(18 January 1960) The latest Cato Manor outbreak. (Enormous township outside Durban). My attitude has been altered by reading a book by a Cape Town lawyer, Harry Bloom called *Transvaal Episode*. It is about a riot in a location in the Transvaal ... conveys the panic of the white men and of the police and the sheer hatred which is built up. The remarks in today's papers about Cato Manor might have come out of the novel. 'My God! They're stoning us. Come to our rescue.' And the remark overheard by a reporter as they brought the bodies of the policemen out of the location under the cover of sten guns. 'My God! They'll pay for this!'

Cato Manor and this mine disaster illustrates so well one of Marquard's observations in his book *The Peoples and Policies of South Africa* that SA is a colonial power [throughout southern Africa.] The greater percentage of those trapped in the mine were not even South African but Basutos and Portuguese Africans.

Macmillan's 'Winds of Change' speech
(3 February 1960) Not every day one happens to have lunch with a person who is going to be talking to Macmillan within three hours. I was looking for Randolph Vigne in the *Contact* office but he had not arrived. I started talking to Patrick Duncan the Editor who suggested we send out for some lunch.

(7 February 1960) The hopes of the Nationalists and the worst fears of the liberals were firmly [reversed] by Macmillan's speech [to the House of Assembly 3 February 1960]. Verwoerd and Co obviously hope that they had managed to keep Macmillan captive and that he would not want to risk losing South Africa from the Commonwealth. Liberals were afraid that it

would be Britain again voting for South Africa against the United Nations of the world. The grinding of teeth and the relief has been colossal. The sophistication of Macmillan's speech with quotations from Donne and St Paul (not to mention Selwyn Lloyd) is something quite unknown in South African politics. Albie Sachs thought it above the heads of most of the MPs.

Verwoerd, according to Adderley (Delius's name as parliamentary correspondent), grew steadily more pale and tense, and stumbled his way through the opening words of his reply. Kenneth Mackenzie (*Spectator* articles) was saying at Randolph Vigne's last night that V. had only been given a rough outline of what M. was to say and not a copy of the speech and so the shock was pretty great ... Davie, the *Die Burger* columnist (much respected as portrayer of the most reasonable Cape Nationalist views) was extremely worked up yesterday. Phrases such as 'the crisis is now', 'this is what our forefathers have prepared us for', 'we must stand fast in the hurricane of world abuse'. The Nationalists have yet again had it brought home to them that they are alone. The thing that has also shocked them is that Macmillan has pointed out clearly that it is not just Britain but all the members of the Commonwealth who decide whether to invite SA back into the Commonwealth [if it decides to become a republic]. This is what holds them back from holding a referendum next week (there is a canvassing campaign getting under way by liberals to register the quarter of a million unregistered voters by the end of February so that, should Verwoerd announce a referendum for August, at any rate all opposition votes will be on roll.)

Joy Millar behaved in a way calculated to incense all Afrikaners. [In her dramatically flowing dress] she rushed through the police and right up to Mac's open air Rolls Royce and called out 'What a woonderful speech!' right across Verwoerd who was sitting on her side of the car. She is the most ... impulsive woman. I wonder if Mac would have been surprised if she had said 'Love to cousin Cuthbert Alport!' [Her cousin who, after being a Minister for Commonwealth Relations in Mac's government would become High Commissioner for Rhodesia and Nyasaland.]

In every other country in Africa Mac has seen the leaders of the main parties. But he has not seen the ANC [not even Luthuli]. On Friday he met the Coloured councillors. The leftest he was allowed to go were the Liberals; Margaret Ballinger, Representative for Natives and the only Liberal in Parliament and Patrick Duncan. [It should be noted that although Macmillan told parliament that they would have to follow 'The Winds of Change' that they did nothing of the sort. They just made things worse and kept power and apartheid for 30 years until after the Berlin Wall fell in 1990

Liberal Party party

(7 February 1960) Last night there was a Liberal Party party at Randolph's house. Congress today so Peter Brown, polo playing chairman, was there. I met Tim Holmes a pleasant chap who was at Trinity at the same time I was at Wadham. He is just about to start law at UCT after two and a half years running Natal hotel at Underberg under the Drakensberg after his father died. [Father was nicknamed 'Stately Holmes'.] But sadly I feel that the Liberals are not very dangerous. This is of course part of their pleasantness. Not politicians but humanitarians. However the liberal network of journalists do get South African headlines into the world's press.

Trans the River Kei

(16 February 1960) I leave for the Eastern Province on 27 February. Today I reach the state of opulence of having two cars. I take over the office Dodge for the week before going. It amuses me to think that a year ago the conception of ever having a car was beyond my thoughts. Now I have two.

(18 February 1960) Eastern Province visit builds up. I have written to a large number of schools to warn them that I am about to appear. Spencer Chapman, headmaster of St Andrew's, Grahamstown, has invited me to lunch (author of *The Jungle is Neutral* about the war in Malaya). Pahl, the Inspector of Schools in the Transkei, is going to help me work out an itinerary when I get to Umtata. (Randolph says that he is perhaps the least shady of the school inspectors in this country. Each of them seems to have his name on a school course and schoolteachers in his area think he will give a bad report when he inspects if his course is not being used).

(4 March 1960, Umtata) Happy journey down to Umtata with Mary and Louis (African medical student) returning to university in Durban and Pietermaritzburg. We took a gentle three days travelling 776 miles to Umtata [in convoy with Mary Kirwood in her mother's Morris Minor with me in the OUP Dodge.]

Spent Saturday night at George and the second night at King William's Town. Each time Louis could not stay at the hotel and we took him to friends. At George he stayed with some Methodists in a little house in the location. Very different at KWT where he knew the son of the richest African in the town who owned the local bus fleet and is featured in the *Bantu Education Journal* as an example of 'what the Bantu can do for himself'.

(Bantu Education Department are the most cleverly two-faced propaganda machine in SA.) As Mary remarked this man's superb enormous wide-roofed bungalow would probably be the first to go up in a location riot.

White Girl, Black Man

Back to the journey down. As we drove Louis came alternatively between cars as a passenger. We stopped for enormous picnics and petrol. Everywhere garage attendants were asking Louis in Xhosa if he was Mary's or my servant and when they found out that he was a student they were effusive about how 'We need trained men' and gave us super service.

We called in at Grahamstown so that I could quickly drop some things I had brought up for Wally and Ingie (as in Aunt Iris.) Looking back on it I think they must have been flabbergasted especially as at that time Louis was travelling with Mary. Actually I did not really notice their reactions because I was busy unloading. But on talking with Mary afterwards I realised quite how shaken Ingie and Wally had been. I am becoming a bigger and bigger exhibitionist and love watching other people's reactions as they watch Mary or Sally or me with Africans. Mary is delightfully open-faced. One time at the location in Cape Town, Langa she was asked by the white policeman if she was going to have supper with the people she was visiting. She said she thought so. The police officer sneered. Randolph Vigne in talking about this thought that he would have denied it and said he was 'taking his boy back home' because that would be what the policeman wanted to hear; this was partly because of the coward in him and partly because of any consequences it might have for the African.

Jappies and skappies

One of the amusements of South African life is telling stories about the illiterate behaviour of '*jappies* and *skappies* in the perlice force'. Everybody seems to have got huge amusement out of my encounter with the Criminal Investigation Department (CID) in Cape Town when I applied for a pass to visit schools in the native reserves of the Transkei. They asked me 'Are you a communist or have you ever been a member of any communist organisation?' Not too bad and at least a matter of plain statement of fact. But also 'What is your opinion of communism?' I had to sit on a smile which was bounding up my throat. 'Oh well! I suppose they might as well stay in Russia.' This was read back to me as 'In my opinion the communists can stay in Africa.' But the last laugh was on the *jappies*. When I arrived in Umtata I went to collect the permit. At that moment they discovered I was British and therefore that I would have to apply through Pretoria. So that was that. One of the Inspectors came with me to see if the Chief Magistrate could find a way round it. It was maddening. Pahl, the Chief Inspector and author of various Oxford Xhosa books, had helpfully planned three daily itineraries into the rolling green hills which I could see from my windows at the Savoy Hotel in the town. But these lands were forbidden because it would have reflected badly on the Education Department if I was caught. The chances of being asked for my permit were about 100 to 1 and if I had made no approach for a permit everything would have been all right.

Best occasion so far was when I arrived at an African school in the middle of a sports day with black girls in gym slips. These little girls had directed me in the first place and had arrived with me in the Dodge screaming with laughter as they were recognised by their classmates. I left with the staff singing, very well, *i-Jubili*, a Xhosa song published by Oxford.

Duncan Village outside East London this morning depressing with quagmire roads in an inch of rain. (named after Patrick Duncan's Governor-General father). The Location Manager in his office surrounded by barbed wire with floodlights high on standards – like a prison camp. Conversation overheard in Location office 'Those buggers shouldn't be there. Boot 'em out. Can't you deal with the bastards. Who gave them the authority?' and at the end 'Well seeing as it's you Peter, I'll do it.'

Far more English than England
(6 March 1960, East London) I have just got back to Dolphin Hotel on the coast near East London after spending week-end in school-encrusted Grahamstown in Ingie's charming and chaotic house. A green swimming-pooled town with Saturday afternoon cricket matches on every field; boys in Kingswood black and red ties, boys with St Andrew's crosses, and St Aidan's boys stopping their cricket when the vespers bells ring ... far more 'English' than anywhere in England ... By the way Grahamstown has South Africa's oldest surviving newspaper called *Grocott's Daily Mail.*

Ingie and Wally have moved into an extraordinary and very South African house. A long white-railed stoep in front; rooms scattered around so that you have to go outside to two of the bed-rooms. The chaos was added to by the fact that the African servant had had to go to hospital, there was Miss Somebody or other who had to use the same bathroom and also until the end of the month a junior English lecturer at Rhodes University in another room. He has the only front door key. This lecturer is quite a lively person who was at Pietermaritzburg under Geoff Durrant and Christina van Heynigen. Without telling him I knew Mary Kirwood he started telling me about the women's residence where Mrs Kirwood is the warden. 'Yes she runs the women's residence, or rather her daughter does ...' Which I can well believe.

The capture of Fort Hare

(12 March 1960, Grahamstown) The last two days have made me really feel that I am at the battlefront. Yesterday I was at Lovedale teacher Training College and Fort Hare University College at Alice and today I have been some of the time at Rhodes University in Grahamstown.

Beynon, the Principal of what was Lovedale Teacher Training College, launched off into a tale of woe as soon as I appeared. These people have no reason to know that I am liberally minded but I suppose that they think that, as Marquard's assistant, that I must be. By shuffling and bureaucratic wangling the Bantu Education Department have made it necessary for this [renowned, historic] college for Africans to close ... The government does not like the Scotto-British traditions and tried to break these and in doing this broke the whole college. Beynon told me that he had been reprimanded for carrying out a tradition of some years whereby he gave a tea party for his staff which is naturally mixed. Dugard, the Director of Bantu Education for the Ciskei, arrived and muttered from behind his glasses 'Tea parties? Tea parties? This must stop.' Beynon said that the directive must be in writing but he was told that this could not be. An Afrikaner member of his staff had reported him. The whole apartheid policy is breaking up the goodwill which has been built up over years and suspicion and distrust is breaking into everything.

At the Lovedale Bookshop I heard more about the textbook racket. Via Afrika is one of the large Afrikaans presses which has boomed since the war and has several National Party cabinet ministers on the board ... Via Afrika play on the fears of the African teachers. They have a van loaded with their books and not only a representative but an ex-inspector of schools. The Teachers all remember him with dread and do not know that he has left the government's employ. The Africans are afraid of losing their jobs if they don't buy the books. This chap Dugard plays a racket. A chap called Barnes has written an English course. Dugard, as regional director, has advised on it. Result: Dugard's name is quite as large as Barnes's on the front. The teachers play safe as he is their ultimate boss and use the Dugard and Barnes book.

I visited the new Afrikaner Rector of Fort Hare who has been keeping his trap shut after some pretty pathetic appearances in the press. Initially he thought that the Oxford University Press was a newspaper. He has banned the SA Students' s Union (NUSAS) from the campus 'because they were in opposition to my moves.' He is an ex-Inspector of Schools and looks like it in a somewhat avuncular manner. Inspector of Schools is an important position here when the government wants to impose central authority.

After lunch ... I visited the Lovedale printing press. White, the Works Manager used to live next door to Aunt Iris and Uncle Iver, who was bursar of Fort Hare. His attitude was that anybody who took a job at Fort Hare this year was suspect. This was the attitude of Hundleby, the Principal of St Matthew's, formerly Church of England mission school, who was offered, without asking for it, 'the professorship of English' at the new Zulu college. He wondered whether it would not be a good thing that somebody from the [liberal] side of the fence should be there. In the end the renowned African academic, Z.K. Matthews persuaded him that he would have been considered to have gone over to the enemy by the Africans after years of teaching them. ZKM had put this into practice for he had resigned as Vice-Principal of Fort Hare within two years of his pension.

Burrows, sacked Principal of Fort Hare and now in the economics department at Rhodes University, showed me a letter from Ngcobo, who resigned from Fort Hare even though he was offered an Economics professorship. He was telling Burrows that he had been told by the Deputy Minister for Bantu Education to expect to have his application for a travel permit to go to University College at Salisbury refused because he was considered to have given the government a slap in the face by accepting a professorship at Salisbury when he had refused a professorship at Fort Hare.

35,000 Africans March on Cape Town
(30 March 1960) I am sorry that I have not managed to write in the last eight fantastic days since Sharpeville. Actually it is in the last four days since arriving back in Cape Town that everything has happened. It all seems so unreal.

On 26 March Wednesday the Africans marched on town. Anthony Millar, whose BP offices are among the tallest in Cape Town, could see people coming in their thousands along de Waal Drive from the suburbs and the locations. They were – thirty or forty thousand – going to the police station in Caledon Square [they had left their passes at home and were offering themselves to be arrested] ... It was symbolic that they should have ignored Parliament. Somehow I was just gaily ignorant of the whole proceedings. I was in Parliament Street and did not notice the troops. Everybody seemed to be walking around as usual in the lunch hour. A helicopter was noisily roaring around and I admired it swing its red body round in front of the Mountain.

Back in the office Miss Williams rushed in at about ten past two saying that Baker the printer had rung up advising us (from the distance of eight miles south at Wynberg) to pack up office as others were doing and if necessary he would come up to fetch Miss Williams and Marquard. Marquard was not going to be rushed. He had been where I had been in the town and had bumped into de wet Nel the Minister of Bantu Affairs and Administration coming back from the scene of the demonstration; he made some remark to LM about the case of of the economics lecturer who had got a job at Salisbury and had been refused an exit visa. [which I had just been told of in my visit to Fort Hare] He was quite unperturbed. The only things to reach us at the top of our building was the sound of the helicopter and the fact that at about three o'clock the automatic telephones got jammed with calls ... from people saying they were coming to collect their wives and others and that they were packing up work. A quiet panic and a red helicopter against the mountain. A State of Emergency was declared.

[Patrick Duncan, Peter Hjul, and Randolph Vigne and the NUSAS activists from the University of Cape Town had all summer been in close contact with the Pan-Africanist Congress in Langa and Nyanga townships. On 26 March 1960 some 35,000 Africans marched into Cape Town. Philip Kgosana, the young PAC leader, led them down the de Waal Drive motorway into Cape Town. The police and army had surrounded Parliament with armoured cars. The marchers filled the four streets round the enormous police station which occupies a whole block off Caledon Square in Cape Town. The marchers had left their passes at home and were offering themselves for arrest. The police were paralysed with indecision. The police had guns but they had no form of public address system to talk to the vast but non-violent crowd. Patrick Duncan, having fought an election in Sea Point, at his own expense, knew where he could rent a loudspeaker van. This enabled Terblanche, the head of police, to broadcast a message to the crowd promising a meeting for Kgosana and the leadership with Erasmus, Minister of Justice. Philip Kgosana, in the great traditions of non-violence, persuaded the crowd to return to Langa and Nyanga. Patrick Duncan, son of a former Governor General of South Africa, had provided his leadership and his training in crowd control in the British colonial service to save Cape Town from a massacre which would have dwarfed Sharpeville. It could have sparked a revolt which the apartheid state would have used extreme violence to crush. That, of course, might well have led to revolution.]

Cape Town leads the country
(30 March 1960) I was back in Cape Town at a moment of great hope. The rumours had it a bit wrong; that passes for Africans had been altogether withdrawn. As it was the police had merely admitted that in effect the law was unenforceable for the time being.

(3 April 1960) With the one exception of the Cato Manor outburst in Natal and the shootings in Sharpeville and Langa there seems to be a feeling that the government have got the situation in control in every place except Cape Town. This is the first time that liberal easy going Cape Town has led the country.

The PanAfricanists here have even adopted the ANC idea of non-violence. Apparently people on the demonstration [the great march] on Wednesday were impressed by their leaders that they must be non-violent. Kgosana and the other leaders spent the previous night going from door telling everybody that there would be a march and impressing them that they had no weapons but non-violence to meet Saracen armoured cars. Sticks and stones would be useless. [Kgosana, who did not know Xhosa had coined the chant in English 'Ab-sol-ute Non-Vi-ol-ence'.] Kgosana, the 21 year old student, led them in shorts. They good naturedly let cars with white drivers crawl past. The police chief agreed that they would allow him to see Erasmus the Minister of Justice if he got the 35,000 to return peacefully.

At 6 o'clock that evening Kgosana was arrested. 'Treachery' boomed Randolph. 'I do not believe that they can have been so stupid' was Marquard's reaction.

Don't strike but 'Stay-at-Home'
(30 March 1960) There was general feeling of hope among Liberals yesterday at the success of peaceful demonstration. News today is that Langa and Nyanga (Xhosa for Sun and Moon) townships outside Cape Town are surrounded by troops.

(3 April 1960) I wrote on Wednesday and told you about the beginning of this week of great strain. I feel as though I have been on the go for the last five weeks. Randolph Vigne is organising great food distribution schemes for Nyanga and Langa. They are sorely short of money as they have not been working. The Liberal Party in Cape Town has got together £1000 this week but this cannot go on. The locations are surrounded by troops and police and those without passes are stopped on the buses and so that anybody who burnt their pass is in captivity. The sad thing of course is that the uncompromising Africanists are in command as they say they are not

going to stop until passes are withdrawn and their leaders released. Chief Luthuli, long-time head of the moderate and non-violent African National Congress, asked the Africans to go back to work on Tuesday. There is a great call for a 'Stay at Home' tomorrow and the white shopkeepers think that the Coloureds are going to stay out now. The Africans do not think they will for one moment. In District 6 there are walls painted with 'Don't betray us'.

'Banned Amy' is arrested in the night
(30 March 1960) At 4.30 the Argus came out with first list of the people arrested at 2.00 and 3.00 this morning. It was known that for the first time that several prominent Liberals had been arrested. Up till then there had been speculation. It was supposed that Patrick Duncan and Alan Paton had been arrested [but it was not the case]. The usual people farther left had been seized, several of them not for the first time; communists, near communists, Congress of Democrats, ANC leaders and so on.

Among them was a girl we had been at the cinema with the previous evening. Sally and I went with Albie Sachs, lawyer son of the SA Trade Union leader. With us was a girl known as 'Banned Amy' because she only managed to get banned from taking an active part in politics a long time after other people such as Albie. Amy Rietstein is a bit of an exhibitionist. We had listened at her flat to the news on the radio with details on the banning of the congresses; she had pulled out a Congress rosette from her handbag and Albie said she would have to destroy that soon. She said she had a free afternoon from school the next day and that she would have to get down to clearing out all the incriminating evidence. On the way home Albie cleared out his house and gave us all his Congress of Democrats (COD) pamphlets to send over to friends abroad. Anyhow we left 'Banned Amy' at her flat at Sea Point at 11.30 and at 2.30 she rang up Albie as her lawyer to say that she was being arrested and that the police had no warrant as there were emergency powers in operation (the State of Emergency was proclaimed this afternoon). Her reaction to a cockroach which came out from under her coffee table proves that she will find all the grime and dirt in prison pretty awful.

(30 March 1960) A week-end of quiet excitement at the Sachs while the details of the food and so on were arranged for the four students who had been arrested. Three men and one girl who had been caught by the police in Windermere African location distributing 'Stay at Home' pamphlets. The girl had never taken part in anything political before. She was nineteen and called Beaujolais.

(3 April 1960) In fact the State of Emergency forbids the papers to publish the names of those arrested. (In fact it is an offense to pass on the names although everybody does.) People can be spirited away by the police and locked up for years without any news being allowed in or out. In fact the police seem to be acting reasonably in Cape Town. The detainees all see one another and 'Banned Amy' was allowed to send messages in and out because she is the only woman. This was taken away when she was caught writing the Freedom Charter on the wall. All of them were furious because she was their only link. Now the link has been restored and they have asked for a tennis ball. They do not seem to be allowed to read and their lights are turned off at 7 o'clock.

Only an hour or two more of freedom
(3 April 1960) A mad-cap coloured chap I know was arrested yesterday; he had been distributing subversive literature and it appears fairly certain that he burnt down one of the coloured councillor's houses. At the Library I bumped into his room-mate who told me how he had been just about to remove his shirt at the Charge Office, before being taken to the cells, when they changed their minds and said that they would investigate his case and tell him later if it was necessary to arrest him; he told me that he thought that he had only an hour or two more of freedom. Meanwhile Bach was being exchanged for Mozart on the record counter, and everybody was more relaxed after the week's worries. There was a sickening feeling that because the situation was under control there was a total lack of appreciation of the causes.

Shoot the kaffirs and they would come back to work
(3 April 1960) White South Africans keep talking about 'these savages'. One grocer near here said – I could hardly believe it- 'It used to be said that the only good nigger is a dead nigger.' He said to one of Joy Millar's liberal friends 'It will soon be all right. You know what I would do with whole lot of them?' He then proceeded to make a tommy gun noise. Randolph quotes one shopkeeper as saying 'They ought to shoot the whole lot of the kaffirs and then they would come back to work tomorrow.' Another friend of mine says that the men in the shipping office where he works talk about guns. An outburst like this brings out all the worst in people.

Meanwhile I get on with work and enjoy being back at typography while the helicopter flies over. One goes on with careful spacing of words, and demands for less shiny ink and hatching up new ideas, conceits and excitements of typography. I have spent the week-end thrilled to bits with the proofs for Marquard's book.

Bad police, good policeman
(4 April 1960) Today has seen a new and hideous move. One had hoped that the police were going to behave reasonably as they had seemed to be doing so far…helicopters and bombers scattered 'Go Back to Work' leaflets on the locations. Result: 40,000 out of 60,000 workers returned to work. The police had won with the help of hunger. Gideon, our messenger, said paraffin had been stopped and there was nothing to cook with.

Today they have acted against 'intimidators' [pickets] with absolute thuggery. Right in Cape Town the police started beating all Africans. Some of them were messengers at work. The police were armed with all sorts of home-made weapons: sticks, rubber coshes made from car tyres. Patrick Duncan [shouted] from his taxi 'Stop it you swine!' The policeman yelled 'This is a State of Emergency. We'll lock you up.' A Sergeant appeared and Duncan said 'Tell your men to stop behaving like that.' A string of abuse and threats of imprisonment flowed.

When Pat Duncan reached his office he rang up head of police Terblanche and said he ought to stop his men behaving like that. Terblanche, a reasonably moderate policeman, as good as admitted that his tougher deputy Rheeder was in control. He promised to ask Rheeder to stop. Terblanche said 'I have been through hell during the last week'. Pat Duncan said that he was going straight to Parliament to get Mrs Ballinger, the Liberal Native's Representative in the Senate, to bring it up. 'You will do me no disservice' said Terblanche 'if you get it brought up in Parliament'.

Police sadism on the streets
(9 April 1960) Last Monday's move by the police has been the worst and most terrible thing yet in South Africa. For the first time the police used public and brutal sadism. The deaths at Sharpeville and Langa seem mild in comparison. There have been many different reports of this obscene development. This sort of thing undoubtedly happens in isolated spots but when you have a police force [beating up Africans just because they are Africans] in the centre of a city within two minutes of Parliament then it is being condoned officially.

Nevertheless Erasmus, Minister of Justice has in parliament defended the police conduct as legal:

1. <u>He says that that the police are only allowed to use regulation batons.</u> There are several people whose word is trustworthy who say that the police have all sorts of home-made weapons such as rubber coshes made out of motor tyres. This is typical of the police attitude that they can take the law into their own hands.

2. <u>Erasmus says that the action taken by the police to clear intimidators off the streets is legal under the third article of the Emergency Regulations.</u> This says that anybody who is 'endangering the peace' must be told in a loud voice that force can be used to remove him. Many pieces of supporting evidence show that this has not been anywhere near followed. Mrs Petersen, a responsible member of the Black Sash, says that she saw an old man who was sitting on the kerb being talked to by a policeman. They then laid into him and left him bleeding. She asked the man what he had been doing. He said that he was resting on his way to hospital. She took him in her car to hospital and was followed by a police van. She was told off by the police.

3. <u>Erasmus made the wonderful remark that if people were attacked they could lay a charge.</u> Joe Louw, journalist and photographer, tried to lay a charge. He was attacked outside a police station. The policeman in the charge office said that he could do nothing. Swart, previous Minister of Justice and now Governor-General, had all police numbers removed to protect the policemen from 'frivolous charges' so that you cannot now identify them if you want to lay a charge.

'You <u>have</u> arrived at an <u>amusing</u> time.'

I think, I hope that South Africa cannot go as far as Nazi Germany because of people as brave as Mrs Petersen and Patrick Duncan. The general impression is that they have not arrested Patrick Duncan because he had talks with Macmillan. Anyhow he is going to publish in the next issue of *Contact* the pictures of police chases which the *Argus* dare not print.

(9 April 1960) More people have been arrested. Randolph thinks that the government believe that the Africans cannot have been clever enough to have run the last affair themselves and that they are looking for white leaders. I slept last Tuesday night at Randolph's because Gillian Vigne is ill and Randolph is not sleeping at home to avoid night arrest.

He made a remark I greatly appreciated yesterday. 'You <u>have</u> arrived at an <u>amusing</u> time.' I was so glad that he used 'amusing' because I feel slightly guilty about finding it so entertaining when people's happiness and lives are at stake. But there we are. I am quite honestly enjoying it all, although with a feeling at one moment of gloom and the next of hope. We were by the sea at house of friends some twenty miles away. An English girl who was there said 'South Africans are always sympathising with me being here at this time, but it is so exciting.' This is the longest and most amazing fortnight I have ever lived through.

(15 April 1960) I have just got a letter saying [Ralph's journalist friend]

Rufus Gibson envied me. Well he might. We keep saying 'Who would be anywhere but South Africa at this moment?'

Who shot Verweord?
(9 April 1960) I thought that somebody was pulling my leg when I was told at dinner last night that an attempt had been made on Verweord's life. It is all a bit useless. Under the emergency regulations the name of the man cannot be published. My first guess when I heard was that he was a white man. [Pratt was a rich English South African farmer] … Killing Verwoerd would be about damn all useless as he would be merely martyred as one of GOD's and Afrikanerdom's saints and the whole Afrikaner nation would man their laagers in defense of God's Chosen People. Everybody said that nobody could be worse than Malan, than Strydom … and each time they are worse.

A safe stronghold OUR God is still
(9 April 1960) I had great amusement on Wednesday Van Riebeeck's day, a public holiday. I worked because of the backlog of stuff after getting back to Cape Town. Ten floors below is the Van Riebeeck statue. Celebrations with rumbustious teutonic bands. They had just got to 'A safe stronghold OUR God is still' when the SAAF red helicopter drowned them out with its roar and it started to rain.

(15 April 1960) All is calm ostensibly, and the police are chiefly concerned with trying to keep up the idea that there is an Emergency. De wet Nel has said that there is a return to normal. *The Cape Times* asked whether this meant that the government considered the present set-up normal or not. Certainly they have now got it just about as they want with high percentage of white, coloured or native leaders locked up without any charges. Mind you de wet Nel was able to say one week after Sharpeville … that 'race relations have never been better.' You can hardly believe the wish-fulfilment which goes on among Afrikaners, although the English-speaking South Africans, like most human beings, are pretty good at it.

Give up politics or give up job
(4 April 1960) Poor Randolph Vigne has been faced by his firm Maskew Miller Publishers with giving up his job or giving up politics. Meanwhile Gillian Vigne is in bed warding off a miscarriage. Their maid arrested. 'Must pay her off', said Randolph 'because cannot afford another.'

(15 April 1960) Randolph Vigne has lost his job at publishers Maskew Millers, or is in the process of doing so. The Special Branch came and asked

his directors if they knew how involved he was in the Liberal Party? His directors have given him an ultimatum. Apparently a few years ago he turned down an offer of a job at Longman because they insisted that he would have to stop his politics. At the moment he is rather despondent about the whole thing.

(15 April 1960) A thing of personal good has come out of this crisis. For the first time I have felt that I have really broken through on a personal level with Marquard. We are always having discussions about the latest news and there is always a new batch of rumours to weigh up. Cannon thinks our politics endanger the Oxford University Press.

Sandcastles for the prisoner's daughter
There seems to have been an immediate reaction in the press in England to the arrest of Myrna Blumberg, the *Daily Herald* correspondent and wife of Kenneth Mackenzie … Sally and I spent an entertaining afternoon on the beach with Randolph and Ken plus Piers Vigne and Ruth Mackenzie, both two and a half. Four adults all making paddling pools and sandcastles and talking politics and journalism. KM was saying that all the eleven women detainees in Cape Town are in a dormitory together, and that his wife Myrna (Blumberg) gives lectures on Shakespeare and the others give lectures too. Meanwhile her little two-year-old is motherless. Two women with children a month or two old have been let out.

Just a bit of beating up the locations
(22 April 1960) A general feeling of nothing has happened because everything in town has returned to its normal pitch. In fact the police go on beating up the locations and arresting people; 1,569 arrested in Cape Town seems a fantastic number although we knew it was going that way. Marquard, as representative of the Institute of Race Relations, spent the week at SABRA (A National Party institute of race relations). He was refused admission to the closed session and this got into the paper. He said that that the hardening in re-thinking since last year had been remarkable. 'Last year some of the resolutions might have been put before the Institute of Race Relations in one of its more conservative moods.'

I have spent a pleasant week. Marquard's *Peoples and Policies of South Africa* has arrived and he is to give me a signed personal copy on Monday. My jacket looks powerful and I hope helps push it; it might do well at this time in England. OUP London have ordered my jacket for the worldwide market…This is a slight victory as it is by no means a foregone conclusion.

The whole direction of South African history has changed
(30 April 1960) This week I got at last got down to dealing with the report about my Eastern province visit I have to write. After looking at the twenty-six pages of single spaced typing I had made of individual visits, I decided to show them to Marquard even before editing them. It turned out to be just the thing as he said that he was not only interested but amused and that they gave him a very precise idea of what I had done. He suggested in some detail how I should build up my report for him and for London. With coming back right into the middle of the crisis I had almost forgotten the whole trip. ... It seems no time at all since I came back and yet in that time the whole direction of South African history has been changed.

Outflanking the Special Branch
(15 April 1960) Tremendous game with *Contact* this week [the edition with *Argus* pictures of police violence]. All copies wrapped as they were printed for posting on Tuesday. This was all done in secret in a house in Rondebosch.

On Wednesday the *Cape Times* announced that *Contact* following a raid by the police ... had suspended publication. Marquard said he thought it was the last thing that Pat Duncan would do. I thought it was strange as days before I had been round with Pat Duncan to the *Argus* offices to see one of the deputy editors who had several photographs of policemen chasing Africans. Sure enough it was a ruse to keep the police off and to continue without getting banned, as the other left wing papers have been. But this grand ruse has been foxed by the post office who have invoked the 'objectionable literature' clause in their regulations and done a quite illegal thing of consulting the customs ... So now 11,000 copies of *Contact* have to wait in the Post Office over the week-end till the customs man gets back from a fishing week-end. ...

Secret packing parties
(1 May 1960) On Wednesday it was packing copies of the latest edition of *Contact*. To avoid the possibility of it being seized by the police they were packed in three or four parties across Cape Town. Conversations over the telephone went like 'Where's the party?' 'Who's bringing the drinks?' Our party was in the house of Hans Fransen a Dutch friend who was not there because he proof-reads in the evening for *Die Burger*. Then the printer appeared bringing eight thousand copies. At about eight o'clock a vague collection of mothers and children arrived and it was all chaos. The man who was organising it did not seem to be getting anywhere so I piled in:

'You and you take that pile, please.' 'You and you count, please' and got them into a chain production system.

Murderers, rapists and banned politicals
(1 May 1960) Horrifying sight of the full lists of the detainees taking two-thirds of a page in the newspaper. It seems that ... the total of people arrested as a result of the disturbances is about twenty thousand. Apparently the list published is a hopeless mess, at least in the Cape. They have just mixed up everybody. There are convicted murderers and rapists mixed up with uncharged political detainees. Some of the detainees are not mentioned such as 'Banned Amy', whom we were with the evening before she rang Albie Sachs to say that she was being detained. They have moved the detainees out to Worcester which is about eighty miles away, but where apparently the accommodation is better. The trouble is that all their friends and relations have a journey there and back of 160 miles for their weekly visits.

Starving dependants
(1 May 1960) We are again taking food to the dependants who have lost their breadwinners. Dependants of the detainees. Dependants of those had lost their jobs because of the State of Emergency. Dependants of those who had been jailed for various offences because of the State of Emergency. Five European doctors have volunteered their services free for dependants of the detainees. It is winter and it can be cold.

This morning we went out, Tim Holmes, Sally Morgan and myself, to take food to a dorpie about fifteen miles from Cape Town. This particular collection of huts, where about fifty families live, is in the sandy Cape Flats; which are flat although there are dunes with a considerable amount of bush and scrub and trees. Twenty-four of the families are considered starving and we are taking combined Liberal Party and Quaker food to them. My car got stuck in the sandy road and we had to lay branches and everybody pushed to get it going again. Some of the men have not been able to get jobs. Several of them lost jobs at the time of the disturbances. One of the men who was helping push had just come out of prison after a month; he had been put in prison because he was not working; the police version was that he was taking part in the 'Stay at Home'; his version was that he had not got a job to go to.

(20 May 1960) Today we visited some of the worst slums I have yet seen. Ironically originally they were in better-built houses than the shanties. The little pondokkies were usually smart and shining inside with lace mats on the table. We walked through 'Zabo's House' with its boarded up windows

and rotten floors a great fug was generated in all the rooms with a charcoal stove. The woman pathetically thanked us so very deeply.

Monday evening was well spent. Tim Holmes, Sally Morgan and I went out to Windermere which is one of the uncontrolled slum districts where there are sacking shanties and pondokkies. (They all had a magnificent view of the Mountain just as everybody else does in Cape Town, rich or poor). We did the form filling in one of these shacks. It was dusk when we entered and it looked as though the last glimmers of light were filtering through the sacking walls. But it was warm and, as one's eyes got used to the paraffin light, one saw that the walls were papered with sheets of golden 'Lux' soap packets. Ironical juxtaposition.

An example of the gross callousness of apartheid in action. I arrived at *Contact* one lunch hour. There was a black woman nervously crying in a chair with a wheezing child. Her husband was picked up at the time of the emergency and he was found to be in arrears for tax and so he was shipped off to East London. He was not given a chance to collect warm winter clothing. Moreover his wife was just left with three children. She was found starving by Black Sash.

One of the witnesses in the Langa enquiry was seen to be shivering by Judge Diemont 'Are you nervous or cold?' he was asked. 'Cold' was the answer for he only had a shirt on. Diemont ordered the police to find him a jacket. An hour later when he had finished giving evidence the jacket had still not yet arrived.

A sort of diplomatic immunity

(21 May 1960) It turns out that the Cape Town Liberals have secured for themselves a sort of diplomatic immunity. When the Special Branch list was sent to Erasmus, Minister of Justice, Terblanche (who had been suspected all along of being a good policeman and not a political one) objected to the inclusion of Patrick Duncan, Randolph Vigne and Peter Hjul (the Cape Chairman) because he thought that they were the last bridge, the last contact with the Africans. And so it is that they are still free.

But the Special Branch have kept on trying. Sauerman and another policeman spent an hour and a half trying to pin a charge on Patrick Duncan. Or at least they gave up after about an hour and they just had a chat. Sauerman had begun to realise that Pat was not a communist. Certainly Patrick Duncan is so open that his real beliefs, which are not treasonable under South African law, were of no help to the Special Branch. When eventually they got up to go PD said that he appreciated that 'You chaps are doing a difficult job! You know that when we are in power we shall need men like you.' Sauerman's reply was 'Well, so long as I get my pension.'

Dying hours of the old Senate

(20 May 1960) I was having drinks with Cecil Higgs, the artist of seascapes and seashells, and with Dieter Bertram and Dirk la Cock (Black Rod at the Senate). Dirk was describing the dying hours of the old Senate thirty of whose members will not return. It is being packed to ensure a two-thirds National Party majority. It was a tremendous free for all with party whips out of control and all sorts of people who had not given a speech trying to make a last desperate bid to remain. The last surviving Boer war veteran stood up who had not spoken in all his time there (He had sort of been put there instead of giving him a pension). He is eighty and very frail. He gripped the bar in front of him and the veins in his neck stood out and he was shaking with emotion and he started out on an attack on the 'liberalistic jingo press'.

After drinks and dinner we went off to the House of Assembly where the Minister of Justice's vote was being discussed on green leather benches under a sodium bathe of light. It was the best free show for years. Everybody was true to form. The Minister of Justice frankly seemed embarrassed. He answered only in generalisations about the State of Emergency. UP leader Sir de Villiers Graaf put on a good parliamentary display in his pullovered suit. We had de Wet (who had at the time of Sharpeville said 'Only one killed!'). He came out with a long whining attack on the English language press and a suggestion that all editors should be told that if they did not conform they would be sacked. Sir DVG said that 'Goebbels would have a worthy disciple.' One man who looked like a frog croaked away '*Wit man ... swart man ... wit man ... swart man.*' Anthony Delius was an extra member in the press gallery. He may not speak but he shrugs his shoulders, grins and walks in and out continually as though to make a point.

The silent march of the ten thousand

(20 May 1960) Here we are supposed to be in a State of Emergency and the MPs have gone off to Pretoria to join the celebration of fifty years of the Union of South Africa. A solemn march is being organised through Cape Town to the sound of a muffled drum, led by people like Marquard and Archbishop Joost de Blank; it will be to a meeting of rededication when people will pledge themselves to trying to make a better job of the Union in the future and not to celebrating a hideous failure.

(5 June 1960) ... the 'march of the ten thousand' as it is now being called. Everybody gathered at the bottom of Adderley Street and were formed into five hundreds, six abreast. The Liberal party was providing marshals, five to five hundred with white armbands. The moving thing was the silence

in Adderley Street as we walked up with the sun on the back of our necks. The procession was silent but so were the surrounding crowds, so quiet that one could hear individual remarks like one woman who said 'Why are they looking so sad? I thought that they were celebrating Union.'

The Drill Hall off Grand Parade was absolutely packed with peoples of all colours and the Archbishop announced after we had been there about a quarter of an hour that the procession was still coming up Adderley Street, at which there was an outburst of clapping for the minority felt that they were the majority for once. Unfortunately nobody outside could hear the overflow loudspeakers. We slipped outside to see what was happening and there was an enormous patient crowd in the sun. The thing was to keep the crowd there at all costs until the speakers could come out and address the crowd. The rededication was read out in Afrikaans and Xhosa and then all of us who had the dedication sheets read it out in English ... then ' a safe stronghold our Lord is still.'

Eventually Centlivres arrived; he is a former Lord Chief Justice, and like Marquard and Braam Fischer was a Rhodes Scholar at New College, Oxford. He has no real speaking manner and his efforts to be heard over the portable loudspeaker borrowed from the Black Sash were hopeless. So one of the Liberals, a Byronic young man who was delegate from Natal to the Liberal Congress last week, read it for him while Centlivres stood in his hat at the foot of Boer War memorial and smoked his pipe. Davies, with the blood of the non-conformist valleys in his veins, made the speech not only audible but exciting. Cheers and clapping punctuated the speech and rounded off every cliché.

Cape Town put on fireworks two miles out to sea on two South African Navy destroyers so that everybody could see the display all round Table Bay. Joy Millar and I managed to get Mrs Collier, her redoubtable mother aged 80, up and over the roof and onto the flat roof over the stoep. There we drank brandy and were thrilled to bits that we were going to be disappointed. There was an occasional splutter on the horizon. The only good bang was when the navy dropped a match on seven rockets and the whole evening's entertainment went up at once. Darkness descended.

Tremendous Optimism about the Speed of Change
(25 May 1960. *This is sole surviving letter from James in SA to Clare.*)
How nice to get a happy bouncing letter from you full of freedom from Rowntrees cocoa ... And so you have a pale blue car too. How I should love to be at your party for 'Hurrah! Here I am in the South.' and I am sorry that you cannot be a few thousand miles closer and go the Liberal Party

party which should be killing as we have got hold of the jazz king [Dollar Brand/Abdullah Ibrahim] to give a show and my goodness this show will be something for fifty-year-old well-meaning upcountry Liberal Party delegates. Randolph Vigne thinks they may well be shocked.

Randolph is off to the Transkei this week hatching plots against all the government-run chiefs. Actually it is all very fascinating. There is tremendous plotting going on for the Liberals are the last remaining link with the banned African Nationalist Congress and the banned Pan Africanist Congress (PAC).

As you may know, for the first time they have locked up Liberals everywhere else in the country but not in Cape Town. Apparently Terblanche the local police chief saved them (Randolph Vigne, Patrick Duncan, Peter Hjul). When the Special Branch provided a list for the second round of arrests they were on it. Terblanche told Erasmus the Minister of Justice that their names should be removed as they were the last remaining white contacts with the Africans and it would be hopeless to lock them up. As well he might for Terblanche knew that Kgosana, the 21/22 year old PAC leader in Cape Town who led the 30,000 march of Africans into Cape Town, went up to the *Contact* office each day to see Patrick Duncan to talk over tactics. He was the policeman who promised that the PAC leadership that they would see Erasmus if they got the crowd to disperse. Terblanche's word was over-ruled by tougher police officers and Kgosana and his colleagues were arrested that evening …

There is tremendous optimism about the speed of change; I wonder if they are right. Somehow I think that two years is a bit soon but it may be so. They have left an awful lot of active people around even if they have skimmed off the top layer. Every Sunday we (i.e. Sally, Tim Holmes and myself) take food to thirty-three families on behalf of the Liberal Party and the Quakers. These are the dependants of those who have been seized under the Emergency or who have lost jobs in the Stay at Home. We have to go out sixteen miles to Eerste Rivier which is a collection of pondokkies in the sand on a farm. But when we get to Windermere, the great uncontrolled African slum, we have to take with us the local Pan Africanist chief as safe conduct. These are the most terrible slums in the Cape (apparently Cato Manor at Durban is far worse where the sewers seem to have a penchant for overflowing into the streets). Rotting boards on the floor, holes in the walls, no windows, just walls papered with sheets of Lux toilet soap packets (irony) loaded with women, children and the sweet smell of sweat and cheerfulness.

I must tell you about Sally Morgan's affair with Joe Louw, the Cape Coloured photographer of mixed race. To begin with they were going to go to Ghana to get married. But they are both too insecure for each other and quarrelled like mad. Then they were no longer going away to get married but they started living together, or rather, sleeping together. Anyhow they went on until rumours starting circulating and everybody got concerned lest they were going to have on their hands an Immorality Act case [with potential imprisonment]. Then Joe went off on political business to Durban and I went off to the Eastern provinces. When I came back Sally had been warned, as also had Sally's parents in Bulawayo, and they were being much more careful. The affair came to an end in the face of police warnings and watchings, just as it had grown up in the first place to a great extent because of the 'dare to' circumstances. Sally has as good as admitted that it would never have happened but for the illegality of it all. Still it was tremendously interesting.

One Man One vote
(30 April 1960) Have I told you of the split in the Liberal Party over whether the Party should go for a progressive franchise or a total franchise? The old Cape Liberals such as Marquard argue for just about what the new Progressive Party advocate: a progressive franchise. On the other hand in the Cape the younger members of the party are in control now, such as Randolph Vigne and Pat Duncan, who advocate total enfranchisement. They, and their like in Natal, say that we cannot get Africans to join the only non-racial party if all members are not treated as equals. I must say that before coming to this country I was inclined to the progressive franchise but that I am now willing to consider total enfranchisement.

[Rebecca West, journalist who had reported Nuremberg trials of Nazi leaders, has just paid a three month visit to South Africa and published her provocative feelings in the London *Sunday Times*.] She said the Liberal Party is 'rich in individual benevolence and fatuous in its aims' as 60% of the Africans are illiterate. But what the whites mean by illiteracy is stupidity. And yet lots of these so called illiterates use three or four languages daily. And the enfranchised men loose off sten guns in the name of preserving the 'flame of civilisation.' (Gosh, one is sick to death of this phrase in this year of celebration of fifty years of the Union of South Africa.)

I thought that Banda of Malawi's remark was quite good: if you did not let Africans practice the vote they would never learn. So I finish in a muddle, not really happy with Randolph saying that there will, must be, a black government in a few years. Of course the problem is 'excruciating'. So is the whole problem of the West's relations with the rest of the world. That problem is magnified abnormally in South Africa.

Liberal Party is the only bridge with the Africans and coloureds
(6 June 1960) The Liberal Party Congress, this year in Cape Town, was a fascinating occasion. I had not joined the Party because I had not felt that it was quite right for an outsider to do so. Anyhow I wanted to attend the Congress so I got Randolph Vigne and Peter Hjul to propose and second me over brandy the night before.

The opening meeting was public and chiefly aimed at showing that the Liberals were not going to be intimidated. Alan Paton told a story about how the Natal Liberals in Pietermaritzburg jail had decided that they were going to get him inside as well. So they were going very ostentatiously to throw a message over the wall while out in the yard exercising. On it was to be written 'Paton. For God's sake, hide the revolvers!'

The Congress was dominated by the franchise issue. The compromise accepted was that the 'The Liberal Party ... aims to have the idea of a universal franchise and a bill of rights accepted by the people of South Africa.' The discussions became fierce on a grey Sunday afternoon in the (Jewish) Temple Hall. It was argued that it was no good being worried by the franchise issue any longer. Any timid people would join the progressives.

The Africans at this time started giving powerful speeches pleading with the conservatives in the party to compromise as the radicals were compromising and not to leave the words 'universal adult franchise' out of the statement of Liberal Policy. One old bearded African, who only spoke Zulu and came from Charlestown where he was chairman of the Liberal party, had his speech translated for him. He had two hundred members in his branch ... and if he had to go back and tell them that the Congress had turned down the universal franchise he would lose them all ... As long as the franchise issue is wrangled over in the Liberal Party the Africans could only suspect that the whites in the party were only concerned with the continuance of white domination in South Africa. ... The Liberal Party must be preserved as the last remaining bridge politically between the whites and the Africans.

Independence is coming on the borders of South Africa
(30 April 1960) Marquard has been most approachable lately and since the crisis began I have got on enormously well with him. He told me today that he would like me go to Basutoland for a week in June to attend a conference on the teaching of English.

[Before independence Basutoland (to be Lesotho in 1966) and Bechuanaland (to be Botswana 1966) and Swaziland (1968) were called the High Commission Territories. As they were British territory the political exiles could find sanctuary. Basutoland was the backbone of the Drakensberg mountains and a country of supreme Alpine beauty. I took every chance to go there for the OUP. I visited the Morija Printing Works. It had been the apprentice shop for Hans Schmoller, a Jewish exile, who after the war became renowned as a leading typographer at Faber. He had at the beginning of the war bought them from Holland the only font of a van Krimpen type in Southern Africa, which I used for book of poems in Sesotho by B.M. Khaketla a woman poet. All the typesetting and printing work was done by Basotho and their work was amongst the best in southern Africa. I had some atmospheric evening times there; I never expected to be taken to the Basutoland Dance Championships.]

Oh where, oh where is Roma?
(26 June 1960 Lancer's Inn Maseru, Basutoland) Here I am in this amusing island in the centre of South Africa, on British protected soil where none of the land is owned by whites. There is a pub here at the Lancer's Inn where men and women, black and white drink together. (Sesuto for donkey is 'donkey' and there are lots of them in these mountains).

I spent a delightful week-end at the new Roman Catholic University College at Roma. I had met Peter Walsh, a Wadham South African Chemistry Lecturer, when he was passing through Cape Town. I was trying to get through to him on the hopeless telephone when a young history and English lecturer from Roma overheard my efforts and introduced himself to me. He was called Arthur Jenkins (although he now calls himself Hilary since becoming Roman Catholic, although everybody still calls him Arthur.) He was another of these impeccably English South Africans. We spent a pleasantly discursive Saturday afternoon and he urged me to go out to Roma because he was sure I could find the Walshs and could in any case use his bed as a last resort. He gave me very careful directions about getting out along the mountain roads. 'It is all straightforward except that after the bridge you turn left. Otherwise you will find yourself arriving in the royal village.' (Paramount Chief was at Corpus, Oxford.) After the bridge there was a road to the left so I took it. After going up this road through drifts (fords) in the setting sun I started to wonder if this was all right. I asked a Mosuto where was the Roma mission. He pointed up the valley. The road deteriorated and I asked another Mosuto in European clothing the way to the University. Oh yes, I had to go back most of the twenty miles to Maseru before finding the correct turn. It was all like the Atlas in Morocco. It turns out I could not have asked a worse question. Any mission church is called Roma Mission because Catholics rule the territory. If there is a road up a valley there is a Roma Mission.

I had a truly entertaining Sunday with Peter Walsh and his wife who had been a nurse at the Radcliffe Infirmary. He was enthusiastic about getting Sotho plays to perform and was asking about writing among Coloureds and Africans at the Cape.

Exiles in the Drakensberg
(26 June 1960) on my last day in Maseru I met the various political exiles at the Basutoland Congress headquarters – right from African National Congress to plain communist. Khumalo the leader of the ANC in exile came out officiously to meet me. I met Khaketla President of the Basutoland Congress Party and the Editor of the paper.

One of the most interesting was Joe Matthews, son of Z.K. Matthews ex-Vice-Principal of Fort Hare. He was given a tip-off about a police raid in Durban, rang all his friends and then went back to bed as he did not think it would be that night. Then he was arrested. His lawyer appealed for habeas corpus. The Crown kept saying that the Judge must know that a State of Emergency had been proclaimed. 'I certainly do not.' 'But your Lordship must have heard it on the wireless and read it in the papers.' 'I do not listen to the radio or listen to the papers.' The legal performance was all because the *Government Gazette* did not arrive in Durban until Wednesday evening on the 6.30 plane from Cape Town. The Judge was a stickler for legal detail and as the *Gazette* had not arrived he did not officially know. They were released at 5.45. They did not go back to prison to collect their belongings but took the first plane to Bloemfontein and thence drove to Basutoland.

Exit, pursued by a white man
The last evening I went up to Leribe which is sixty miles north-west of Maseru to visit Collingwood August, who was Assistant Editor of *Contact*. I arrived after dark after a drive of sixty miles over roads where the stones leapt up against the bottom of the car. I arrived after dark and only had the name of the Anglican parson who is a Mosotho. I was taken all round the town through the thick frost under a glaring moon by two young members of his congregation who were passed on from place to place after place until we got to the right place. The August family are living in a furnished room. To get to it you have to pass through a catacomb of other people's rooms, one of which was crammed with people listening to a professional crooning trio slickly moaning a song and we crossed the stage behind them. Exit, pursued by a white man!

Eventually we found Collingwood August and the priest invited us back to the rectory where a bottle of communion wine was opened. Later there was a powerful knock on the door and a Mosotho member of the Basutoland Mounted Police came in and very politely started asking me questions. He was thrilled to find I was from England and told me stories about his training at the Hendon police college in North London. After he had gone the priest told me that his visit must have been because he saw my Cape Town number plates and immediately came to enquire thinking that I might be engaged in IDB (Illicit Diamond Buying).

Collingwood was chased out of South Africa by the police. Later his wife and children went up to join him. They were pathetically happy to see me and I was glad that I had gone to see them because I had originally intended to drive to Bloemfontein that evening so that I could start back early to Cape Town the next morning. Collingwood, highly trained mathematics teacher, was out of a job. He is suspected of being a communist. The school principals, as an excuse for not giving him a job, say 'You have too high qualifications.' Patrick Duncan has written to friends to say that he is a Liberal. The blacks are hostile to him because he is a Liberal.

(26 June 1960) The journey from Cape Town to Bloemfontein was quite an experience. The distance is about 650 miles which took me about eleven hours. I had a look at the map of England and I worked out that that this would be Land's End to past Edinburgh. It is more than the length of French Morocco. I then came back 800 miles all the way from Leribe Basutoland to Cape Town in one day – the poor car collapsed with burnt valves the next day in Cape Town.

Publishing in the mountains

(5 December 1960) Since my visit I have also been making various moves in the field of Sotho publishing; this has brought me in touch with Daniel Kunene a charming man at UCT who is an expert on Thomas Mofolo [whose novel *Chaka* appeared in Sesotho in 1925 and in a censored English translation in 1931; I was to commission Dan Kunene to retranslate from the full original Sesotho for the African Writers Series].

I again met B.M. Khaketla, the Basutoland Minister of Education, at a lunch party that Pat Duncan gave at *Contact* for some of the clerics who were down at the Cape for the Anglican synod. Khaketla has written a novel in Sesotho and translated it into English and is going to send it for OUP to consider. We are to do a book of his wife's Sesotho poems. While in the Basutoland colonial administration Pat managed to encourage two rival parties to develop along their own lines, so he launched democracy in the country. [His brother in law D.V Cowen wrote the constitution for Basutoland when it was becoming independent as Lesotho.]

When the Globemasters roar South
[For obvious reasons I did not write in a letter about this and have rewritten it from memory in 2018]
Patrick Duncan would come and leave South Africa through Basutoland as a way out to Europe and America. He had a store in the South run by Joe Nkatlo and would cross by Sotho pony into Sabata territory in the Transkei where the name Duncan became synonymous with the Liberal Party.

One time he was away from Cape Town for months. Tim told me that I must go one evening to Pat and Cynthia's house not far from Muizenberg on the Indian Ocean side. Tim said that I must not mention the meeting to anyone. I was excited and running late but, when I drove off the southern end of the de Waal Drive motorway, I was stopped by the police. I feared the worst and was relieved that it was only for speeding. I almost thanked the policeman for the ticket.

At the house Tim Holmes, Peter Hjul, Randolph and myself were taken silently up the ladder to the loft because Pat thought that it was unlikely that the Special Branch would have bugged up there. He then gave, with great excitement, a blow by blow account of his journeys in Congo, West Africa, Britain, Europe and America and especially of his visit to the United Nations to try and get them to invade South Africa to remove the racialist regime. He had started from Basutoland in a light aircraft with mud on its wings. He was intoxicated with excitement and told us that he was sure that he was convincing military men in America that they could and should liberate South Africa. Tim and I afterwards delighted in one of the excited phrases he used on that occasion: 'When the Globemasters roar south…' The Globemasters were the most powerful US military transport planes which could carry tanks and bridges. He had come a long way since, on crutches, he was beside Gandhi's son at the head of the non-violent Defiance Campaign march in 1952. He was soon to leave South Africa for good as he had come to the conclusion that change in South Africa was not possible without the use of violence.]

Congo thrown to the winds of change
(10 July 1960) The SABC is going wild with joy over the mess-up in the Congo. It is frightfully sad. South Africans (white) fail to draw the obvious conclusion. The Belgians have kept responsibility away from the Congolese. Now in one irresponsible gesture they have thrown everything to the winds. The SABC adores reporting in full gory detail how many nuns have been raped today. In South Africa the missions have seen that there is a developed democratic sense. All the forms of 'Chairman', 'Votes of Thanks', 'Votes' are

punctiliously observed. The Nats would wish for a return to tribal despotism under the chiefs. [About this time I came into Pat Duncan's office and he had managed to get through on the telephone to whoever had taken over in the latest coup in Leopoldville in the Congo and he was interviewing the man in his best Winchester French.]

[In 1959 R.N. Currey won the South African Poetry Prize with Anthony Delius and Sydney Clouts and in 1960 was invited to give lectures at universities round South Africa. Stella Martin Currey, also born in South Africa, was much in demand as well for her lectures on playwrighting and writing for TV, which the South Africans had made sure they did not have.

James Currey's own letters pause. He drove his parents round South Africa and this gave him a idea of the country and his own family. During five years in South Africa it was only in Ermelo that he met ordinary Afrikaners.]

South Africa in three farms
(Ralph/Andrew, Cape Town, 2 September 1960) It has been an exciting and interesting tour apart from the shadow of the referendum overhanging the country [about whether South Africa should become a Republic]. I've given too many lectures, seen too many people – relatives – university hosts. You'll know from Stella that I've given between 25 and 30 lectures (including one speech, not planned, to the Settlers Day crowd of 4000 at a rugby ground in Maritzburg – my golden words reported all over the Union!). We have gone unarmed among a strange variety of Phipsons, some more like Wild West characters than I have ever seen.

We have visited three extraordinary farms:

1. A once fortified farm in the 1820 Settler country outside Grahamstown, where a young African with a completely ochre face got off a bicycle and failed to tell us where we were.

2. Boston, up towards Underberg from Maritzburg, where my mother Edith Vinnicombe spent her childhood with Mary Phipson while her father and mother trekked and built churches. It is still in the Phipson family and they entertained us royally with turkey especially killed for us. We specially liked the great waggons [used by the family not only on the farm but also for transport riding from Durban up into the Transvaal and on to Rhodesia when it opened up. Clare and James found a wagon still there in 2012.]

3. Mtubatuba in Zululand where Cecil Kennedy lives in two luxurious rondavels or pondokkies and, out the profits of Africans working in his sugar cane, keeps race horses.

Another cup of tea and more photographs
(Stella Martin Currey/ Andrew, Ermelo, Transvaal, 10 September 1960)
Ermelo is the place where the Curreys had a very happy time from 1917 to 1921 and R has written about it in quite a lot in his poems. He wanted to see it as it is now. John Currey, in typical fashion, wanted a better manse and the new one is really charming: lots of ground, a big barn, oak trees and paddock. The Dutch Reformed parson (at school with Ralph); his house is like a bishop's palace. He looks old enough to be R's grandfather in spite, or perhaps because, of the luxury. Everybody exclaims on R's youthful looks.

When they were at school together there were almost as many British and Australians as Dutch. The town is now twice the size and is very much more Afrikaner. The three of us had tea in the mayor's parlour with the very Afrikaner mayor this evening. Great honour! I began to realise how the poor Queen must feel after looking at about 500 portraits of mayors – or perhaps only 50. Still it is very interesting for R. to be here and he ought now to be able to write his BBC commission about returning to SA.

Early Morning in Vaaldorp; a touch of the monumental
(3 September 1961) Robert Robinson in *The Sunday Times* wrote about the broadcast on The Home Service:

'… this account – no, not an account, it was the re-creation, the thing itself – of a childhood passed in a Boer village, somewhere on the veldt, was of the highest quality. The author (R.N. Currey) spoke his own narrative – he had the ruminative confidence which is never tedious because it arises out of experience thoroughly digested – and his words bore upon those attitudes to life which are the sources of South Africa's political system. The provincialism of the Boer – the narrowness of the brutish timidity which nourishes his fear of the stranger, whether he be English, Irish, Belgian or African, in short 'the laager mentality' emerged without the author making the point; his form was semi-dramatic, but the characters never seemed to be propping up the narrative. Mr Currey is no propagandist. He almost chanted his words, fully aware that he was speaking something out of the ordinary but never giving you the impression that he thought that <u>he</u> was out of the ordinary. (The contrary supposition lies at the heart of 'the poetry voice'). His script reminded me of Patrick White's great Australian novel *Voss*. It had a touch of the monumental.

A Boer Republic
(10 October 1960) On 5 October 1960 there was the referendum about whether South Africa would become a republic. At 7.30 a.m. the anti-

republicans were in the lead. The 8 a.m. news shattered all hopes. Cape Times placards were 'Enormous Urban Vote will not Make Up for the Country Yeses'. The result will with any luck bring change sooner. Patrick Duncan is in jail as expected. Argus reprinted lengthy story by Patrick Duncan concerning his lengthy visit to Pondoland. I have sent an article on the situation in the Transkei and the sit-in movement to *The New Statesman* which will be rejected as usual. There are advertisements for the new lit-art mag *Contrast* with your name as forthcoming contributor.

Commonwealth Classics
(14 October 1960) I have also been reading Nadine Gordimer's *The Lying Days*. I am enjoying intensely this semi-autobiographical first novel about growing up in a small mining town book because of the accuracy of the observation. I find her more likeable than Doris Lessing who I must have another look at. Dan Davin, a New Zealander at the Clarendon Press in Oxford and a novelist in his own right, has put an idea to John Bell that he should run a 'Commonwealth Classics' alongside 'The World's Classics'. [Nadine Gordimer's second novel *A World of Strangers* was about a young British publisher coming to South Africa. It was published in 1958 and I was several times asked if I had come to South Africa in 1959 because of it. I only came to know of it after I arrived.]

'Hocus Pocus Vatcher'
(25 October 1960) Duncan and Paton both have their photographs in *Drum* this month. It is very unusual that *Drum* ever has a picture of a white man at all. This is the week of Vatcher – a lecturer in international affairs at Stanford who has written a massive study of propaganda for OUP in the States. On previous visits he has only met the white political establishment from Verwoerd downwards, but no Africans except Luthuli. He is a personal friend of Adlai Stevenson and Kennedy. He is in SA to help President Kennedy with background. But he realises how important black opinion is becoming. Excused himself from dinner given by a United Party MP so that he could meet two Pan-Africanists at Randolph's. [The big-name dropping became suspicious and an American diplomat said to Randolph 'Oh, you mean "Hocus Pocus Vatcher!".']

Skewers through their cheeks
(31 October 1960) I organised a Liberal Party party; this time it was a Malayan Khalifa Party which was a rollicking success. The Cape Malays do all their flagellation in time wailing and beating drums and tambourines.

They have razor sharp swords which they swipe down on their arms leaving wheals but no cuts. They carefully skewer little seven year olds through the cheeks. After the second performance at midnight one or two of the more exhibitionistic Europeans started putting skewers through their faces but they bled a bit. We had three visits from the police. We stick to wine and beer and the Africans know that they must dissociate themselves from their glasses. Whenever the police came they were faced with a mass of guests and they left with enormous pattings on the back from all and sundry: black, white, purple, scarlet, orange, primrose hands.

Sitting it out in 'sit-ins'
(22 November 1960) The Liberal Party in Cape Town has been doing a little questioning of the social colour bar in Cape Town. ['sit-ins' as in segregated America]. A lot of non-Europeans use the OKBazaars but they are not allowed to sit down although they can be served at the counter with stuff to take away. So it was decided that on Saturday morning at the height of the morning's rush in the shops eight or so non-white members of the Liberal Party would go and sit down in the tea-room at the OKBazaars. This they did. The idea was that, if they were pushed out, thirty or so white members of the Liberal Party would walk out in protest. One of the coloured waitresses was about to serve Mr Cromwell Nododile, a very respectable sixty year old African who is one of the Vice-Presidents of the Party, when she was stopped by the manageress. There was a bit of a discussion and everybody stayed put. Fifteen minutes later the Special Branch arrived. Whether they had been previously informed or had been sent for it was impossible to say. Anyhow they included the chief of the Cape Town Special Branch, who hung around in the women's dress department next door peering through the racks. Eventually the place was closed twenty minutes early and forty Liberals all went out grinning at the Special Branch on the way.

'Sit-ins' hit the headlines
Stanley Uys, political correspondent of the *Sunday Times*, was there together with the *Argus, Cape Times, Drum* and *Golden City Post*. They have all given it between five hundred and twelve hundred words. Today Tuesday the *Cape Times* came out with it on its second main headline. The OKBazaars is not in a Group Area although the whole of South Africa is called a 'Controlled Area'. A special proclamation was gazetted a month or so ago against mixed eating and bioscopes [cinemas] but the whole situation is a legal tangle.

We have all been painting the new Liberal Party offices white in between descriptions of how Tom Walters, one of the Liberal lawyers, got a donkey across the bonnet of his car and found it too heavy to pull off and had to drive standing up until he found somebody to help him. The laughter kept the painting going. The summer winds have been starting and the whole place has been steadily buffeted each day. Anyway means it is not too hot.

Jamming self-service at the OKBazaars
(5 December 1960) The Sit-In Campaign has gone forward with ever-increasing attention across the Union. Every Saturday for the last three weeks there have been Sit-Ins at the OKBazaars. The Saturday before last we jammed the self-service queue for two hours. The amazing thing has been the lack of hostility and amount of sympathy; one man, a very ordinary English-speaking man said 'The non-Europeans have got their money ready I've got my money ready. Why can't they serve us?' This week at the OKBazaars one young Afrikaner said he was about to assault a 'Kaffir' but was told by management that he would be flung out if he did not quieten down.

'Sit-ins' go posh
Last Saturday we met at *Contact*. The 'sit-in' objective had not been disclosed. Half the forty moved off to the OKBazaars followed by all the Special Branch who had been waiting outside. Ten minutes later we left with some of the reporters and none of the Special Branch. Kenneth Hendrickse and myself were the only people who knew where our twenty were headed. We surprised ourselves by getting into the Bird Cage coffee bar at the poshest store Stuttafords. Ken and I lead the way into the Bird Cage. Ken is good-looking but is very obviously 'coloured'. We picked up cups of coffee to our surprise and paid the cashier. To our astonishment they were accepting everybody's money and Africans with ham sandwiches were walking through and having their money accepted. It was a rousing sight. People who were already sitting at tables did not seem to object and the whole incident passed off except that Ken, who had gone back into the queue, was stopped the second time and got into an argument with management.

After about twenty minutes, our point having been made, we moved off to CTCBazaars which are a shoddy branch of OKBazaars. The clientele is 60/70% coloured; one goes through the Malays, Africans, Indians, coloureds and then one gets to the squalid tea-room where everybody looks pallidly white as they drink soda fizzes and slosh coffee. We were refused service, complained to the Manager who referred us to his next boss at the OKBazaars. We then went off to the OK where the rest were being refused service and the Press and Special Branch were waiting. After some twenty minutes Neil Ross, the organizer, said that he would take everybody away if he could discuss the legal position with the management on Monday. We have it from the highest Group Areas Authority lawyer that the law as it stands is bad law and that prosecution would fail.

Was it the heavy brigade coming to beat us up?
(13 December 1960) I have been in photograph on the front page of *The Cape Times* and *The Golden City Post*. [The delightful open-air cafe under the trees in the Dutch East India Company Gardens was run by the Council. There was no colour bar but only whites are going there. A dozen Liberals of assorted colours went on Sunday afternoon to test this and, as was correct, nobody was refused service. We were sitting with tea under the waving shadows of the trees when I heard the crunch, crunch, crunch of feet on gravel and thought that it was the heavy brigade coming in to beat us up. I spun round and FLASH went the camera of the *Cape Times* photographer. On Monday morning I was on the front cover looking very startled. [A fortnight later I was walking along the sand dunes at Hermanus with Uncle Iver who said 'Was that you on the front of the *Cape Times*?' 'Yes!' I said, blushing. 'Don't tell, Aunt Iris!' he said.]

How dare you ridicule apartheid?
(5 December 1960) I suppose you saw in the English press that *Contact* was fined a total of £500 by the Nat magistrate who in his summing up said that the newspaper had 'ridiculed apartheid' and attacked that honest man the Minister of Justice Erasmus. Within almost the same two days the *Port Elizabeth Evening Post*, and the neo-communist paper *New Age* had their cases withdrawn by other magistrates who allowed that no summons could be issued after the repeal of the State of Emergency. Pat Duncan is appealing.

No rain for five years in the northern Cape
(13 December 1960) Had a fascinating Saturday. Tim and I with two other Liberals went 200 miles north to the drought-stricken areas of Namaqualand to see [and report for *Contact* on] what was happening to the Coloureds who had been left without livelihoods when the sheep were railed to Natal and the OFS. The sheep were saved. The humans were left. At Van Rhynsdorp we found one coloured woman living under a donkey cart with three minute kids. She had come from where there had been no rain for 2 years. It had not rained elsewhere for 5 years. What a conception! Unfortunately one of

Tim's shock absorbers got broken on the terrible roads in the blasted heat.

Conspiracy at the Ovambo barber's shop
[Randolph was building up his lifelong commitment to Namibia which, under the name of South West Africa, was until 1990 ruled by South Africa under a mandate from the United Nations. The Liberals in Cape Town were building up an alliance with SWAPO (South West Africa People's Organisation) who were predominately Ovambo from right up on the northern border and into Angola. It was to prove a crucial area for infiltration. Patrick Duncan saw Angola as key to the liberation of South Africa.

Many of the Ovambos worked in Cape Town – especially in the docks - and one of their social and political centres was a barber's shop on the main road out to Sea Point. Tim said that we ought to go there to have our hair cut so that we could talk to them; barber's shops are the great talking shops for African men. It was initially rather awkward in that they felt that they had to go out of their way to sterilise their equipment.

Their leader in Cape Town was Andreas Shipanga who had been educated at an Afrikaner mission and spoke Afrikaans so fluently that officials assumed that, dark black though he was, he must be 'coloured' that is of mixed race and therefore entitled to an identity card rather than the *Dom Pas* the Africans had to carry. He decided to apply for an identity card under the Afrikaner name of Andreas Cloete. He got a photographer friend to smear margarine on his head and face, bring in very strong photographic lights to produce such a shine that his identity photo showed his skin as very light. He appeared before the Group Areas Officer whom he addressed humbly in Afrikaans. There he was standing on the other side of the desk deeply black. The official didn't look at him but looked at his photo and stamped his application for an identity card which legally classified him as a 'Coloured'.]

1961

Good parties for the Nuwe Jaar
(3 January 1961) I am sorry not to have written for such a long time. I hope that you had a happy Christmas. I went town to Hermanus for Christmas and did not dislike it as much as last year and had some most enjoyable swimming.

This is the last evening of holiday which, with the exception of last Friday, has lasted from two days before Christmas. Not only is the day after New

Year a holiday but in the Cape but also *Tweede Nuwe Jaar* (the Second of January) because the Coloureds have their great jamboree taking over all the streets from District Six to Green Point. Anyhow it has been a pleasant and useful change.

There have been some good and not so good parties. One at the house of an architect member of the Liberal Party, Ferdy Nolte, was chiefly marked for me by the enormous argument I had with an architect about the redevelopment of the docks called the Foreshore. One person said to me 'You were the only person at that party with any consistency. I left the party and came back an hour and a half later and you were still in the same place arguing with the same man.'

We also had an impromptu Bach concert. Do you remember in Wynberg going into the Dutch chap Hans Fransen's house? He is a Bach addict and we started taking different parts in the Brandenburgs and the Matthew Passion and Cantatas and other things. You remember the pretty street of single storey houses where Hans lived? About a fortnight before Christmas the whole street had another party. This time there were about five hundred people there at one time or another and the police parked their van at the end of the road and two of the constables were found asleep in one of the houses the next morning. At one stage in the evening June te Water rode up the street on a white horse in black tights from head to foot with a black mask. [June te Water is the daughter of Charles te Water former High Commissioner whom I had visited when I first arrived.]

I suggested to Marquard that Hans Fransen might be a possible for the Oxford University Press where we are looking for an Afrikaans-speaking person to run publicity. He is a proof reader on *Die Burger* at the moment and so is a member of the Liberal Party under a pseudonym and wants to change his job. Anyhow he and Marquard and I had a pleasant lunch together. One positive thing came out of it as he is engaged at the moment on a programme of photographing Cape Dutch houses and is wanting to get a book together and to raise some money. Marquard knows all these do-good cultural organisations and if he feels the photographs are promising enough he will try to get a publication grant from the Molteno foundation or some such group. Then we might publish it for Christmas next year.

We had a Liberal Party party in the Malay house where we had the khalifa party. This was for New Year. Unfortunately a crucial mistake was made a midnight when we all went out into the street to sing in the new year and all the local '*skollies* and riff-raff' came back in and, as they say, it all 'became rather out of hand' and we finished earlier than we had meant to. About thirty of the most active members moved on to Peter Hjul's house in Sea

Point. One of the cars had broken down and so I was landed with taking eight people home before going on to this sub-party. We got going to the strains of a chap called Samson who is the messenger for typesetters which sets *Contact*. 'We Africans are always asking too much of the white man.' Eventually we found ourselves shedding people about ten or twelve miles out in the southern suburbs in places like Vasco da Gama and Parow. At one place we went down a great many dirt roads to some sub-dorpy on the Cape flats called Tweevlei. I was now left with one pleasant bearded Xhosa chap Shibi Ndlumbini who works for Longmans and a girl who had taken this rather long way round to Peter Hjul's party. We lost the way back to the main road and got bedded in the sand. We had a hilarious but rather hysterically worried forty minutes trying to get free. Reversing and going forward merely meant that we went down to the axles in the sand. Then we started laying bushes behind and reversing. This failed and so we really got down to work at digging a great ditch out with our hands from the back wheels up to the front. I raised the sharp ends of branches under the tyres and then others cross ways and to our relief the car juddered and then lurched out onto the hard road again. Then we got stopped by the police taking Shibi back into Langa township. I was polite and could not think of anything to say but the truth: 'I have just been at a party with this friend and am giving him a lift.' The policeman was quite civil and said 'Go on' which I did not expect ... as it is strictly speaking illegal for outsiders to enter the locations after dark.

Sign away your children to the Pope
(5 January 1961) Tim Holmes and Sally Morgan back from getting married with full Roman Catholic nuptials in Underberg in Natal. Sally seemed to enjoy it like mad which is all very amusing (But perhaps after her drifting life she seems to need something a bit more conventional.) They had instruction from a priest who said things like they should not sleep together when drunk or the child would be an idiot. How anybody can laugh and joke about it all and then be married by them and sign away your children (she says Tim won't make her keep her promise).

Christmas Card and East Indiaman
(17 January 1961) I had a letter from Mary Kirwood in Natal saying that she had failed the politics part of her final exams though she had got a second in English. This is ironical as she probably knew about real politics than anybody. [She has decided] to go on with the visit to Europe which she hopes will give her a bit more balanced an outlook on South Africa in which

she is too emotionally involved.

She and her mother seem to have liked my Christmas card so much that they took it out visiting with them. They [showed it] to Dr Hans Meidner, university man and prominent member of the Liberal Party in Natal. The Meidners said, according to Mary, 'Talking of good typography have you seen the book on the Grosvenor, East Indiaman?' Mary says 'Our pride immediately soared.' It is pleasant to have such biased supporters. It was the first time Mary had seen my cover. Joy Millar last night was talking about the how she had been discussing the dust cover for her forthcoming book on Cape Town with her publisher Bill Kerr of Longmans. 'I don't think he liked it when I produced your Grosvenor book and said I thought that was a good idea for a jacket.'

I was not arrested
(23 January 1961) I suppose some news of the fact that 12 sitters-in were arrested has percolated through to the English press. I would have been if I had not been down at Kommetjie. As for your exhortations about lying low I see no reason for them really except that it is possibly not altogether right to fiddle around in another country's affairs. But while I am living in the privileged society at the expense of the non-whites (so-called), I must do something. I am, after all one of the people who can suffer least having no dependants and a British passport.

Anyhow the point is that we do not consider that we are even breaking the law of the country with 'sit-ins'. On Saturday they had their names taken and then were told that they were under arrest – a quite unnecessary procedure in view of the fact that we were quite open about the whole matter. They were taken to the police station and were not allowed to phone our lawyers. One woman at the restaurant had asked, however, if there was anything she could do and she had been told to contact Barney Zackon one of the Liberal lawyers. Time 11.30 a.m. They were finger-printed and interrogated. They were told that they not need to answer the questions put to them and most of them answered 'No Answer' to everything including race, colour. They were put under stupid school discipline and were not allowed to talk and were yelled at when they laughed by one or two of the nastier police. On the whole they were treated reasonably except that they had no food.

Peter Hjul and Barney Z. arrived about 2 p.m. having got together £400 bail in spite of the fact that the banks had closed. Eventually at about 4.30 p.m. they were released. The charge was that, under the September 1960 Group Areas Act Proclamation, they were 'illegally occupying premises'. This is a foully prejudiced charge in that it means that the whites must get off and it will be the blacks and coloureds who will be found guilty. Dyson, the expert on the Group Areas Act who is to represent them, is confident that the law is so bad (legally) that they will all get off anyhow and that the government will now have to make a special law. Anyhow this morning in court they were formally remanded and their bail was reduced to £15 each from £25. Everybody is pleased that the case is coming up now and that the publicity will underline the hopelessness of the government's legal advisers.

Is there any hope?
(23 January 1961) Every now and again one feels that there's simply no hope. It so happened that several arguments and discussions over the weekend made me feel this way. One gets the panicky feeling that every month the situation goes further and further towards the point of no recall. Then first thing this morning Professor Cowen arrived with another batch of proofs of *The Foundations of Freedom* with its proposal about how to build an integrated society in SA. He was despondent. He says South Africans are just too backward in their thinking and their absolute assumption in every thought is of the complete inferiority of the non-whites. He mentioned that Duminy, the weak Principal of the University, has just forbidden the medical graduates from having a graduation dinner together because he is afraid that the non-white medics 'will get drunk and miscegenate.' Professor Brookes at the congress of the Institute of Race Relations last week said 'I apologise to all my African friends for having always urged moderation. I apologise … I was wrong. Moderation has got them nowhere.'

It is so easy to escape. There I was down at Kommetjie on the Saturday morning talking with Mavis Orpen about New York and Dylan Thomas and Greek statuary while seven of my friends were being arrested. Sylvia Sypkyns and I swam three times on Saturday. Once before breakfast, once before lunch and once before tea. She went to the Primary school at Ermelo and stayed in the girl's hostel where she used to jam her hat on her head every now and then, pick up her bag and go for a sleep walk. She was taught of course by Miss Pateman (who had taught Ralph from the age of 10).

Would I go to Rhodesia?
(4 February 1961) Marquard came into my office me in and said 'Do not make your mind up about Rhodesia yet. I am quite certain in my mind now that you should stay in Cape Town with David Philip [when he comes back from the new Salisbury OUP marketing office]. Of course London and Cannon may disagree. I think that Marquard already feels that he can trust my judgement in practical matters. I gather, indirectly, that he may have

been a little influenced by an evening at his house not long ago when Sir Basil Blackwell was there. The evening finished up with Blackwell inviting me to visit them any time I visit Oxford or get started at the Clarendon Press.

(21 February 1961) The Censorship Bill was turned down because of big opposition by Afrikaans presses who have Cabinet Ministers on their boards and saw how it would be more difficult to make cash. Cannon refused to see how impossible the Bill was. He had told me personally how the Bill would make it easier for OUP.

A swimming pool shaped like Africa
(21 February 1961) Spent a lot of the week-end finishing *Contact* for the printers. Pat Duncan has been away and Tim Holmes's father has just died so that Peter Hjul and I have been holding the fort while Randolph has been trying to find out the truth about the stories of the police in the Transkei using shocks to get confessions to the murder of a headman. He phoned through some good stories just as we were trying to put *Contact* together, out at Pat Duncan's house. Pat has a swimming pool in the garden shaped like Africa and we swam before supper.

The Royal Navy illustriously plays to a segregated audience
(21 February 1961) The aircraft carrier HMS *Illustrious*, without its coloured ratings aboard, was in Cape Town [to drum up support for keeping South Africa in the Commonwealth]. The Royal Marine band is playing for three nights at one of the cinemas, which non-whites cannot enter except as cleaners. So the Liberal Party bought 10 tickets. A mixed bunch of sitters-in went this evening. I have not heard what happened. They counted on being turned away. We have sent a telegram this afternoon asking Grimond [head of UK Liberal Party] to ask the British Government if it is aware that a band of the Royal Navy has been hired to play to a segregated audience when it could have been hired to play at places where all races can go. I hope that it causes a prick.

Make the best of a white job
(21 February 1961) We had a Liberal Party Forum on Thursday evening where Stanley Uys correspondent for *The Observer*, was speaking…He says that the Progressive Party performance in the house this session has been frightfully disappointing. Up until the policy declaration on the franchise people had felt that there was a touch of idealism and bravery about them. But now they have voted with the government on the Republic bill. They

say let's all get together to make the best of a white job. They have made no stand on the fact that the majority of the country were not consulted.

The Great Decimation
(4 February 1961) I have sent you a copy of the little booklet *Decimal Coinage in a Nutshell*. [SA is about to decimalise from Pounds to Rands.] This was going so fast at 500 a time ordered by telegram that I had the great experience of ordering a reprint 4 days from publication, although we still have not had any big Transvaal orders. My hard work on publicity I hope will pay off. We sent off forty publicity copies to newspapers and two hundred to schools. I wrote letters to contacts in newspapers suggesting it would go best in the gossip columns and it has indeed appeared in several of them.

(21 February 1961) We have just suffered what David Marais the cartoonist calls the 'Great Decimation'. D-day was the day of the beginning of Rand and Cent. Up until Tuesday everybody had been practising and the shopkeepers had little jokes about asking for money in decimal coinage. Since Tuesday everybody has reverted to £sd because the new currency is simply not available. They have only minted cents and half cents and it seems as though they are too few to go round. Lots of businesses decided that it would be easier if they only took cents and then they ran out. Everybody with anything to sell has made sure that they are not going to lose and a lot have just exploited the situation .... Even the government has joined in as a one cent stamp only does the work of a penny stamp now so that you only get 200 cent stamps instead of 240 penny stamps....But still it is a measure which I hope that England follows.

King Kong is bigger than Cape Town
(21 February 1961) Everybody is wildly interested on the left wing, and not only on the left, about the Black African musical *King Kong* moving to London. I do hope that it is a success. We will then have the government claiming it as a triumph for the Bantustans. It really looks as if it is going to be a hit (what with Mrs Anthony Armstrong-Jones a.k.a Princess Margaret at the opening night.)

(21 February 1961) There is an interesting if slightly sentimental article in *Drum* headlined 'Fringe-country; where there is no colour bar.' The opening picture is of mixed guests at the wedding of Arthur Jenkins who I met on the way to Roma University in Basutoland.

Brave liberals in the Malay Quarter and in District Six
(6 March 1961) Yesterday we had a 'Strydag' för the Cape Town Liberals to outline plans for 1961 and to whip up a bit of enthusiasm. This has meant a week of trying to visit all the City branch members. As the majority of them live in the Malay Quarter and the District Six it is pitifully revealing and some of the hovels and the stenches that one skirts round are pretty ghastly although in the middle of this urban desolation practically all the party members have clean and decently, if cheaply, furnished rooms. It takes quite a lot of bravery for some of them to join because there is considerable opposition to the Liberal Party as being white controlled and just another form of disguised white domination. I have got myself the job of organising some sort of small study group within the party to study points of economic doctrine and how to work out the details of Liberal policy in South Africa.

Catching up on London
(6 March 1961) It has been most interesting over the last ten days catching up on London a bit. Randolph's twenty-five year-old second sister Thea is in South Africa for a holiday. (P.S. 10 March 1961) Apparently she may be going to marry Paul Thompson, one of my most brilliant Oxford contemporaries, who got a congratulatory first after being shoved in jail for Official Secrets Case because he revealed things in *Isis* which had horrified him while doing the Russian Course in National Service. It has been enjoyable to talk of Bergman's Swedish films and the Coal Exchange, the Barbican and the *Times v. Guardian*, of comprehensive schools and class. She says she is her parents' biggest disappointment. They are conservative United Party and do not quite know what they have sired; Randolph full time for the Liberal Party, Thea a socialist, Phoebe a UCT student who knows all the Black men and Coloureds. The one redeeming personage is, sister Pamela who married a very safe and prosperous Mr Brown.

Hop on a Vespa
(10 March 1961) Yesterday was a day full of interest. In the morning we rushed out to Stellenbosch to go to the marriage of two of our friends… Annette had a beige brocade dress with an enormous bow, green to complement her red hair. It was all rather delightfully fresh. It took place in the little Anglican church on the Braak in the midst of Saturday market. The reception was held at Lanzerac, in the blue morning with white staring walls.
(10 March 1961) Then in Cape Town I went on to a party given to raise

funds for the sitters-in. Their case has been remanded again and their bail finally returned. The government obviously wants to keep them tied up under charge until the new amendment to the Group Areas Act comes through and then the police will abandon this case.

Then some of us went on to another party with a bit of a difference. This was the weekly hop organised by the South West Africans to raise cash for the Ovamboland People's Organisation (They are all also members of the LP and very moderate.) It was held in the garage of a large firm of wholesalers. A little Vespa transporter with the name of the firm written all over the side used to pop in and out loaded with drinks or loudspeakers. We got huge amusement out of this; the owner of the firm would leap out of his posh bed in his posh Constantia homestead if he knew what his delivery wagons were being used for in the early hours of Sunday amid the dirty newspapers of District Six. The 150 people all sat on benches round the concrete floor; when the music started they would all leap to their feet and jive and Kwela furiously; when the music stopped they all promptly sat down.

Cowen's secret mission to the US
(10 March 1961) Professor Cowen has been in US on a secret mission with several opposition figures. He started the week by telephoning Marquard at 7.30 a.m. after getting back from America with loads of complaints about his page proofs. Marquard was furious and told him he could take his page proofs elsewhere if he would not stop interfering with the technical side of publishing. This disciplined him a bit but nevertheless meant an average of three phone calls a day from him, his wife or his secretary. He is so conceited that he cannot think that his is not the only book on the go. He thinks that it is so saleable that that he is already talking of a paperback edition although we are going to be doing all right if we get through its 3,400 hardbacks.

Kicked out of the Commonwealth
(6 March 1961) There is naturally intense interest in the Prime Minister's conference [and whether South Africa will be thrown out of the Commonwealth]. The general feeling is that South Africa will not be kicked out completely. There is feeling among most Liberals that it would be better to be out than in; Verwoerd has shown that he will not move especially over the latest demand by the moderates for concessions to the coloureds. I think that Nehru, Sandys and Macmillan will work out a compromise.
(22 March 1961) Benny the liftman said 'We've won'. The Africans are thrilled; for them it's recognition by the world-wide group of nations. The English South Africans are blind with fury; for them it will mean emotional

and economic losses. Judging by the SABC, which has over the last week more or less lost all pretence at impartiality, the government wanted South Africa in the Commonwealth club. But now they have been kicked out they have now exploited the feelings of the anti-British and anti-Kaffir Afrikaner; the visit to London of Verwoerd is rendered on SABC as a triumph and a crowd of thousands hysterically cheered him at Jan Smuts airport in Johannesburg on his return.

In Pietermaritzburg [in British-supporting Natal Province] work stopped for a couple of days and there were groups of people in the town standing around talking about nothing else. On the other hand there are certain English South Africans who say 'Oh well! Perhaps we are better out! The Commonwealth isn't what it was with all these other natives [i.e. Africans from newly independent African countries].' An Englishwoman the other day was quoted as saying 'The only difference between now and when Smuts was in power is that the niggers have money.'

I personally feel that it is essential for the Commonwealth that South Africa is out. I hope that people will be brought to their senses by being hit in their pockets but (a) I am afraid that Macmillan is under trading pressure in England to make it an easy settlement and (b) that this second rate set of country bumpkins will become more and more extreme at the bottom of Africa. The steady loss of capital, brains and trade will merely put them into the position of a third-rate nation instead of a first-rate small nation which is leading the whole of southern Africa. The general feeling here has hardened into one of gloom. I think that Verwoerd is one of the few who is not a fool; he knows that he has to go on without compromise and apply every ounce of prejudice to maintain his power. But as for the rest of these people in the Cabinet they are just farmers in Sunday suits.

Sit-in jail!
(21 February 1961) We have had a period of terrible interior feuding over the sit-in trial. The Citizen Group, who are Marxist coloured intellectuals, have recently joined the Liberal Party en masse. One of them called Kenneth Hendrickse is quite a friend of mine. They have insisted that the trial must be conducted on a purely political basis with great speeches. The lawyers and the executive of the party in the Cape say the political implications will come out from the legal conduct of the trial and that the object is to get the people off.

(22 March 1961) More of the sit-in people were arrested on Saturday. The first case has been twice, no thrice, remanded because the police have no case under the law as it stands and they are trying using 'awaiting trial' to

stop those individuals sitting-in while an amendment goes through the House of Assembly. This time they tried some pretty nasty bullying tactics; they arrested Neil Ross who was not even in the restaurant but was waiting outside to see what happened.

Drumming up a new magazine
(4 April 1961) I have now found out the exact situation over the new newspapers and magazines. Tom Hopkinson (he leaves *Drum* next month) is starting one with American backing which is going to be a *Life* for Southern Africa and should probably become the world's best in this televisionless country where the visual potentialities are so terrific. Bailey, the owner of *Golden City Post* and *Drum*, has inherited mining wealth and is difficult. He advertised for a new editor for *Drum* before he had even told Hopkinson. The first H. knew was when he saw an advert in the *Sunday Times*. Anyhow the important thing about this new paper is that it will not just be for Africans or whites but for both. A tremendous positive step. In at the right time with the rising middle class in Rhodesia especially, not to mention Ghana.

The Treason Trial is stopped after five years
(4 April 1961) The main occasion this week has been the stopping of the Treason Trial with all charges withdrawn. [1956-1961; 156 people including Mandela, Tambo and Alex la Guma]. Rejoicing is mixed with horror at the waste of so many valuable people's lives for five years …

Patrick Duncan is suppressed as a communist
(4 April 1961) I do not know whether the English newspapers have noticed that Patrick Duncan has been banned under the Suppression of Communism Act from attending all meetings for a political purpose of more than 2 persons. Ironically he has often been accused of defeating the common cause against apartheid by his fearless showing up of the manoeuvrings of the SA Communist Party. Also banned was Joe Nkatlo, Vice-President of the Cape Liberal Party, who left the SA Communist Party over their official line towards the Ribbentrop Pact of 1939 when the Russians signed up with Nazi Germany (he was told that the Germans were running a capitalist war of no concern to world communism) and then changing sides when Germany invaded Russia in 1941 (he was then told that it was a national patriotic people's war).

(6 July 1961) I was down at Kommetjie today and we heard the BBC's 8 o'clock news with its recording of Russian astronaut Yury Gagarin over

London crackling over the ether. The SABC news started tonight with the announcement that the NATO allies are 'preparing for war'. Suddenly it all seemed so far away and yet close because of this person flitting round the world. Everything here which is so important to us seemed suddenly so parochial. (Wikipedia says 12 April 1961)

Africa Day on the Grand Parade
(19 April 1961) Last Sunday we had the most successful meeting that the Liberal Party have apparently ever held in the Cape. Three years ago the Liberals held the first Africa Day meeting [celebrating independence in Africa]; last year the State of Emergency stopped it. We Liberals were anxious to establish outright this year to be the people who held the meeting on the Grand Parade in front to the City Hall and just down Hanover Street from District Six. So in order to stop there being a whole group of rival meetings in various corners – as might well have happened – we decided to hold a rally at which we would have speakers from all across the left. This was arranged with some good diplomacy and most left or lefter wing organisations sent speakers with the exception of the Progressives. We had ANC, PAC (or rather members of the ex-PAC or ex-members of the ex-ANC as they now have to be legally described while the ban lasts – it has just been renewed for a second year). Others giving speeches were one of Huddleston's 'meddling Priests' called Father Macbride, Albie Sachs of the Congress of Democrats, somebody from the Coloured People's Congress, Liberals Hammington Majija and Eddie Daniels (also secretary of the Coloured People's Convention, the new move for united action by the coloureds), and Liberal Mrs Eulalie Stott (National Chairwoman of Black Sash and recently elected to Cape Town City Council). Cape Town Liberal Peter Hjul ran the occasion as a rousing and magnificent chairman.

The temper of the crowd was excitement mixed with good humour, even when it rained half-way through the meeting. Roars of applause for the whole two hours as they stood packed together. Estimates varied from 3,500 by *Die Burger* (inevitably) through 7,000 by *Argus* and *Cape Times* to 10,000 by *Contact* (Tim Holmes inevitably). Anyhow it was an enormous crowd mainly, although far from exclusively, non-white. Stanley Uys, *Observer* and Joburg *Sunday Times*, was carefully examining the Special Branch through the back window of one of their two Fords. He swore that one of them must be writing Chinese because he was only writing about one word in five directly up the page.

One of the features of the meeting was when an ex-member of the now-banned ex-ANC made a final appeal for money. Collectors had already spent forty minutes weaving through the crowd. Suddenly some-one threw a penny and then everybody began to throw cents, pennies, tickies and half-crowns at the platform (the back of a lorry). All the speakers had spoken in front of a eight-foot high map of Africa painted by me on two of the bed-sheets Tim Holmes took with him to boarding school. This sheet map was also carried through the crowd and people threw money into it. The total collection was nearly £70. There were fifteen pounds worth of pennies and cents. It cost nearly £50 to organise though; 2000 hand-outs, 250 posters (Two of them 'Come and celebrate the Coming Freedom' are still strongly glued to the builders' hoardings outside the new Union Castle offices – although there have been several attempts at ripping them down.) [I was to use sections from the photos of the crowd on my paperback cover design for *African Nationalism* by Ndabaningi Sithole.]

Shaking the Progressives
(29 April 1961) Cowen gave the Hoernlé Memorial Lecture at UCT this week, which is normally a staid occasion. It shook the people who had recently left the Liberal Party and gone Progressive to hear his call for universal adult suffrage. Cowen's book came out this week and everybody in my immediate circle has been discussing it. He has rather spoilt the effect by announcing that he is taking up a professorship at Chicago University; it is felt that he is ratting by leaving the struggle in South Africa.

I went to see the tame Richardson version of Faulkner's *Sanctuary* last night. Before it there was a film on Henrietta Szold who did a lot with refugee children from Germany for Israel. It was quite powerfully although a little sentimentally told. It was full of shots of Hitler and pogroms and refugees and split families. It was followed with rapt attention and there were tears and handkerchiefs all around. The end was greeted with great clapping. I wondered what percentage of that all-white audience really drew any parallels with what was happening to non-white families within ten miles of them. At the end of the *Sanctuary* film the large beautiful negress clasps the white head of the heroine with her hands. The cinema was full of shifting people.

I enjoyed the BBC Caribbean talks you made for Hank Swanzy [Henry Swanzy the creator of the formidably encouraging weekly writing programme called 'Caribbean Voices' and widower of artist Tirzah Garwood whose first husband had been Eric Ravilious.] I see Julian Mitchell has written a novel. Second Wadham novel of my time after David Caute. I have written 8 out of 22 chapters of my first draft.

We had a Liberal Party concert of African music on Friday. Choirs, dancers and penny whistlers. Inevitably the choirs arrived late. Then there was one extra which had come uninvited and very grudgingly had to restrict itself to two songs instead of the usual 20 minutes.

'Shame!' the classic South African remark of a woman last night passing a wreck of a car which had rolled itself to bits.

Strike against the Republic
(29 April 1961) The concern at this moment is whether the 'stay-at-home' by Africans and Coloureds at the time of the Republican celebrations at the end of May will succeed. This strike has been called by the ANC ('strike' is of course an illegal word in South Africa). *Contact* is prone to supporting it although the Liberal Party is divided as to whether to support an event which has been called by the Commie-influenced ANC. I feel that it is the only sort of weapon left although I do not know whether in fact this particular stay-at-home is being sufficiently well-organised. Lots of whites say that it will only lead to violence; I suppose a certain number violent incidents will take place and the Africans will burn a certain number of schools and churches. Such is the sadness although it is obvious that the sooner a change can be made the better will be the result in terms of a balanced society.

'A war footing'
(29 April 1961) But the laager mentality is with us. It was announced by the Minister of Defence in the House of Assembly this week that the South African Defence Force (not external but internal defence – a militia rather than an army) is to be brought onto 'a war footing'. As Anthony Delius put it the government is arming itself against four-fifths of the inhabitants of the country.

(20 May 1961) One cannot decide whether the government are scared or whether they think that, by banning all meetings and calling out Civilian Defence Units, they are going to frighten everybody. They seem determined to create a crisis. They are … like kids trying to keep the centre of attention at a birthday party. They keep bleating that nobody is going to spoil their fun at the end of the month when they have their Voortrekker Republic fest.

The government has in effect banned all political parties left of the Progressives. We have been forbidden to hold ordinary committees. We have to ask the magistrate for permission for everything. This in effect means all legal means of expression by non-whites has gone until 26 June 1961 at least.

Last night we were having a quiet and small party in town when we had the benefit of the attention of Van der Westhuizen, the head of the Special

Branch in Cape Town, two constables and Grobler, a young Special Branch man. We had rung up the magistrate that morning to find out if we had to have a permit. We were told that it was all right as it was a private party in a private house with private invitations. Van der Westhuizen, a horrifyingly small man, not in stature but in character, ... was talking to Neil Ross and the Liberal Party Secretary Val Hutchinson, who were running the party, when lawyer Barney Zackon came over and said could he help. Van der W. immediately lost his temper.

Intimidators with dispatch cases
Erasmus, the Minister of Injustice, had made a remark in parliament about how you could see how many 'intimidators' there were around if you took a look at the number of dispatch cases in African hands at a Sea Point bus stop. The *Argus* did a mock serious spot check in the brief cases of ten Africans, Coloureds and Europeans at Sea Point bus stops; all they found were garlic sausage, insurance forms and copies of the *Cape Times*. I said within Grobler's hearing 'Anybody got a dispatch case?' He took the jibe but had a 'doing duty' attitude and was very polite.

Anthony Delius thinks that this government will he out in three months. Or so he said at a party at the Millars on Friday. From his observations in the House of Assembly he judges that they will go. Too much to hope I am afraid. They just do not seem to have anybody of sufficient standing in the caucus to challenge Verwoerd and Erasmus who are supported by the numerically superior Transvaal....

Glad you liked the Cowen book. It is very readable stuff I think. I have been busy on covers for the paperback edition of *African Nationalism* and for *Tshekedi Khama of Bechuanaland* and with publicity for a book from the Clarendon Press with the timely title *The Fall of Kruger's Republic*.

The 'stay-at-homes' go back to work
(29 May 1961) Today [the stay-at-home] was the great disappointment we rather expected. The spirit, which they had only a fortnight ago, had gone out of the Africans. The Pan Africanists, who ran the march into Cape Town last year, issued a 'go to work' call on Saturday – the wretches. They said the communist-influenced members of the ANC were running it, which was probably true. Anyhow I think the ban on meetings meant people lost enthusiasm and started to think about losing their jobs. Plus the constant police intimidation.

Things simply aren't bad enough at the moment. A *Cape Times* reporter who was at Langa 5.00 a.m. this morning said he was horrified by the ordinariness of it all. People did not look guilty going to work. They did not show any hesitation. He began to wonder if they had something else up their sleeves for later in the week.

Anyhow the Afrikaners are all going ahead with their jollities to mark the establishment of the Republic. Randolph and I were talking today about how amazing it is that they are going ahead with their festivities as though the Republic will last a thousand years. I suppose that the celebrations would annoy people like ourselves if we were not so absolutely confident that this republic will be smashed before too long. One of Randolph's headlines in *Contact* this week refers to the 'First Republic'. Unfortunately one is pessimistic about the length of time involved – perhaps ten years and each a year nearer bloodshed and chaos.

I went to the House of Assembly last week to hear Verwoerd answer Sir de Villiers Graaf's questions about the emergency measures. He showed such contempt for parliamentary procedure that he did not answer a single question but simply made a statement. Lawrence (Progressive) was shouted at by Nats when he rose on a point of order. Klopper, doddering old speaker, at times practically censors Progressives. He has read, he boasts, the bible 24 times and he behaves like he had.

Smuggling Contact equipment into Swaziland
(Early June 1961) I have just spent a week on leave driving round the Union to drop people and things. Went up to Pietermaritzburg then via Ermelo to Swaziland then back via Johannesburg to Cape Town. 2,500 miles in a Volkswagen Combi. All very rushed but interesting people.

[For some reason, perhaps the Post Office reading his letters, this was all I told Ralph and Stella about this eventful journey. What follows is written from memory in 2018:

A year after Sharpeville there was a tremendous build up for weeks before the planned stay-at-home which was to take place on 28, 29 and 30 May 1961. Strikes were illegal so, in order to produce the effect of a 3 day General Strike, people were urged to 'stay-at-home' and not go to work. Pat Duncan anticipated that this trick would provoke ferocious reaction by the government and he feared that *Contact* would be closed down by the Special Branch. He asked Tim Holmes and myself to move the journal some 1,200 miles across South Africa to Swaziland, which was still ruled by the British. Tim was to set up an office on the farm of an exile friend near the capital Mbabane. Pat Duncan asked me whether I would I take a week's holiday from OUP so that I could drive his Volkswagen Combi loaded with all the equipment needed to re-establish the paper out of the range of the

Special Branch. There were boxes of editorial and reference files and the addressograph plates to print out the names of the subscribers. Ibraham Abrahams, the Cape Malay general factotum in the office, would drive up with me and would stay behind there setting up the office. Tim Holmes would a few days later drive up in his Morris Minor, which he would need if he was to run the paper in rural Swaziland for the foreseeable future. The distances are formidable though the good roads are tarmacked for fast driving. Somewhere coming over the top of a rise I rammed a sheep breaking its back. The impact drove in the bumper on the front passenger side and bent in the bodywork against the wheel. Ibraham and I pulled it away from the tyre and we drove slowly into the next dorp looking for a garage for running repairs. There was suddenly a loud bang on our VW Combi. A car under garage test was driving out of town when a wheel hub came spinning across the road and dented the middle panel of Pat Duncan's Combi. One was of course nervous about lost time and being questioned by the police. The mechanic led us into his motor repair garage. I bartered with them that we would forget the damage to the paintwork if they yanked out our bumper and secured it. A deal was done and a repair was cobbled together and we were off again with no sign of police. We reached Carolina in the Eastern Transvaal and nervously approached the Swaziland international frontier wondering whether it would be manned after dark. Would South African police border guards be suspicious of this heavily-loaded van crossing the frontier at night? Ibraham only had an identity card and I had a British passport. Maybe he would have to circumvent the border post on foot. Desperately tired one was relieved that there was no official there and we headed for the capital Mbabane. The Central Hotel was half-way along the main street. The British manager viewed us suspiciously and said to me, as though Ibraham was not there, 'What nationality is he?' That was easy. I said 'South African' but what he really wanted to ask is 'What race is he?' He showed us our room in the grounds and as he left he said 'I'm as much against these nazis as you are but I must ask you to take breakfast in your room. Some of the people here would object.' I said that we would keep out of sight. When room service was charged on our bill I asked for its removal.

The next day we went out to the farm and Pat Duncan's exile friend showed us the outbuilding for *Contact* and with great relief we unloaded. Later after lunch I set out on my own to drive back to Cape Town. I planned to drive until midnight and then kip in the van. As I was driving across the highveld south of Johannesburg the name Klerksdorp began to appear on the traffic signs.]

PostNatal Exercises
(Early June 1961) Stayed with [Ferdie and Helene Nolte] who used to be in Cape Town and are now living in Klerksdorp, a gold mining boom town. They used to be very active in the Liberal party in Cape Town. He is an architect and has gone up to K. for a year to supervise the building of an extension to the town hall. From the word go he has been under observation. He wondered how the council had managed to fix them a house so briskly when there is a great housing shortage and he is pretty sure that that it is so that the people opposite can keep an eye on him and his wife for the police. One day the brother of their maid, who is a treason-trialist and used to be an organiser for the ANC, arrived in a truck which he drives for a firm of wholesalers. He was there for only two minutes but within five minutes the local Special Branch Volkswagen came cruising around. The night I arrived the light in the house opposite was on, even though it had been off earlier.

Ferdie was fined for entering a location without a permit and failing to stop at a stop sign on the way out; he had been taking an African back who was teaching them both Xhosa. Immediately he was fined the hot-heads on the Council started to agitate for his removal. This attack picked up last week when they heard that he was one of those raided throughout the Union by the police. I arrived two days afterwards.

I did not get there until 1a.m. I had rung up at ten minutes past midnight in a fit of social doubt about asking them at that hour whether I could stay with them. They were thrilled to see me so that they could tell me all about the raid and we sat talking until 3 o'clock while I had scrambled eggs and brandy. Helene Nolte said she was so relieved to be able to talk to somebody because there are so few people to whom they can. They are both Afrikaans but if anything that makes it worse because they have rejected *die volk*. Helene's father was such a British hater that he once sent a case of his apples to Hitler as a token of his esteem. The letter personally signed by Hitler is carefully preserved. She grew up in an atmosphere of waving Vierkleurs on the Voortrekker Hill in Pretoria. Anyhow raided they were. One policeman spent a long time reading her POSTNATAL EXERCISES (Helene had recently had a baby). I suppose he thought that it was disguised military plans for invading the Transvaal from Natal.

12 days in detention without charge
(Early June 1961) Peter Hjul, Randolph and others were all raided on the same night as the Noltes. In fact Liberals were raided for the first time in Cape Town. They were visited everywhere else except in Pietermaritzburg. The aim seems chiefly to intimidate; it was given out to that it was to find

documents to do with the stay-at-home at the end of May. Anyhow there is a feeling of waiting in the air. Mandela, ex-ANC man who is one of the organisers, told Norton who is Editor of the *Cape Times* that even if the stay-at-home did not come off then at least it had achieved the mobilisation of army and police. Threats would achieve this until the authorities thought that they were crying wolf and then they could strike.

The blighters are trying to do their best to avoid entering the republic with a State of Emergency. One of the worst laws is being rushed through Parliament. It will enable them to lock up people not just for up to 2 days before a charge is laid, as now, but for up to 12 days. They are making it possible for them to call out the army without calling a State of Emergency.

You really feel that are in the police state
(10 June 1961) You begin to feel that you really are in the police state when you go to visit a friend and find that at that very moment he is being escorted out of his flat by four Special Branch plain-clothes men. At the same time another of your friends has simply disappeared for three days. Both things happened this week.

Tim Holmes and Ibraham Abrahams were arrested by the police coming out of Swaziland with the *Contact* equipment. Tim was transferred at 1.30 a.m. by eight sten-gunned policemen from the border police station to Ermelo. The next day he was transferred to Carolina where he was interrogated by Major van den Berghe who was specially sent down from Pretoria because some papers were found on him about a joke anti-republican demonstration. They wanted to know where the paper had come from. Tim saw that the alternative was that either they were going to hold all the *Contact* stuff or that he must give the name of Tom Walters in Cape Town.

Tom Walters was arrested on Friday. He was allowed to go, escorted, to tell his wife whom he had just left taking the kids round the Model Railway Exhibition. He lives within sight of me in a flat on Hof Street. I happened to see that his light was on when passing at about 8.00 that evening soon after I had heard the news. I rushed up thinking that he was on bail but found that he was just coming out escorted. I tried to pretend that I was going upstairs to the next floor but Greef, the nearest Special Branch man asked me what I wanted. So I said to Tom 'I saw your light on and came up.' 'Well I am afraid that I'm otherwise engaged' he said with a stiff smile.

(23 June 1961) Tim and Ibraham have had their case discharged. The police were determined to find something even though the paper they found on Tim was clearly a joke. Tom Walters is still on trial for incitement.

Graphic Arts
(10 June 1961) So Colchester has got its University College. Where is it going to be? Tell Tom Hart [who has given style to the Colchester printers Benhams] to get a Graphic Arts Department, there being so few. The interest in typography would justify it. I must say that I feel that the newest university colleges do seem to be bringing independent ideas. The new courses at Staffordshire and Brighton, which break away from London Teutonism and from the Oxbridge system, are to be encouraged.

I am going to see Cecil Higgs this afternoon to discuss the children's book on Leonardo da Vinci. I have learnt a lot from *Their Secret Ways* [illustrated by Francois Krige] and hope that this is going to work out pretty glamorous for Christmas. Joy Millar's book on Cape Town should be ready for Christmas (Longmans not ours).

Africans give English a lift
(23 June 1961) This has been a week of Marquard being on leave revising his book *Peoples and Policies of South Africa* for a paperback edition. I am going on leave just before he gets back so he asked me to leave notes for him. He made a remark which amused Miss Williams and myself: 'I don't want to make any decisions while you are away ... I mean about which I don't know the background.' This last remark a hurried afterthought.

(23 June 1961) I am going up to the Liberal Party Congress in Durban from 8 to 10 July and then I am taking the other fortnight of my holiday. (By the way I suppose you did get a letter in which I mentioned having been all the way up to Swaziland or did some blighter in the Post Office remove that?)

'The distinguished South African poet R.N. Currey' was mentioned on a programme on the SABC (beg its pardon 'Radio South Africa', although the address given for competitions is Radio South Africa c/o the SABC). Henry Howell mentioned your [R.N. Currey's] three forthcoming programmes in discussion on 'What can the SABC do about the standard of spoken English?' I heard a previous discussion about how could one secure the future of English in South Africa. Frightfully patronising attitude about Afrikaans getting on all right and English in difficulties. I kept muttering 'What about the Africans?' Finally Nadine Gordimer swung in with the main reason why she was not worried about English – it is the Africans who are helping to revivify and revitalise English. She mentioned hearing a young South African in America at Harvard fluently discoursing with some eminent literary authority. It turned out to be Lewis Nkosi, the young Zulu writer on *Drum* who is at Harvard. There were ten seconds of silence afterwards and then they got back to discussing English vis-à-vis Afrikaans.

I had a letter this week from Sally Morgan in New York. She told how Lewis Nkosi, a Japanese girl and Jolyon Nuttall a reporter from Natal had been at her flat and left at about 2 a.m. They were beaten up by a gang of thugs who told them that they did not like seeing a white man walking with a nigger. The ironical thing of course here was a white South African with a Black South African in the free land of the USA and then ... Like the story of the American who got off a plane in independent Accra and said to the nearest black man 'Say, what does it feel like to at last be free?' The answer came: 'I don't really know. I'm from Alabama.'

Delight in the Transkei and its history
Randolph and I spent this morning walking round Lion's Head and up in the wild places behind his house, talking about the tribes of Pondoland and their history. He has an antiquarian's delight in local history. He is becoming more and more knowledgeable about who is related to whom and who pretends to what chieftainship. This means that he is able to get on with Chiefs on his visits. I put it the wrong way round. He was interested in these things first and he enjoys talking about them.

[Randolph asked me one time, when he as was slipping off for more political work in the Transkei, to come and sleep at Clifton House. Gillian Vigne was expecting their second child, Lucy. They had a servant during the day except on Sunday so could I sleep over on Saturday and Sunday? I went off with a walking group to the mountains on Sunday. Inevitably Lucy started early. Gillian was in the bath saying 'I am bloody well not going to have this baby until Randolph gets back from the Transkei.' By the time I returned Lucy had won. Their friend Dr Kok lived just down the steps below Clifton House and was later to save Gillian from dying with asthma.]

Taking off into the New Africa
(6 July 1961) Our magazine is really getting under weigh now. We have been in a state of indecision and deadlock about what to call it. Yesterday Saturday, just before we had an editorial meeting, I put together four suggestions for the design of the headpiece on the front cover. In thinking them out I worked out a new title *The New African* which has connotations that we are all Africans who live in Africa. It has an echo of the name of *The New Statesman* and the radical left. There was immediate agreement after weeks of disagreement. Also my idea for the headpiece was immediately accepted. It has what Randolph calls the 'clothes-hanger men' which I used on Cowen and the typeface Standard Expanded which is very fashionable at the moment and which is widely used in *The Observer* and the new *London Magazine*.

Our plan is to have one or two established names like Paton, Delius, Cowen writing some of the articles and then to get young people in university and liberal circles to write provocatively and constructively. We are paying 3 guineas a thousand words, small but something; nothing for the Editorial Board. Also reviews of African Kultur books, films on Africa, gramophone records, art, history etc. Starting date 1 January 1962, issues once a month, 16 pages *New Statesman* size selling at 1/6 a copy. If we can get rid of 500 copies we will make a small profit. No advertising to begin with but subsidy from mysterious English source. If we can sell 200 or 300 one pound subscriptions we should be all right to begin with. I think we should be hard-hitting, provocative and funny/satirical. We should be able to grow to 24 or 32 pages. Anyhow it is exciting and badly needed especially since *Africa South* has gone into exile and lost touch with South Africa.

I have just been reading the manuscript of a novel sent to the OUP by an African called Fula who signs his letters to us 'African Novelist.' I look at fiction partly for *The New African*. Also Rex Collings is starting in OUP London a new series called Three Crowns with literature from the Asia and Africa. OUP has a strange self-denying ordinance that it does not publish novels, but that it does accept short stories and plays. Fula's novel is called *The Lure of the Golden City* and is all about a country girl being seduced away from her betrothed whose *lobola* bride-price cattle have already been driven into her mother's pen. His description is given by one of her seducers: 'You don't go with that man of rags and tatters do you? With the toes of his shoes turned up waiting for mealy porridge?' The conversations are full of animal and country similes and comparisons which are probably in many cases direct translations of everyday speech which sound vivid in English. It does give an idea of migrant life in Johannesburg.

Police road blocks in the Transkei
(31 July 1961) We had a cheerful two-day journey in my pale blue Hillman from Cape Town up to Durban for the Liberal Party Congress. It was quite hard going but nevertheless driving shared with Val Hutchinson meant that it was one of the most comfortable journeys I have made. Most of the Cape delegation went in two Volkswagen Combis and didn't stop. In their thirty hour journey they went through Grahamstown at 3 a.m. while I was asleep in our relation's Ingie and Wally's rather nice house.

I had been asked by Randolph to pick up two people in Umtata and when we found them they told us that Randolph's car and the Combis had gone through ten minutes before. One of the two was a brother of Chief Sabata Dalindyebo with whom the Liberals are working against the government stooge Paramount Chief Matanzima. [The Liberals were successfully to help Sabata's party win the popular election in Transkei.]

At about 2.15 in the afternoon we came across the whole Cape Liberal caravan which had stopped for a break in the middle of the Transkei. Three little boys with donkeys had had their beasts commandeered and pictures were taken of Mr Tabata and others on their way to the Congress on donkey back.

You will remember the long straight national road down from the high point at Brokkes Nek near Mount Currie. Right down in the far distance one could see the junction for Kokstad and one vehicle standing there. It was a police Landrover and it was waiting to stop us. The policeman had the number of my car on a piece of paper. Unfortunately our passenger had lost his pass a few days before but had reported it to the Chief Magistrate. The policeman uttered the dread words 'You will have to come along to the charge office.' This meant certain delay and possible imprisonment for him. I said 'But surely that is unnecessary, officer! He knows his number, he has reported the loss.' Luckily this country policeman was reasonable. He took all our names and addresses and asked us whether we knew where a certain CA car was and he gave Randolph's number. We said that the car had gone back to Umtata and would not be coming along that night. This apparently worked for the police did not stay but went away. Sabata's brother remembered seeing the 'information officer' for his Xhosa tribe (an African 'government agent') near my car and thought that he must have taken down its number and told the police to find out with whom he was travelling.

At Umzimkulu we stopped for petrol near the frontier before going into Natal. There was another police block and we were rather afraid that they might be cussed and arrest our chap without his pass. At that moment a large Cape Town American car drew up and a little African got out and started boasting about how his brother was a chief and how his brother was there in the car. We decided that the best way of getting across the border into Natal was to apply apartheid to our cars; so Sabata's brother got into the large blacks only car. Neil Ross and I climbed up onto the bank and saw to our great relief the American car go past the police without being stopped. Our whites only car also was not stopped. Randolph was later stopped at this point but he and the three Africans were allowed to go after their names had been taken.

Never on Sundays
(31 July 1961) The Liberal Party Congress got through some solid business.

It revised its economic policies and made them welfare state ... The land policy, civil rights policy, the education policy were revised and considerable organisational plans were made under the restrained leadership of Dr Hans Meidner, chairman of the Natal Division. Although he has been in South Africa since his early teens he is still teutonic although with an endearing laugh at himself on occasion. His extreme organisational demands were toned down. At one of the Maritzburg meetings opposing the Republic he got carried away and he harangued the audience with 'Ve must defend the Breetesh vay of live.'

The Congress was all conducted against the chaotic background of Durban's Indian Quarter. On Sunday a stream of Indian weddings took place in the same building and girls with gay silk trousers under their skirts trotted up and down stairs and a band (Indian though it might be) played the theme song from 'Never on Sundays' while the garlanded bride and groom walked round the guests receiving congratulations. Meanwhile Indian children on nearby rooves were being led in singing by a shirt-sleeved man with a violin. SA railways only stopped a pile driver to let a train pass.

Occasionally Alan Paton would make a debate turn with great skill as he weighed in from his seat at the back. One of the most contentious points was brought up in the education debate in which it was suggested that private schools should be allowed to practise racialism but they would not get any state help. This was immediately attacked by those who said that all forms of racialism must be stamped out immediately citing John Stuart Mill 'You can tolerate anything except intolerance.'

The voting for universal adult suffrage [one person one vote] was approximately 170 to 2 (both also members of the Progressive Party). There was fear in Liberal circles that the convention was going to be conservative ... but in the Liberal Party now the attitude is that it is too late to discuss clever franchises in South Africa. The balance must be achieved by constitutional organisation and a true understanding of basic factors such as the conservatism of rural tribalism and the radicalism of the town Africans. It is an exciting time of new realisations and re-orientations. (And we are starting a provocative 16 page journal.)

The most frightening piece of news is the sacking of Erasmus, the Minister of Injustice, whom we have all considered a lying two-faced blighter. But he has Cape outlook and he did not use his powers to ban this Liberal Party Congress....Vorster who follows him is a self-confessed Nazi who was interned during the war and does not see why he cannot intern everybody else. It really looks, as Cowen was predicting, as though with the Republic Verwoerd is reaching for new extremes of personal power.

A sheep for the pot, a fleece for your back and a pound for your pocket!
(31 July 1961) Neil Ross and I had an eventful journey up to Maseru in Basutoland. I ran into a sheep and broke the poor wretch's back. We managed to get hold of the African peasant farmer who was working in his mealie patch; he was reluctant to come out for, when he saw it was white men, he assumed that would mean trouble for him. I wanted him to despatch the sheep and I was anxious to give him some compensation. Then an Afrikaner farmer drove up and he explained to the peasant what had happened in a man-to-man way with great politeness. The peasant said he did not want anything. However his eyes lit up at the sight of a peace offering of a pound. Neil Ross told me that what the farmer had said to the peasant farmer in Afrikaans was 'Well old man! You have a sheep for the pot, a fleece for your back and a pound for your pocket! I think you are lucky!'

After dark we left Ladybrand, still in South Africa for the last leg of 24 miles across the frontier to Maseru the capital of Basutoland. We set out on appalling roads (some of it was undressed sand in which you would have stuck if you stopped) and about three quarters of an hour later we came out over a rise and there were the lights of the town before us. 'I was just about to suggest that we turned back' said Neil. I said 'It looks very neat for Maseru.' Five minutes later we arrived back in Ladybrand.

I stayed for five pleasant and cheerful days with Peter Walsh and his wife and three kids, all under three in good RC fashion. Roma was on vacation but many of the lecturers were there. Apparently quite a tussle for power is brewing up between the Oblates and the Laymen who consider that the priests do not know enough about running a worldly university as opposed to a seminary.-

Paperbacks for Africa
(20 August 1961) Business is very bad. Anthony Millar, working for BP, says that a lot of garages are in difficulties. The General Motors Assembly Plant in Port Elizabeth has laid off workers and stopped work in its car shops for two weeks.

Thank goodness I am employed in the field of ideas because this is just the sort of time to provoke thinking. I am having a private campaign with the Oxford Press to try and persuade the South African branch to face up to the problem of distributing books outside the normal channels so that the newly literate classes can easily get hold of the new series of paperbacks. The OUP in London in association with the Africa Bureau is producing a new series of books called The New Africa Library at two bob a nob (10p) with difficult ideas such as economic and constitutional organisation explained in straightforward terms for somebody in Standard VI at the top of elementary school. We are in Cape Town are publishing a series of Practical Books which explain in straightforward language Electricity in Your Home, Household Maintenance, Dress-Making and so on.

Africans hardly go into bookshops. So Tim's and my idea is that an enterprising bookshop should be encouraged to start a mail-order business on a restricted catalogue of perhaps a dozen cheap paperback titles from Penguin, Oxford and whoever else is interested. That the publisher should give a special rate of discount and that the bookseller would sell multiple copies to agents for cash with no credit. The agents would make a bit for themselves by selling to friends in mine compounds, at bus queues, door to door. For a start *Contact*, the popular liberal newspaper, would probably give us the names of all its agents to write to and there would be advertisements for agents in African newspapers. It would mean a considerable amount of hard work to start with but at the moment I see it as the only way. The communists get their books from Progress Publishers in Russia distributed by the agents for *New Age* magazine. Anyhow Marquard seems initially to be behind the idea and my memo is going to the Publisher. I see it as of vital importance in the battle for democracy in Africa that these sorts of books should be distributed.

(17 September 1961) On Friday at lunch-time I gave a short talk to a Liberal Party Forum on the problem of (a) providing books for the new Africa and (b) of distributing them. This has helped provoke considerable thought. By 3.30 Joe Daniels, the Business and Distribution Manager of *Contact*, had written a two page foolscap screed with some good, some wild ideas.

(17 September 1961) Later that afternoon Marquard told me that Cannon had agreed to forward my proposal to the Publisher (the Managing Director in London). Marquard says however that 'Cannon is not convinced that the market exists.' People as astute as Randolph and Tom Hopkinson are convinced it does. (Tom Hopkinson was editor of the famous illustrated magazine *Picture Post* in London and then of the renowned *Drum* in Johannesburg.) But Cannon doesn't really want to bother to stir himself to find out if it does. Anyhow Nelsons apparently are bringing out a series of Teach Yourself books for Africa. Penguin's Modern Africa Library and Oxford Three Crowns are aimed at the new market in the rest of Africa; the market already is starting in SA. But both Marquard and Cannon are doubtful about the mail-order idea which I consider the most important. Tim has ideas of starting a new type of bookshop in Swaziland using Liberal Party members who have had rotten deals as packers and messengers in

the book trade because they are black. It would basically be a hawking, colporteur, mail order establishment. [Later a teacher at the non-racial school at Waterford in Swaziland started a mail-order bookshop specialising on slipping banned books into South Africa. He found that the list of banned books in *The Government Gazette* gave him an order list to make sure that he got in extra stock from London because of the extra demand across the border.]

(3 October 1961) Today I interviewed Marquard about the series of Oxford books for Africa for a short news item for *Contact*.

(2 December 1961) Last week the new manager of the SPCK bookshop was in from Johannesburg exploring the idea of setting up a chain of shops for selling books to Africans (not just religious tracts). He immediately went for the *Tshekedi Khama* and for *African Nationalism* covers 'as being the sort of thing he was looking for'.

(3 October 1961) Marquard sent my suggestion about a collection of South African short stories for World's Classics to Hudson the Editor of the Series. In Cape Town we are doing a collection of short stories for South African schools which Hudson thought might do for the Series as the stories seemed to be 'non-contentious'. I ask you, a 'non-contentious' book of South African short stories for the world market and, moreover, not a single story by a non-white. Marquard immediately agreed with me that OUP should approach Nadine Gordimer [she was to win the Nobel Prize].

(3 October 1961) How very good about Andrew and [getting a poem into the] TLS. He is very lucky indeed in the frightfully limited market. I know it only too well. We are continually getting manuscripts of poetry by people who seem to think they can get a book published although they have never had a single poem published in a magazine or paper.

Vote Vigne!
(20 August 1961) After a great deal of discussion the Cape Liberals have decided to fight a seat in the general election (as they are in the Transvaal and Natal). The question is whether it is politically wise to associate with the 'white tribal parliament.' Anyhow Randolph is our candidate at Constantia. As he said 'God! I never expected it to happen to me. Or not before we had a non-racial set-up and I would be some black man's election agent' Anyhow he has got an OK history for snobbish Constantia; head-prefect at St Andrew's private school, Oxford and the right accent, so he might persuade some of them that Liberals are not just a lot of bearded freaks. We are having non-racial platforms at meetings and non-racial canvassing in

our continuing battle to narrow down the area of difference between the races.

(26 August 1961) This has been the first week of Randolph's campaign and I have been canvassing on two evenings. Only one door slam from a retired chap with an English name who waited long enough to find out that I was neither Progressive nor United Party (UP). Randolph came across people who did not know there was an election and others who had not the foggiest which parties were standing. We also had a meeting on the Grand Parade which, though not as successful as the Africa Day one, attracted about a thousand people; Randolph made a rather good off-the-cuff crack. Verwoerd has said recently that his 'Granite-wall policy' is similar to Churchill's policy against Hitler. Said Randolph 'Dr Verwoerd and Churchill are not alike. They do not look the same. They do not speak the same. And as far as I know Dr Verwoerd is a non-smoker.'

(17 September 1961) On Thursday in his election campaign Randolph gave the most interesting political speech I have ever heard. He talked about how well versed the Africans in South Africa are in democratic procedure and how the Progressives rightwards have policies which are so full of fear that they are self-defeating. Anyhow it is certain that the Nats will get back comfortably. P.S. Aunt Iris's remarks are still as dreadful as ever about 'the munts'.

(3 October 1961) I have been designing an election manifesto for Randolph. It is beautifully folded so that it says on the outside 'South Africa is a wonderful country' and when the voter opens it up it says 'Ruined by Politics'. [Rather sadly Randolph turned down Terence Beard's suggestion 'Constantia is Vigne Country.']

(22 October 1961) You will now know that the general Election was almost entirely as expected. Slight Nat gains, one Progressive victory ... Randolph lost his [Liberal] deposit but got 1,115 votes in conservative Constantia. Anthony Delius said that he was surprised that we got over a thousand with such an honest policy. Anyhow we had had no hopes and were quite satisfied as we had used the campaign as a propaganda period to, at least, place a few doubts in people's minds.

I spent the afternoon at one of the polling stations and enjoyed the day although I had not expected to do so. The contrast between us and the United Party was enormous. The great majority of their helpers were frowsty and very very middle class women in their fifties and sixties. Our helpers were well-dressed professional men of all colours mostly in their thirties and twenties. One United Party man came up to me and said to me: 'If I were you. I hope you don't mind. It's only friendly advice. But I don't think it does you any good having a Native on the table out front!' We had all sorts of slogans we chanted such as 'Vote Vigne for the future. If you want a future!' Whenever a young person appeared I said 'Young people vote for Vigne.'

There is some gap in the Electoral Law in South Africa because I, as a non-citizen and non-voter, could legally be made a sub-agent to collect postal votes. This amused me greatly. In this capacity I was sent along, with Randolph and Neil Ross, to the Magistrate's Court to see the verification of postal votes ... several of us then moved to the centre of Cape Town to see how the Progressives were doing ... and on to the Magistrate's courts for the announcement of the Sea Point result where Progressive Professor Sakkie Fourie was expected to lose to Jack Basson, who is a cheap flashy man with film-star looks fighting for the UP. [Just at the moment the Returning Office was about to make the announcement recent news came through of what was to be the sole Progressive win of the night at Houghton, Johannesburg by Helen Suzman. It was an historic moment. Twelve sitting MPs had left the United Party in 1959 to form the Progressive Party. She was to be their only MP from 1961-74 and became renowned as she could use Parliamentary privilege to say things which nobody else could say legally in South Africa.] At last it was possible in all the excitement to announce that Basson had been elected for the UP. Neil Ross shouted naughtily for 'Three cheers for the monkey who got in!' Basson advanced down the steps screaming that he would sue him.

Councillor Eulalie Stott then suggested Alan Paton, Val Hutchinson and I should go off to the see the news editor of *Die Burger*. So we arrived as a self-invited party of Liberals....Later in the night Paton got down to one of those rare Liberal-Nationalist arguments (everybody is usually too polite and just assumes that the other person does not speak your political language). (continued 30 October 1961) Alan Paton finished up by saying 'Shall I tell you people how to buy 20 years more power.' 'You talk about "Buy"' said the news editor 'Don't morals come into the question?' 'O yes, as always. But if you want to buy yourselves 20 more years power put up the wages of the Africans by 50%.' In fact industrialists are already busy on plans, let alone the government. As we left the news editor joked: 'It's a good thing they took away your passport!' Anyhow it was a fascinating occasion....one of those properly bilingual conversations in which English slipped into Afrikaans and vice versa.

Next birthday in England?
(10 September 1961) Your very kind birthday present has now turned into a long-playing Kwela record full of penny-whistles, singing and trombones

which has the real feel of Africa about it ... It was the first time I have ever had to work on my birthday ... I'm thrilled with the picture of Alice Martin in Finland who looks terrifically pretty, very lively and very Martin.

(20 May 1961) I have had a letter from Parnwell, the Deputy Publisher in London. He says that I shall definitely have leave from April 1962 and I shall have some time working in the London office. Yippee.

(10 September 1961) Your remark about your hoping I would be back for my next birthday was unfortunately ominous because the wretched Cannon, just back from London, had a talk with me about my leave which was expected to start in April 1962 ... I shall now not be having leave until July 1962 which would indeed mean that I was in England for my birthday in September. Well, that's not so bad except for the feeling of being pushed around. The schemer Cannon goes on to suggest that my home leave should be six weeks only; he said 'I only took 6 weeks although I was entitled to 2 months.' Anyhow in addition I get a month in the London office...It turns out that Ken White, who has just been enticed out here from the warehouse at Neasden, has been promised 3 months after two years ...Unfortunately my rotten Parnwell contract, which I had so much trouble fighting over, does not specify how much leave. I know that with Neale and Marquard I shall be able to work out something reasonable.

(3 October 1961) You will be relieved, as I am, that I shall have three months home leave and a month in the London office. I can only say one thing about Cannon is that he lied to me. After going to see him again this week, after talking it over with Marquard, he said I had misunderstood him and that he had never suggested 6 weeks! ... I had suspected him before because he had said 'How does that suit you?' with a sly look. I can see that I am going to have to play on his snobbery a hell of a lot when he takes over.

A swift publishing tour round Africa
(10 September 1961) Anyhow Cannon seems agreeable to my round trip of Africa en route to and from Europe, which will mean a matter of stopping off at several places en route for a couple of days thus: Salisbury – (OUP office); Brazzaville, Leopoldville, Ibadan – (OUP) Accra (OUP), Dakar, Casablanca and then back by Tunis, Nairobi (OUP). You can stop off en route for no extra fare. I'll have to cover my expenses where there is no OUP office. I will get non-leave days for my visits to OUP branches where it will be most useful to discuss and exchange ideas.

(3 October 1961) Tim Holmes and Pat Duncan are also at work on a new idea of a Pan-African Press Agency. The idea is to be agreements with other smaller journals throughout English and French-speaking Africa so that we

pass to one another stories and photographs collected in our publication if wanted in other areas. Initially it will probably be one office in Nigeria, one in Tunisia, one in Dakar, one in East Africa and of course one in South Africa. My round trip may come in quite useful time for liaison work.

(3 October 1961) It is terrible how quickly one's perspective changes. From here the Russian-American war-mongering has seemed a mere academic exercise….One gets obsessed by the stupid little set-up here. [The Cuban Missile Crisis was to be in October 1962 while I was working in the London office.]

(8 October 1961) P.S. What a fine person Conor Cruise O'Brien sounds from his *Observer* profile. These new international civil servants are giants. Civilised servants who write and think creatively as well as administratively.

Primitives are very rare
(16 October 1961) Randolph, Tim and I decided to arrange a small exhibition of paintings by a Nyanga school teacher called Gladys Mgudulana. This is in the *Contact* board room. We had an official opening which was pleasant without being pretentious. We invited all the local 'art critics'. The *Argus* was good. *Die Burger* was tremendous; their art critic bought one, the editor Piet Cillie bought another, the editor of *Die Huisgenoot* another. It was also reviewed on the SABC, she sold fourteen paintings and drawings. Cecil Higgs was thrilled: 'She is a real primitive; primitives are very rare.' When *Die Burger* had such a favourable review Marquard, who had been away at the time, said 'Have you seen this African's paintings?' I asked if he had noticed it was in the *Contact* board room and told him that I was on the hanging committee.

The New African takes shape
(26 August 1961) This is the letterhead for *The New African* with its clothes-hanger people. Anyhow it gives people the impression that we are serious and in existence.

(3 October 1961) Then I have been laying out a dummy for *The New African*. I also, in a fit of desperation at nobody else doing it, took upon myself to write a blurb for the journal which, to my great surprise, has been passed with practically no changes by Randolph, Tim and Neville Rubin.

(16 October 1961) *The New African* begins to take shape… Delius, Mboya, Sithole, Brutus, Paton … we are working on building up the initial 350 subscriptions.

(16 October 1961) We are thrilled about Luthuli and the Nobel Peace Prize. It has put the government into choosing whether in spite of his ban they let him go to Oslo, or whether they follow Russia and Nazi Germany and refuse him a passport. *Die Burger* says it will be worse to stop him. Liberals hope that the government are stupid enough to do so. We arranged a non-party meeting yesterday in the Drill Hall off Grand Parade to celebrate.

(12 November 1961) Yesterday morning I had a most enjoyable time with the printer discussing *The New African*. To my great pleasure he on the spot ordered the Standard Expanded type that I wanted from Germany.

(2 December 1961) We are now getting towards the first issue of *The New African* and are overwhelmed with articles, although as usual we are still looking for the really outstanding one. My chief job is now coming along, that is the layout and production of the magazine. We are getting copy set already on galleys for stock-piling.

(2 December 1961) One of the most interesting art books I have ever seen arrived this week; the work of Sidney Nolan the Australian artist. Tim got me to order it for him. There is a fascinating series of pictures of Kelly the outlaw; did you see the exhibition in London four or five years ago? For intense colours and exciting shapes this is terrific. Makes me look at South Africa. In one painting there is a picture of Kelly with his square iron mask simply melting into his horse like a centaur.

There is a most entertaining introduction to the book by Colin MacInnes. One very good remark about 'a certain European who "discovered", as we European choose to say of things which are millennially ancient…' This is so right. Randolph pointed out a Cape Times review of our book *Townsmen or Tribesman* which said 'Little is known of the African townships in South Africa'. 'What'do they think the inhabitants know? exclaimed Randolph 'Nothing?'

(31 December 1961) *The New African* is now in its first page proofs and going for final correction before printing on Tuesday. It is a pretty heavy first issue and too much politics but I think it promises not too badly. It has just got to be a lot more entertaining and amusing.

(15 January 1962) The first *New African* is off the press. I have sent you half a dozen copies over and above your subscription to pass around to interested people. It is rather stodgy and severely political. To sell it must also be far more entertaining. Though one cannot tell what people will like. In this first issue there is a piece by Leslie Rubin who was Liberal senator until he went to Ghana. He wrote a rather boring and sentimental piece about going to a conference on Africa at Boston – or so I thought but Marquard, Pat Duncan

and Tom Ngwenya all thought that it was wonderful. No, but really it must be a journal people want to read.

Across the immorality line
(8 October 1961) I have almost finished the first draft of my novel ...Three of my women friends have had involvements across the colour line despite the legal risks [which could even lead to jail under 'The Immorality Act'].

(16 October 1961) Your letter about Mary Kirwood visiting Colchester arrived yesterday ... Coincidentally on Friday evening I met Jerome Gallo again. Jerome is a brother of Mary's friend Ernest. They are a very nice catholic family whose father is Principal of the Langa RC School. Jerome is a teacher at the Cowen Secondary School in New Brighton, Port Elizabeth. Jerome was taking a leading part in a Xhosa play which was being put on at the Little Theatre. A friend Mongi Ndibongo had arranged for three of the players to come out to Randolph's for a drink after the play. The last time I saw Jerome, believe it or not, was on the afternoon of Sharpeville. I took a copy of *Evening Post* with its headlines into New Brighton.

I like him much more than Ernest who is rather a bitter person. One can understand it of course ... I saw a lot of him with Mary in Durban. He was then very active in the ANC because so many of the leadership had been locked up or had left the country and he has thrown up his degree work (?law) for politics. Sylvia Sypkens, the delightful Afrikaans friend of Mary's from Ermelo who is a lecturer in English at Durban, says 'Ernest is part of what we will come to call "the lost generation" in South Africa.' She means the brilliant young Africans who sacrifice all their long range ability and the chance of getting trained (which will be vitally necessary) for the sake of the immediate political struggle.

(16 October 1961) When I was in Durban [Mary took me to meet Ernest just afterwards] he was failed on his driving test. Mary had already told me that he was not willing to take any advice about his driving which was very dashing and selfish. He was completely convinced that the only way to pass was for money to pass, partly because that was the done thing and partly because it was the only way of counteracting his black skin. But still he is very well informed though Russian sympathetic. As you say I hope that Mary gets through this all without too much damage to herself.

There will never be a revolution in the summer in South Africa
(9 November 1959) After beach at Clifton on Sunday we moved in on Randolph and his protesting wife Gillian at sunset and did their washing

up. Went on to jazz club in District 6 where everybody who writes for *Africa South* was gathered. Editor Ronald Segal has had article on British concentration camps in Boer War accepted by the *Spectator*. [A visit to this jazz club was to become a regular Sunday night feature. We were all deeply taken with a pianist called Dollar Brand who had grown up in District Six. When he took to Islam he changed his name to Abdullah Ibrahim and has become known internationally by that name.]

(12 November 1961) Summer has suddenly hit us with a hot week-end and I have been on beach today and yesterday. We were on the non-racial Glen Beach (one of these Cape survivals where nobody worries about anybody else). We were lying on a rock and underneath were four coloured men with a guitar strumming songs in the sun. There will of course never be a revolution in the summer in South Africa.

(12 November 1961) Last week we had a Liberal Party week-end school. This was the first we have had in the Cape. The idea was to get about 25 people away from Cape Town to discuss party policy and organisation. We were lent a deserted farm house on the Karroo about 150 miles away from Cape Town. It was a wonderful place in a deserted valley with great shelving boulders coming down diagonally. Six of us were staff and gave lectures and led discussions. When we were not lecturing we cooked for everybody. And then in between times there is much talking and discussion. We went on Friday evening in cars and combis and came back on Sunday afternoon. Anyhow it was very good for everybody's morale and the whole thing is likely to he repeated a couple of times this summer.

(2 December 1961) By now one casually accepts the sun day after day. And thank goodness that here it is practically never uncomfortably hot. The weekends tend to get beach orientated; and the Cape beaches are so pleasantly small and varied.

The vote is not all that important
(12 November 1961) Where there is money it staggers one. Several years ago Anglo American commissioned Sir Theodore Gregory, the economist, with the job of writing *Sir Ernest Oppenheimer and Anglo American*. He had flat, car and salary and must be sorry to have finished now; all 250,000 words of which we are publishing for Anglo American for a fat fee. Wilson, the Public Relations Chief, seems to have all the time and staff at his disposal to make himself a nuisance. 'We have prepared several manuscript copies for the press.' Grand waste. 'I'll fly down to Cape Town next week to discuss it with you'. Not only totally unnecessary but a positive nuisance.

(14 December 1961) Marquard and Cannon and I had lunch with Wilson,

the Anglo American Public Relations Officer who had flown down to Cape Town. Self-important but not nearly as bad as his letter. Always talking about 'Harry' (Oppenheimer that is) and 'the Oubaas' (Smuts that is, for Wilson was Head of Information during the war). Lunch divided into Marquard and Currey versus Wilson and Cannon. Very quiet and restrained agreeing to differ mostly though I could not forgo one or two darts. At the moment when he threw up 'Well, the vote is not all that important.' LM and I chimed in: 'Well, there is only one answer to that; why bother to hold it back?' He was throwing up some remarks about how the African states were certain to fail economically (not one, or several, but the whole bang lot).

(14 December 1961) I said to Marquard afterwards that 'I hardly feel that it is really worth bringing up such subjects with such people.' He replied 'Oh! We couldn't let him get away with that sort of stuff!' Cannon contributed that he was in favour of 'bringing back flogging' to combat 'the crime wave' in Britain. Anyhow we managed to get good control of the production and the typeface and paper.

(14 December 1961) Katanga/Congo naturally occupies a great deal of interest. It is neighbour to Northern Rhodesia which seems relatively so close to CT. The SABC is taking advantage of the attack to build up anti-United Nations propaganda; I have just heard a histrionic man glowing over the rapes and the bombed hospitals which all goes to show.... Gosh it really is a mess but the wretched Tshombe is not being helpful by attacking the UN. The pro-Tshombe Katanga lobby in the Tory party is certainly losing all the sympathy among Africans that Mac got with his 'winds of change' last year. Anglo American mining is big in the Copper Belt.

Kidnap and Habeas Corpus
(18 December 1961) Another great legal success against the government. Ganyile, an African political exile in Basutoland, was allegedly kidnapped from the High Commission Territory (British rule, of course) by the home guards of Chief Botha Sicgau one of the chief government stooges in the Transkei, and taken to jail in Pondoland. After a whole year the Transkei is still under a State of Emergency so it seems it is possible for people to be kidnapped and then taken into the area and to be held indefinitely without trial. Apparently Ganyile managed to get a message out of his prison. A writ of Habeas Corpus was applied for on 16 October 1961. On Friday the Supreme Court ordered the Minister of Justice to produce his body alive or dead by the 18 January 1962.

The shocking thing in the whole affair has been the performance of the

British authorities. Pat Duncan has spent a great deal of energy trying to follow it up and has found certain evidence of a sight of the kidnapping (supposed, alleged etc.). Benjie Pogrund of the *Rand Daily Mail* rang up the British Embassy in Pretoria to put Duncan's assertions to them. The reply was 'Mr Duncan's allegations do not warrant serious consideration.' Well PD may be excitable at times but this is a good chance for the British to show black and white opponents of the government whose side they are on. They miss a sitting chance. The Ambassador Sir John Maud was away and some twerp who was in charge has mucked it up. You would have thought that it could do no harm to institute an inquiry.

Next Christmas North or South?
(18 December 1961) A very happy Christmas to you. I wish you were here or I was there. You have never answered my tentative inquiry about being in England for Christmas next year. As you know the discussions so far have been as to what month I can get away. I have been told either the beginning of August or the end of July. It does occur to me that if I come over at the beginning of September I could stay until Christmas and leave at the New Year. Of course the drawback to this is that that CRGS is back early in September and so I would miss your holidays. Say soon what you feel. They have mucked me up once so that they will have to be accommodating to the extent of a month with a bit of diplomatic wangling by me.

(18 December 1961) Christmases here in the past two years have been the only time when I have been homesick at all. I do hope that Aunt Iris will not take too much offence that I have accepted an invitation to go to Kommetjie on Christmas Day. I will probably get out to Hermanus on Saturday and Christmas Eve.

That terrible game Scrabble
(31 December 1961) A frantic week of *Contact, The New African* and jollification. Sunday Christmas Eve was hilarious at Randolph's with Gillian groaning about what a terrible game Scrabble was (having suggested it) or how terrible it was playing it on the floor on our stomachs on the floor (despite having suggested that also) and putting down impossible words and therefore being helped by everybody and winning.

Gillian, Sylvia August and I were making coffee by three different methods at the same time. (Collingwood August is Liberal emigrée who is working in London for Penguin and who is translating *Animal Farm* into Xhosa for us.) The coffee came from the Brazilian goodwill ship which is visiting every maritime country in Africa except South Africa (because of the colour bar which would be an embarrassment to its non-racial crew). Coffee sent by post from Lourenço Marques in Portuguese Mozambique to the Brazilian Consulate in Cape Town (where Gillian is Vice-Consul).

Have you never heard anything about Mistress Lucy Vigne who is now a somewhat wobbly walker with feet wide, with large eyes and a pot belly? Very solemn and very quiet and then when she smiles looks just like Piers. I am sure that I remember telling you that they had selected a Victorian name. You know I wonder if all my letters get through to you. I think we must keep a check although a bore.

(31 December 1961) Then on Christmas day I went down to Kommetjie where there were an assorted douzaine including Mrs Kirwood, as sweet and breathless as ever. It was wildly windy in good Cape fashion. It was a cold Christmas by mid-summer Cape standards with snow on the Drakensberg for the first time for years. Anyhow it was delightfully relaxed day and very happy. Beach-walking and shell-finding and seagull-frightening in great sprays of white across the water.

The Contact Freedom Calendar
(31 December 1961) Then Boxing Day was passed pleasantly doing the Contact Freedom Calendar map of the emerging new Africa. The countries which have got independence are filled in with black and each year the flood of black spreads south towards the white redoubt. This year's is a much more professional job than the first year's. That was fairly remarkable as it was just done with a fountain pen; during the year I managed to get hold of some very clever drawing pens. Anyhow Patrick Duncan is thrilled to bits with it. Stanley Uys, the *Sunday Times* (Joburg) and *The Observer* correspondent, with the local representative of German radio, snaffled copies when they were visiting *Contact* yesterday.

Christmas cards keep you in touch
(31 December 1961) I am so sorry about the 50 Christmas cards not arriving in time for Andrew. They have been greatly admired. Randolph said 'The only off-beat cards we got this year were from the Curreys.' i.e. yours with your own poem as well as mine. Robin Farquarson, mad brilliant young Liberal from Johannesburg (who is having a book on the theory of voting published by Yale), especially asked if he could have one although I had not really known him before. He is the only person brilliant enough to notice the importance that Mary and Joseph are of equal size.

Victor Benjamin, a coloured school teacher who is a large booming character, said that he had it by his telephone away from all the other cards.

Originally I thought the idea up in my head and then told Andrew what I had in mind and he turned out the admirable and very neat little poem. In a way it turned out to be a progress report on my typographical ideas of the year. The little clothes-hanger people were of course used originally on Cowen's book and then they have been used on my masthead for *The New African*.

(14 December 1961) Ian Wright is back from Canada and is working for *The Guardian*. The great thing about Christmas cards is that they keep you in touch ... the printing was a present from my printers and the blocks from my blockmakers. Better bribe than whisky.

(10 June 1961) I had a letter from Roger Pethybridge in Vienna where he working for a short time for the Atomic Agency. He has finished his thesis on Krushchev's rise and submitted it, without much hope, to the OUP. [It was accepted by Allen and Unwin.] He has also written a 'lids off' type of book with the lowdown on the UN Agencies and all the fiddling.

(14 December 1961) Did I tell you that Roger Pethybridge has been asked by his American publishers to write a short history of Russian politics from the war until 1961 – as well as publishing his thesis *The Roots of Soviet Politics* about the way Khruschev was almost toppled in 1957.

(12 December 1961) To my great amusement the other day I picked up a new book in a bookshop called *South Africa 1960* ... It is typical of the book that there is not a photograph of Sharpeville. On the other hand there a picture of R.N. Currey and Stella Martin Currey. It must have been a press photograph taken on the boat in the docks on your arrival.

1962

The British mind at work
(3 February 1962) The Cape Town branch has two new recruits. Alan Cruttenden arrived from London on the *Windsor Castle* ten days ago. He turns out to be a very solid and likeable person. His fostering uncle was a boat-builder at Marlow and his father was a cook. He was one of the first people from Marlow Grammar School ever to go to Oxford. After going down a year later than me he worked for the OUP for two and a half years at Oxford and in London. I think that the job will interest him in Salisbury in just the way that I feared that it would not interest me – that it will be concerned with educational travelling. To begin with he is interested in education and secondly he is pleased to get away from ordinary office

routine. I have done as much as possible to look after him. I was just about completely left alone when I arrived and I rather resented it for the first week although I got involved in the *Caucasian Chalk Circle*. Alan is going for an audition in Julian Slade's sprightly musical *Salad Days*.

The other new recruit amuses Alan and myself – a Zionist Jew called Solly Press who has been to Stellenbosch and Cape Town Universities and worked in a tax office. After two and a half years here from Israel he staggers me by his racial consciousness. He just staggers Alan who is fresh from the fields of English racial unawareness. 'Do you have any particular political leanings?' ask I. 'No, I'm just a jew.' He has a bantering off-hand way of putting things that are seriously important to him. He says about Alan and myself 'Oh, I shall be interested to be able to study the British mind at work…. How does the British mind consider this?'

I suggested that we all go and have lunch at my squash club where the Swiss couple who run it do beautiful steaks, snitzels and chops for remarkably little. 'Oh, is it a very British club?' he immediately asked. I replied 'No! It is actually rather Jewish.' I hadn't considered it before but as it happens I suppose 70 or 80% of the members are Jewish. Ken White, in sales at OUP, and I are some of the gentile members of the club. It is very convenient for me because it is near work and I can get there at 5 o'clock and, having played squash, be back home by 6.00.'

He also got us onto religion and thought that he had a bantering provocative line when he said something like 'Well, what do you think of worshipping somebody whose legal father wasn't his actual father?' Well that was not much good either because my views about the superhumanness of Christ are heretical – just look at my Christmas card with Joseph as big as Mary. Still I feel I will be able to get on with him. Whether he will get on at the schools I do not know – though he seems to be interested in 'selling'. He knows quite a lot about a limited range of subjects and outside that goes blind.

The SA theatre comes of age with Athol Fugard's The Blood Knot
(19 February 1962) Also went to the first run of *The Blood Knot*. [The very first play by Athol Fugard who is now established internationally as a playwright with renowned productions like *The Island*.] Technically a mess. Fashionably orientated. The two blood brothers, one white and one dark, talk interminably for three hours à la Godot. Their talking is Pinteresque. The setting is Wesker – except that they have not even got a kitchen sink in their shack. There is the heavy repeating of the original opening at the beginning of the second act. The press blurb is incredible. It talks

about 'a definite London performance' when Boulting has said that 'he is interested'. It calls it a masterpiece and says that the SA theatre comes of age as the Australian theatre did in 1955 with *SOS Doll*. However the two main characters do come alive and do remain in ones mind for days afterwards.

Carry on Combi
(19 February 1962) We had another of our political week-ends on the Karoo. A grand w/e again. Unfortunately, we had a series of mishaps going and coming back. We four in the Volkswagen Combi I was driving got lost at eleven in the night in the Karoo and went up the wrong track. We bedded down in the Combi and slept so well that we did not wake for two hours after sunrise with the dassies (rock rabbits) bouncing around outside the windows.

On the way back one of the Combis gave up with broken bearings at Touws River. We decided to try and tow it down to a garage in Worcester. I drove on tow behind Tim in the other Combi. Everybody had to get out and walk on each steep hill; eventually at de Doorns we decided that it was becoming too great a strain so they left us and went off to ring garages. To keep ourselves occupied we pushed the Combi up hills and free-wheeled down hills for about five miles. Finally after a hill which was almost too much for us and which we scaled to a chant of 'One Man One Vote' we stopped, stripped off and swam naked in a dam by the side of the wall. Everybody kept down as cars went past. Anyhow we were finally rescued and got back to Cape Town at 1 a.m.

Inventing printed bindings
(18 March 1962) It will be Marquard's last week next week. He leaves by air for England and Greece a week on Monday. Then I and Miss Williams will be in sole charge until David Philip returns from Salisbury on 14 May 1962.

For me it has been an exciting week in production terms. Rustica Press got a local litho printer to print a fine-toned photograph onto white Fabroleen, which is that textured binding material which I used on *Grosvenor* and *Secret Ways*. This is the first time I ever seen it done for a photograph in South Africa; all SA printers said it could not be done. But I have been in correspondence with the Production Managers at Oxford and Methuen and they assured that it was done on a little office litho machine called the Multilith. It is Hurrah! cheaper on certain occasions especially for books which would normally have a jacket. And then we are moving into full-scale litho for the first time. This is a great occasion. The trouble with litho is that you have to big runs to make it economic and when you have paid for the plates to be made the cost then falls rapidly. The artist Cecil Higgs seems thrilled with the idea of doing a special drawing binding for the book of Afrikaans verse.

No room at the Registry Office
(18 March 1962) They are going to build an oil refinery near Cape Town. Most reactions of those who are going to benefit from the petrol is 'How terrible!' I was amused to find that an architect and I were the two people who seemed to be thrilled. We both look forward to the exciting and exotic shapes.

This architect is a Dutchman called Art Bijl who on Thursday married Val Hutchinson, the Liberal Party secretary. The first anybody knew was when Val rang up Barney Zackon, one of the party lawyers, and said that there was a cram at the Registry Offices and that they could not get married. He managed to get them fixed in. Anyhow they are excellently suited. They have known one another, vaguely, for about a year. Val is true to her condemnation of all the fuss over Tim's and Sally's full fig Roman Catholic wedding in Underberg.

I am very pleased to hear about Andrew's poem about von Stauffenberg and the Hitler plot and shall keep an eye open for it in the 3 March *Times Literary Supplement*.

Help from the Congress for Cultural Freedom in Paris
(19 February 1962) I heard on BBC Overseas – just after a programme on Luthuli – that Rick Swanzy has been to Uganda and is going to give a talk about it next week. Is there a hope of getting him to do something for *The New African*. I am writing to him and I wonder if you can forward if you think possible. Our pay is still appalling although there are negotiations under way for Congress for Cultural Freedom money. (Six rands/three pounds for an article of 1,500 words.) We are most keen to have an article a month on another African territory.

The New African is becoming quite stylish
(18 March 1962) Reaction to latest *New African* is that it is the best yet. We have interesting stuff stock-piled. We now have a secretary for one day a week which will mean that distribution will be smoother. Typographically I am very pleased with this issue. I feel that it is becoming quite stylish. This is the first month we have had new and fashionable Standard type such as that used by the *Observer* and *Time & Tide*.

One killed (African policeman) in riots at Langa on Friday, Anniversary of Sharpeville on Wednesday. Tense for police. *Contact* raided on Friday for documents in connection with an article.

A pre-wedding sight-seeing tour
(7 May 1962) Last week-end we had two parties to celebrate the wedding of a very pleasant chap Tulani Gcabashe who has recently become articled to a liberal Party lawyer Barney Zackon. I thought his wife was particularly charming. She was pretty and, above all, socially at ease. African women rarely are, for obvious reasons. Well, she might well have had the chance of learning social behaviour for she is one of Luthuli's daughters. Joe Nkatlo had mentioned that Tulani would like to borrow my car to spend an afternoon taking her round the Peninsula – Cape Point, Chapman's Peak perhaps? I was greatly amused to find out that Tulani had taken her on a sight-seeing tour of the locations and slums just to look around. It gave me great pleasure.

Season of return to the north
(Easter Sunday 1962) Easter week-end. Pleasantly busy with luxurious feeling on Good Friday, as I looked out over the sea at Clifton from Randolph's house, and knew I was usually in my office. Actually I was clearing a pile of manuscripts which were waiting decisions for rejection or a second reader – six in all. My campaign is to get ahead of my work before heading north to England in August.

Do not invest in South Africa
(19 February 1962) You ask about Pat Duncan and *Contact*. Well you probably will have seen the *Contact* Freedom Calendar on the centre fold at Christmas. I am still very much tied up with all that. Maps. Reports on this and that. One of the entertaining evenings lately was dinner at Pat Duncan's with two of Cynthia Duncan's City of London contacts. They were out here scouting round for an investment company. Pat was telling them quietly and diplomatically that they must not invest in South Africa. PD is excellent at this sort of line; his father was the Governor-General of South Africa and he has always lived in establishment circles, knows the conventions and knows how to handle such people. [At the end of the eighties it was the Bank Boycott by the American universities which made it impossible for the apartheid regime to survive. The students marched on campus treasuries to demand that their university did not place their wealth with banks who continued to trade with South Africa. It was inspired by South African poet Dennis Brutus who regularly contributed to *The New African*.]

Patrick Duncan breaks his ban
(Easter Sunday 1962) Patrick Duncan has been confined to the four magisterial districts of the Peninsula, as Luthuli is restricted to certain districts in Natal. He made a statement saying he would defy ban as and when he saw fit. The *Cape Times* ran this as a very small statement; the radical movement have found it increasingly difficult to get notice in the SA 'lying English press'. The SA Foundation mentality has gripped an awful lot of businessmen. The SA Foundation is this organisation of Nat-UP-Prog businessmen who are trying to counter SA's international bad name.

(17 May 1962) Pat Duncan has [broken his ban and] gone to Basutoland. A smart *Argus* reporter saw him in Maseru. He is a great loss. I cannot say more.

Election victory in the Transkei
(7 May 1962) Chief Sabata's party won the Transkei popular election. As expected the Chiefs voted to keep the Bunga (Parliament) in the control of Paramount Chief Matanzima. Randolph was up there arranging for diplomats to meet Sabata and for newspapermen to meet the right people. The Morning Group of Newspapers, which includes *The Cape Times*, has taken up the side of Sabata. [After the election Chief Sabata was sent on his way back home by crowds of Africans celebrating the victory. Meanwhile Matanzima had to slip shamefully away in the opposite direction by police car.]

New censorship comes in
(14 May1962) It is arguable that I should go to the African Writers meeting in Uganda for OUP. Indecision all adds to a terrible listlessness. Together with batch of really tough legislation coming up. Death sentence for sabotage (youths as adults). Close behind comes the Censorship Bill which is one of the main reasons for Patrick Duncan to hand over *Contact. The New African* may find difficulties. The Suppression of Communism Act is to be extended to cover 'non-communists' such as Duncan.

John Cross has, joke, asked me to talk to Colchester Round Table. Tim Holmes says 'You must!'

Last night I was sitting among the burghers of Cape Town and the plump Shell men in the club at Kelvin Grove with Randolph talking plans. English tribal territory. Best place to plot.

Nobel reception in Oslo for Luthuli is full of emotion
(21 May 1962) What should have been a quiet week turned out noisy. Peter

Brown, National Chairman of the Liberals, was down here for a week and on Wednesday we gave a party for him to meet the press and diplomats. Jan Aarse, the Norwegian Consul was talking about how emotional everybody got at Luthuli Nobel reception in Oslo – usually very sedate [The Consul was in July 1964 to be so important to us in providing information to enable the *Cape Escape*].

Several of us were invited on to dinner by Mower, the American Consul [and CIA agent]. Practically everybody is better at getting to know the left in South Africa than the British who are busy being diplomatic – article by me in next *New African* on the South Africa Act going through at Westminster.

(May/June 1962) *New African* week just over. Layout becoming more and more sophisticated. The reaction of so many people has been enthusiastic about lay-out without knowing I did it. I was at a party at the British Embassy the other night where quite a few people seemed to be full of approval. American consul Mower mentioned the journal without knowing I was connected.

(May/June 1962) Everything seems to happen at once. I was going to spend the last week-end (van Riebeeck day on Friday) clearing up various things including letters. And then I was asked to go to Grahamstown for Liberal Party National Committee. So we rushed up and back 560 miles on Friday in a large six cylinder car.

I may be going to Uganda on Saturday
(June 1962) Just a rushed note to say that things particularly hectic because I may be going to Uganda on Saturday for a week to the conference of African Writers of English Expression. *The New African* has been sent an air-ticket for Randolph but his passport has been refused. People are working on the old Parliament boy network trying to get it reversed. Neville Rubin most likely will not be allowed to go by the University of Cape Town because the old ass of a wet principal Duminy falls over backwards about anything which might be un-Boere. I am third in the line-up. It is obviously awkward for me to ask Cannon (Marquard would have agreed like a shot) but one simply does not turn down this kind of opportunity. Anyhow I do not want to ask until Neville and Randolph are definitely impossible.

The conference of African Writers of English Expression is organised by Ezekiel Mphaphlele of the Congress of Cultural Freedom which backs *Encounter*. He wrote autobiographical *Down Second Avenue*. Chinua Achebe will be there and Bloke Modisane. Also Colin MacInnes.

Obviously I am dying to go though it will mean taking a week off my leave and leaving for England a week later.

(18 June1962) Neville Rubin is back from Uganda but I have not seen him. Apparently the well-established literary journal *Contrast* print order is even lower than *The New African*. They print 1,000 to our 1,250. Which is a surprise.

Nearly six months in which to get Clare to marry me
(May/June 1962) Great news. I have heard from London that I am to have 6 weeks leave for every year served. That is four and a half months leave. So with a month in London office I should be in England for five and a half months. Serves everybody right that it is most inconvenient for me to go on leave this year. Cannon, if you remember, tried to get me to take six weeks in all. I hope with any luck to get away in mid-July so that I return in the New Year. I want to go up via West Africa without cutting too much into the Ralph, Hal, Andrew school holidays in August.

(18 June 1962) One month to go before leaving. Most annoyingly I was told today that it is impossible for me to get Volkswagen until 10 September so I shall come to Colchester first.

At the moment working like mad to get things ahead and on their way so not to leave loose ends. A few evenings' work are making an impression. The printers are all rushing things to show me before I go.

Everybody here is in a 'get out' mood. Very sad. Holmes to Tanganyika? Rollnicks to London? Another friend to Israel? They may go.

You perhaps thought I had disappeared in the Congo
(James/ Ralph and Stella Currey, Lagos 25 July 1962) You perhaps thought I had disappeared. Today have reached Lagos from Leopoldville (*ancien Belge*). Long ago at 7 o'clock it seems I downed my café creme in the Hotel La Residence at Leopoldville. Then walked down to 'Le Beach' as the ferry station is called. White UN lorries full of pale blue bereted Swedes, Nigerians, Danes, Ethiopians on the move as usual. At the customs am searched head to foot. Everything in my little bag is searched even the inside of the detergent box. Nothing special. They are just overdoing their independence looking for wonky currency. Ferry across 'Le Stanleypool' as the River Congo is called at this mile wide point to Congo Brazzaville (*ancien Francais*). Eventually reach airport for 11.15 Air France enormous Boeing. Usual business of so much time on the ground to spend so short a time in the air. We come down at Douala in the Cameroun. As the air hostess said so precisely '*Il pleut*'. A real taste of the sultry tropics with rain steaming off the runways. You would have laughed to see me sitting there amidst milling French expatriate families and milling black families with

me reading yesterday's *Times* and *Le Monde*. And the swampy rain forest stretching around.

It is exciting to be in the true Africa. What is the fuss about in South Africa? To see all these attractive black people in their terrific colours with their brown skins making Europeans look insipid. And nobody is badly behaved. And the children if anything better behaved....I have gone quite negrophile on seeing mixing working with such relaxation.

I wrote articles about the countries I visited in The New African. *People in South Africa knew almost nothing about the Francophone countries. Fortunately in those countries they spoke a broader French which I did quite well at understanding.*

The Prime Minister of Angola cuts his well-suited way through the ablutions
(Extracts from article on two Congos in *The New African* November 1962) Brazzaville and Léopoldville sit among the trees on either side of le pool, a mile wide apart of the Congo River. ... in Brazzaville the money is good but the prices are high...In Léopoldville the money is upsetting. It is dream money. There is lots of it everywhere. Bank notes flicker in hands...But it is worth so little.

The United Nations are everywhere. Pale blue berets, pale blue scarves and fawn uniforms make this the prettiest army since the redcoats. The Provisional government of Angola has its headquarters in an old Belgian villa. It has been running the guerrilla warfare in northern Angola which has changed the whole position of Portugal in Africa. Guerillas with khaki shorts squat on the ground to cook. Just over the wall from an everyday suburban road they wash, talk and cut one another's hair. Prime Minister Holden Roberto Leader of the National Liberation Front of Angola (FNLA) cuts his well-suited way through the ablutions ... he is very conscious of being *le premier ministre*. 'Our greatest need is for arms,' he says as though he were discussing coffee plantations or dock equipment. But the only considerable offer of arms would have had Russian technicians attached. 'The second need is for drugs. Against malaria, tetanus and gangrene.'

Soyinka, Okigbo, J.P.Clark & A Dance of the Forests
(Extracts on Nigeria and Ghana from article *The New African* 8 June 1963) In Lagos the buildings skyscraper out of the slums ... This is what the economists call 'the beer, bricks and boots stage' of the economy when local industries are started which do not demand precise skills. Nigeria is almost self-sufficient in 'Star' beer.

In Accra you seem to be able to get whom you want on the telephone ...

In the rickety hot lead atmosphere of the *The Daily Express* in Lagos I asked John Pepper Clark how to get through to Chinua Achebe at Broadcasting House. 'You tried to get Broadcasting House on the phone? But nobody ever gets Broadcasting House.' He tipped himself back with laughter and nearly fell out of the window onto the rusty roofs under rainy season sky.

Segun Olosula, a producer at Western Region television, and I … were just off to see Wole Soyinka, the playwright, rehearsing the 1960 Masques in a new production of his *Dance in the Forests*. Soyinka, Olusula, John Pepper Clark and Christopher Okigbo … are all involved in the Mbari Club at Ibadan, which has one of the most sophisticated lists of plays and poetry in Africa. [Mbari will first publish *Dance in the Forests* and then Rex Collings will publish it in the OUP Three Crowns series.]

In Ghana they are pulling down the slums … blood-red crosses are splashed passover-like on the walls. The marked houses are to be bull-dozed. An official of the Congress People's Party says 'Alternative accommodation is being considered.'

In Accra the association with Russia appears. Nkrumah's one-party state shows an … adoption of Iron Curtain ideas. Black Star parade square, the Black Star shipping line, the national flag with its black star, immediately have Red Star associations.

The Nigerians are self-assured. A clerk in Apapa, the dock area of Lagos, said about Ghana: 'They want to be the biggest, most important country in West Africa; because they know they aren't. We are larger. We have greater riches. I respect Ghana. They are a good little country.'

Snowploughs & the two imperialisms of Russia and the West in Guinea
(Extracts from an article in *The New African* 21 September 1963)
In 1958 Sékou Touré of Guinea deeply offended De Gaulle at the time of the referendum on France's constitution….It was the only French territory to vote for independence. It voted '*Non*' against a continued semi-imperial status.

De Gaulle determined to make the price of independence as high as possible. '*La civilisation française* was ripped out with a malevolence the Belgians never equalled in the Congo. Telephones were dragged out of their sockets; files were burnt; anything too heavy to move was destroyed. By the first week of December 1958 only twenty French administrators and technicians remained out of the 4,000 who had been there at the time of the referendum. De Gaulle purposely smashed the administration to make Guinea an example to the other French colonies.

Russia saw her chance to make a 'Cuba in Africa.' The bureaucratic maladministration of Soviet aid has been an Evelyn Waugh delight for everybody except the Guineans. The snowploughs are but the beginning of a list of trinkets which have piled up on the pretty palm-lined peninsula on which Conakry stands. Two million screwdrivers have been landed for a population of two and half million; there do not seem to be enough screws. A frustrated bureaucrat unloaded a five year supply of paperclips to rust and rot in warehouses for five rainy seasons. There is a field full of bidets but no plumbing.

PART TWO

Clare & James Currey
January 1963-July 1964

Clare Wilson and I married in Cambridge on 21 December 1962. Selections from Clare Currey's airmail letters have been interleaved with my airmail letters to Ruth and Henry Wilson and to Ralph and Stella Currey. Unless stated otherwise letters are posted from Cape Town.

Clare Wilson just before she went up to St Anne's College, Oxford in 1955.

On 29 May 1957 the Oxford International Committee supplied lunch and tea on two punts from the Bardwell boathouse down to the Thames and back. (left to right) James Currey, Roger Meek and Clare Wilson. Clare and James are both aged 20 and the red polka dot dress is the one Clare had been wearing when George Cacanas first introduced them a year before in May 1956.

When Roger Pethybridge had this photo of Clare and James developed he found that he had double exposed the negative. So the ghostly figures of Russian soldiers are to be found at bottom left and of the Kremlin at top right - privileged Western youth growing up under the threat of the Cold War.

We've got a flat! The grand view across Table Mountain from the flat at 101 Kloof Nek Road. We had the top floor architect-designed flat. There was an open fire for which we gathered wood in the forest across the road. There were generous built-in bookshelves and a built-in floor to ceiling wooden desk which immediately became the production and design office for The New African *and for designing maps of Africa such as the* Contact Freedom Calendar of Africa *which is pinned in the corner.*

The view from Kelp Cottage at Kommetjie with the back of Table Mountain some thirty miles to the north. Norah Henshilwood and Mavis Orpen welcomed young people from Cape Town. Below on the stoep of Kelp Cottage from the left: Aart and Val Bijl, James Currey, Judy who married Ivan Drew; in front Tim and Sally Holmes (née Morgan), Mavis Orpen. The photograph below was taken on the stoep six month before Clare arrived but it was the place where Clare immediately felt at home from her first week-end in South Africa.

Randolph Vigne saved the publication of Anthony Delius's satirical novel The Day Natal Took Off. The Cape Times *panicked about publishing it as they thought it would endanger their government contracts. Randolph could not come to this launch party as he was in hiding to avoid being banned by the Special Branch so that the toast to 'Absent Friends' was greeted with much laughter.*

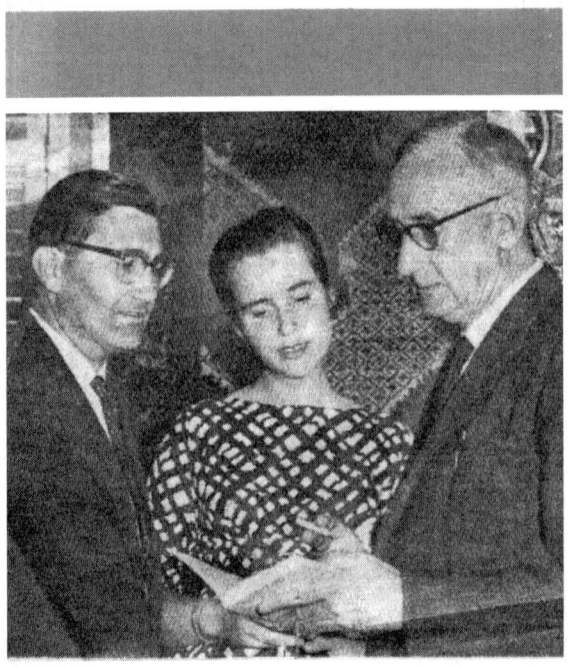

In this Cape Times *photo the author and journalist Anthony Delius is on the left. On the right is Leo Marquard the Editorial Manager of Oxford University Press and a founder of the SA Liberal Party. Leo Marquard had quietly enabled James Currey's political activities to develop and continue. In the middle is* 'Mrs J.M.Currey, who arrived in Cape Town from England recently and will spend about two years here.' *Months afterwards, when people were introduced to Clare, they would mention this photo.*

The Swartberg Pass one of six climbs to the Karoo, the desertlands of the highland Cape.

Clare standing in the vastness of the desert Karoo near where we came across a prison farm with black prisoners cheering a football match.

Clare took this photo of a colour-bar notice outside the tourist Kango Caves. It was later used as an example of constant apartheid notices in J.D.Omer-Cooper: History of Southern Africa, *which Tamsin was to prepare for press.*

The visit of Clare's parents at the end of 1963. Henry Wilson and James Currey on the flat balcony at 101 Kloof Nek Road talking to Ruth Wilson in front of the convertible Morris Minor. It had to be shipped out for their visit from England as car hire companies did not have convertibles in South Africa.

One seemed to so often be on the National Road to the airport or heading across the Cape Flats to the Hottentots Holland and the climb into mainland South Africa. The cooling towers stand near the oldest African township location at Langa from where 35,000 Africans marched into Cape Town in 1960. Monica Wilson, renowned Professor of Anthropology at the University of Cape Town, brought in a research student Archie Mafeje as a co-author of this study of the Langa township. It was considered pioneering because he was asked to study his own people.

Monica Wilson
Archie Mafeje

LANGA

A Study of Social Groups in an African Township

One of the most vivid young writers in The New African was called Jacob Mokgolo who wrote to us with a P.O.Pietersburg address. We planned to head north to Rhodesia through the town and I wrote to suggest a visit. He sent us instructions which turned out to be accurate about direction but gave no idea about the distance of the extra journey of about eighty extra miles. Jacob Mokgolo introduces us to his family; notice the bold Venda designs on the wall.

Below is a view of the village with Jacob Mokgolo and Clare. The family was raided that very night by the Special Branch. We had been naive and did not imagine that every person we visited on our 'great trek' into the colonial Rhodesias and Nyasaland would be recorded in the Bureau of State Security (BOSS) in Pretoria.

James in front of one of the walls of the ruins of Great Zimbabwe. The average white southern Rhodesian did not believe that Africans could have built them and talked about the Arabs or the Portuguese. Whoever built them did not use measuring rods and simple geometry. The buildings themselves are remarkable only in the volume of stone though extraordinary in terms of political organisation.

The Red VW beetle, at the Victoria Falls rest camp, had in Zambia just passed the northernmost point of Clare's and James's 'Great Trek'. Clare and James spent several nights in the little thatched rondavel cooking meals in an outside kitchen with the background sounds of lions and the River Zambezi. James had collected the red VW new in Dusseldorf and had driven to Clare's Hertfordshire thatched cottage and eventually to managed persuade her to marry him and come back to South Africa with him.

The landscape of the Transkei across which Clare and James roared back from the 'Great Trek'. Days later James had to rush with his OUP colleague R.Mynyakama to the capital Umtata to see the first Minister of Education of the new Transkei. The visit in June 1964 was in the month before James and Clare fled from South Africa.

(11 May 1964) We visited Nyasaland in its last days before it became independent as Malawi on 6 July 1964. We had not seen an Independence Office before. Clare's photograph was used for the front cover of The New African *of 11 July 1964, the day we fled via Johannesburg airport.*

We had not met a cabinet minister before. A photo of Clare (left) taking a photo of John Msonthi, Minister of Trade and Industry in Malawi, on the ferry over the Shire river. We had been introduced by Clare's cousin Anthony Wilson (right) who was in the middle of seven years training young people to bring in Community Development across the country.

The minister's Benzi is driven off the ferry

Clare and James spent a night at J.P. Martin's beloved Pilgrim's Rest in the Drakensberg mountains. He first lived at the Royal Hotel (above) where the gold miners used to shout and curse and sing. He moved out to camp in the vestry of the Wesleyan Methodist chapel (in middle). One time he waded across a swollen river with his parsonical suit in a bundle on his head watched by his congregation of miners. Apparently they were betting about whether the padre would survive. The collection was much larger than usual because they had donated their winnings.

Clare looking out of 'God's Window' which is where the Drakensberg range falls away with a vast view across Mozambique towards the Indian Ocean.

1963

Apartheid hits you
(Clare/ Ruth and Henry Wilson, 2 January 1963) Johannesburg. *Apartheid* hits you as you enter the airport – different loos for whites and blacks, different restaurants – one was almost surprised that whites were allowed to see blacks. There are different counters in the post offices, different seats and tables for filling forms at.

Every African has to have a Pass
(Clare/ Ruth and Henry Wilson, 10 January 1963) Spent a most interesting morning with Norah Henshilwood former head of the most prestigious Cape teacher's college. She is a member of Black Sash, a S.A. women's organisation devoted to helping Africans in a rather maternal way (e.g. no African woman can be a member.) The Black Sash runs an Advice Centre for Africans and Norah is there one morning a week. The trouble is nearly always over these passes. Every African has to have a pass; without one whether lost or stolen they're jailed. Then you can't be in the Cape Province unless you are in a job or unless you have lived there for 15 years. So men who work here are more often than not separated from their wives and families who live in the Transkei – that is an area specially for Africans. And an average single train fare costs just under £6. So family life for thousands of Africans is completely disrupted. And of course the husbands find better paid work here than in the Transkei where there's practically none. So there are lots of married people working here but separated from their spouses and children because it's illegal for them to live here with their husbands/ wives unless they too have a job. Can you imagine anything more designed to promote hooliganism and immorality in towns? Of course it is quite true that there is simply not enough room for wives and families in Cape Town. but that's a negative way of approaching the problem and separation is no solution. So few of the people who come to Norah's 'bail office' was she able to help. It was a valuable way of getting to know some of the problems here. [The Pass Laws were indeed central to *apartheid*, which is Afrikaans for 'apartness' or 'separate development', or what had previously been called 'the colour bar'. The Africans had to carry their Pass Books everywhere. The rest of the population had Identity Cards. The 'Coloureds', as people of mixed race were called, and the Khoisan, Indians, Chinese and Malays had to carry Identity Cards so they could prove to police that they did not have to have the *'Dom Pas'* – the 'Damned Pass.' Clare had asked James, as

they were flying into Cape Town, whether they would have to have Identity Cards? No! If you looked 'White' you were all right!]

Publishing for independence

(James/ Ralph and Stella Currey, 27 January 1963) Douglas Milne, who runs Northern Rhodesia Literature Bureau…was full of how much he liked the new Cape Town covers and of how good he thought our production.

(James / Ralph and Stella Currey, 30 January 1963) On Tuesday all the young white men of the office (including those from Salisbury and Joburg) had a meeting with Cannon. To our great surprise everything we wanted was done. It was established that [with independence coming next year] we should strongly recommend to London that an office be opened in Lusaka because Nyasaland authorities strongly refuse to deal with anybody coming from Salisbury. Also Cannon agreed that we should [with Transkei Bantustan being set up] take on an African traveller. I must say Cannon surprised us.

The drift towards violence

(James/ Ralph and Stella Currey, 17 February 1963) The two murders of whites have shaken everybody. But they smell of the inevitable drift towards violence. The 'zones' at Langa are the worst area – that was where the Italian Capetonian was murdered while collecting hire purchase debts.

The Bashee Bridge murders [of a white couple in their caravan] were appalling. The police insist that the motive was not political. But the rumours in the Transkei are (i) that the camp was used by the Special Branch because it has a commanding position overlooking the valley (ii) that the government stooge Kaiser Matanzima was given refuge there when chased by members of Poqo. There was an enormous funeral in Umtata for two lawyers killed in a road smash. Matanzima was tactless enough to attend in a Special Branch car. One of the orators said 'These lawyers were respected as leaders. They come from the people. They weren't baboons on a stick with BA gowns.' Matanzima goes to the Bunga in his BA gown.

The New African has survived a year

(James / Ralph and Stella Currey, 30 January 1963) Terence Beard from Rhodes University said yesterday; 'So you're back to put the layout of *The New African* in order!'.

(Clare/ Ruth and Henry Wilson, 9 February 1963) Jas has been very busy this week-end with *The New African* which he helped to found and of which he is design and production manager. We must send a copy to you by sea so that you can see its Currey design.

Natal takes off
(James / Ralph and Stella Currey, 30 January 1963) *The New African* company is doing a rather an interesting and exciting bit of book publishing [new censorship law going through parliament so speed is necessary]. We are putting out a satire by Anthony Delius called *The Day Natal Took Off*. Frightfully funny. The Nationalist mayor of a *dorp*, who is head of a commission investigating a staggering increase in Immorality Act prosecutions, is caught with a Zulu girl. Natal secedes. [The papers had recently had stories of a 'Back to the Empire' movement called 'The Natal Stand'. Yesterday's *Sunday Times* front page has a report of a Brakpan town councillor who is faced with charges and has been suspended from the National Party.]

The Delius book was being published by Botha, the Progressive Party secretary in Cape Town … He placed typesetting and printing with *The Cape Times* printer. The print manager stopped the presses and demanded a legal opinion. A Liberal, who happens to work at that legal firm, said that *The Cape Times* had asked for a negative opinion to get out of the embarrassment of printing the Delius book (they print *Hansard* and *Reader's Digest* and other profitable work). The five legal points listed were footling.

[Delius appealed to Randolph to get professional support to save the book.] *Cape Times* typesetting is free except for the cost of the metal. Pioneer, the printer of *The New African* and other leftish stuff, has agreed to print for nothing until we have the cash from sales. Delius has agreed to accept no royalties until money comes in. We stand to make £250 if we can clear the first printing of 3,000 copies.

(James, Ralph and Stella Currey 23 March 1963) Delius's book is doing quite well in the Cape and we have sold 2,000 out of the 3,000 we printed. We are now making a profit and if we clear the other 1,000 we should make a clear £750 which will keep *The New African* alive a bit longer. It hasn't really gone in Joburg yet nor, ironically, in Durban.

The Farfield Foundation, whoever they are
(James/ Ralph and Stella Currey, 26 April 1963) *The New African* has just been given 2,500 dollars by the Farfield Foundation, whoever they are. [It turned out in 1967 that they were used by the CIA to launder money for journals in 'the free world' through the Congress for Cultural Freedom in Paris.] So with some modest profits on Delius's book (2,600 have gone) we are finally afloat. We are expanding to 24 pages.

Randolph Vigne takes off
(Clare/ Ruth and Henry Wilson, 18 February 1963) Very busy getting out the book by Anthony Delius. Very exhausting on Friday sending out review copies.

(Clare/ Ruth and Henry Wilson, 22 February 1963) Monday was a hot and sticky night and there was a party to launch *The Day Natal Took Off*. The party was given in an antiques saleroom, such an odd place and there were lots of lovely carpets I was dying to pinch. Lots of journalists and reporters and Liberals and I was photographed by *The Cape Times* (can't think why) with Anthony Delius and Leo Marquard; if the photo comes out and isn't too awful will send you a copy.

The whole proceedings shadowed by the banning of Peter Hjul the Liberal Party leader in this part of S.A. Randolph Vigne was about to be banned too so, when the police arrived at his front door, he dashed out of the back door and went into hiding, first of all at Kelvin Grove, a madly exclusive pro-Empire pro-Queen sort of club in the suburbs! We think now that there's been such a fuss over Peter Hjul's banning that Randolph could come out of hiding for a while but the situation, for all its sickening beastliness, was really rather funny.... Randolph is Chairman of Insight Publications which is bringing out the Delius book: so at the party we had to drink to 'absent friends'.

Peter Hjul has been banned under the Suppression of Communism Act (Can't move out of the Cape Town magisterial district, can't speak to any other banned person, can't go to any gathering whether social or political.) Luckily the rather mealy-mouthed opposition in Parliament have brought themselves to object and to say that of course he is not a communist.

I ban you here and I ban you there!
(Clare/ Ruth and Henry Wilson, 22 February 1963) The Liberal week-end summer school was fun. Marvellous journey there over two mountain passes, beauty upon beauty. Really blue mountains. Three hours there – 140 miles. Remote farmhouse at end of sandy farm track (which took 35 minutes). Very hot, very primitive, but lovely. Talks under evergreens, walks up mountain. No sanitation, water had to be collected from a spring. Very dusty. Jas's talk [about his recent visit to the newly independent countries in West Africa] a great success and I think he will have to repeat it (one and two-third hours, help, my attention alas wandered).

Great barbecue [*braiivleis*] in the open air with chops fried over a huge fire, and songs and toasts. To hell with the government etc. You know 'Old Macdonald had a farm? ' There was an impromptu version about 'Old

Macdonald had a Verwoerd' with a 'I ban you here' and 'I ban you there etc.' Also a de Wet Nel (Bantu Affairs Minister) 'with a Bantustan here and a Bantustan there ... etc.' Lots of ribaldry.

Bans for Randolph!
(Clare/ Ruth and Henry Wilson, 22 February 1963) We are all v. sick at this banning of Liberal leaders. I told you about Peter Hjul and now you will have read about Randolph Vigne ....He escaped the police for 10 days during which he managed to get to Johannesburg and back but knew he wouldn't get away with it for ever and planned, for maximum publicity, to be caught at the meeting to be held in protest against Peter Hjul's banning; this would get lots of publicity as main speaker is to be Alan Paton.

The police Special Branch men (weedy looking individuals in plain clothes) got him outside the hall and were rather surprised at how peacefully the liberals took it; Randolph was given the banning papers (signed by Vorster the Minister of Justice, who was pro-Nazi) and the crowd hissed in a rather frightened way. Only a slightly nervous 'No arguments! No arguments!' from the Special Branch. As Randolph moved off to his car James yelled 'Three cheers for Randolph' and there were huge cheers, followed by three more for Peter Hjul.

Then we went into the meeting. The whole thing made us all very depressed and helpless, but it's made me a Liberal Party member. When I first arrived I was surprised that the press (or the English-speaking press) speaks out against apartheid and it is a relief to find that there is some institution agin the government, but after all this banning one realises how slight is such opposition and how ineffectual. I don't see any reconciliation is possible with this government.

We went to see the Vignes yesterday. I think Randolph's relieved that all the strain of waiting is over even tho' being banned means such terrible restrictions. His wife Gillian, who's a dear and a great joke, was in the lavatory when he was served his banning papers and thought the cheers were for Paton; which led me to make a ditty 'Oh dear what can the matter be, Randolph's wife is locked in the lavatory.' But this is very low. [There were always many visitors at the Vignes and Randolph could only legally speak to one person at a time. So Randolph used to stand in the doorway of his study which ran off the sitting room so that if the police came he could slip back into his study and close the door.]

All change in southern Africa
(Clare/ Ruth and Henry Wilson, 26 April 1963) You ask what does South

Africa think about the break-up of the Federation [of Rhodesia and Nyasaland and the independence in 1964 of Zambia and Malawi]?...People who went to S. Rhodesia years and years ago are fed up and think that Britain has failed them treacherously (most of these people are really rather awful) and wonder what they are going to do as the wealth of the Federation came from N. Rhodesia and S. Rhodesia will find it difficult to stand on its own feet, economically. It's thought possible that it may apply for union with South Africa but she can't do that until she's independent, which she won't be yet a bit. Here the conservatives think it's giving way to the natives, and the liberals think it wasn't planned well enough in 1952 and wasn't worth maintaining.

Solemnly and joyfully one goes on with one's life
(James/ Ralph and Stella Currey, 11 March 1963) The strangeness of the South African set-up strikes one on coming back to the country. In Cape Town especially the pleasantness of people to one another. The fact that a coloured waitress from a café will get out of a lift before a lot of white men because she is a woman and because the men positively stand back for her. And the living of life against a background of ever more frequent bannings, bombings and hysterical statements. This week a Nat MP Greyling accused the Liberal Party of plotting bombs and murders. And then accused it of being a bunch of Jews. But we have had tremendous sympathy because of all this and never such newspaper coverage. Two or three stories a day for the last week.

And solemnly and joyfully one goes on with one's life and every now and again is brought up short by the thought that the books one is designing may be rendered useless by civil strife. Clare and I discuss the various stages of design and choose colours and find great enjoyment in it.

Should The New African take over Contact?
(James/ Ralph and Stella Currey, 23 March 1963) Three years since Sharpeville and the end of the era of non-violence. Special courts are now under preparation to deal with Poqo and saboteurs 'without delays'. Interesting that they still think in legalistic terms; they do at least try you before they shoot you. Patrick Duncan resignation has become increasingly desirable. You may remember that in *The New African* number 3 a year ago that there was an article by him entitled 'Violence or Non-Violence'. At that time he came out in favour of non-violence as he always had done.

(James/ Ruth and Henry Wilson, 21 March 1963) We have been getting support from various quarters and this evening we had a meeting in the office of our accountant. This was to decide whether we would make a takeover bid of £1 for the company which published *Contact*. We spent a great deal of time making motions in the proper language, which was greeted with much mirth. Proceedings were interrupted at one point while Randolph Vigne conducted a conversation over the telephone with his two-year old daughter Lucy.

It was decided that we had better not launch another company because we did not want *The New African* to be killed because *Contact* went bust, or vice versa. And we cannot take over the *Contact* company because there is a 10,000 rand defamation suit against it on behalf of Kaiser Matanzima the government stooge …leader of the Transkei (which is the first phoney Bantustan).

(James/ Ralph and Stella Currey, 23 March 1963) I also was not too keen to be a director as I have far less to do with *Contact* that than I do with the *The New African*. Since then we have found out that the directors do not have, to be resident in South Africa so that all of us are resigning.

Cases will become all the more possible under the Censorship Act when it is inevitably passed (the discussions of this bill have been suitably illiterate). Dr Jonker, one of the most likely chief Censors, says that everybody learns Shakespeare in an expurgated form and they don't notice it and it doesn't hurt.

Carry out the law, however iniquitous
(Clare/ Ruth and Henry Wilson, 6 April 1963) We went to see *Judgment at Nuremberg* the other night, which is excellent – can't think how it got past the SA censors as if you translate some of the nouns, many of things that were said about Nazi Germany could apply to Nationalist S.A. It's a very long film, and on the whole a very fair one, and raises the terrible problem under the Nazis – was their duty only to carry out the law, however iniquitous the law was, or should they have resigned, or….? And of course this is the problem here not only for the judges but for university teachers, etc.

South Africa is about to become a 90 day police state
(Clare/ Ruth and Henry Wilson, 26 April 1963) Really frightful news politically. They've passed an emergency bill which makes South Africa into a police state for everybody. Now you can be held in jail without a charge for 90 days, after which they release you but can imprison you straight away for another 90 days, and so on ad inf. till you satisfy them – any police officer can put you in jug on suspicion. The government must be really scared.

This latest bit of joy which Vorster has thought up really puts the country into the same state as the Transkei which has, of course, been in a perpetual state of emergency since 1960.

One really becomes punch-drunk. At a meeting today Alan Paton said. 'I said a couple of years ago. "South Africa is not a Police state but it is a good imitation of one." I should like to withdraw that statement.' The Special Branch man scribbled hard. 'And replace it with "South Africa is about to become a police state".'

(Clare/ Ruth and Henry Wilson, 26 April 1963) We went to see Alan Paton the other day ... to discuss his musical play *Sponono*, which was performed in Cape Town about six weeks ago. Jas asked all the questions and I took it all down in rusty shorthand and it appears in the next *New African...* The language was rather different from aerial photography. He is a funny little man with white hair and a red face, and very nice.

'No! But you have got to let the Bantu talk.'
(James to Clare, Pietermaritzburg, May 1963) My journey here from East London took a single day. I left at 7 a.m. and reached Umtata at 10.00 a.m. I couldn't find the Inspector I wanted to see so I visited the three schools in Umtata. Then I went up to the Bunga [Transkei Parliament] to see who I could find and bumped into Hugh Lewin a *Golden City Post* reporter who is married to an ex-Liberal party secretary and I went along with him to the Liberal Party office. They were all fuming because the government officials had just been manipulating and stage-managing the whole show. Hugh L. went to Coetzer Deputy Minister of Affairs in the Bantu Homelands and said why had it all been rushed through before lunch. Coetzer said that the motion (about the proclamation about voting and who was to vote in the Bantustan) was all in the Bill which was going through the Parliament in Cape Town. So Hugh Lewin said that the morning's debate in the Bunga would not make any difference. So Coetzer said 'No. But you've got to let the Bantu talk.' I went to the Bunga in the afternoon and they were talking about wattle plantations. It was most noticeable how the line of, mainly white, administrators were controlling the whole proceedings. They passed up notes the whole time. Leibrandt the Chief Magistrate was most noticeable.

Schools on little hills wreathed with singing children
[James was testing his theory of how OUP should market *The Oxford English Course for Bantu Schools*. For five days he plunged into the vast township of Cato Manor outside Durban, where the riots had been, to talk quickly to

the Principals and leave a specimen set of books. Many a school sat on a little hill and was wreathed in singing children. James learnt not to say too often how much he enjoyed the songs because they would put on a concert for him and that would slow down his visiting rate. One day James visited 29 schools.]

On Thursday I went to Edendale outside which is the enormous semi-rural location outside Pietermaritzburg. Six crowded schools. Even the wash rooms in the better schools occupied by classes. On Friday I went into the more tribal area called Swartkops location. This was most beautiful and I enjoyed driving along dusty roads. I bumped into Mr Ali of Shooter and Shuter and we travelled in convoy. They are the biggest booksellers in Maritzburg and very pro-Oxford.

During the afternoon saw Dent who is one of the Inspectors in Maritzburg. The previous day I had seen the most indescribable self-important morons in Bantu Education full of pomposity and seemingly under-employed. But this man Dent was splendid. He is Acting Regional Director at the moment; but there is no hope of his being made Director. He is far too intelligent and has no illusions about human beings whatever their colour. But he is not going to get the top job.

Natal takes off in Europe
(James/ Ralph and Stella Currey, 16 June 1963) Did I tell you that Delius *The Day Natal Took Off* is being published by Pall Mall in England this October. 6,000 copies? Must say that we all think that they are straining the South Africa craze. Review in TLS has brought enquiry about German, Dutch, Scandinavian rights. By the way the great enthusiast at Pall Mall is Colin Legum of *The Observer*. £250 advance. So we are making a bit of money for the freedom struggle.

We are going to have a drink with the Deliuses tonight. He just went to Addis and is all steamed up to do the book which I had first thought of about a year or eighteen months ago and suggested to Marquard; a book, a journalist's book, about the new Africa. A bit of a change to have the view from this end of the continent.

Putting the clock back
(James/ Ralph and Stella Currey, 25 June 1963) We had most interesting dinner with Anthony Delius and his wife. She is just like an Afrikaner version of Gillian Vigne. Also there was Helen Suzman the lone Progressive MP ... She is very tough which reassures one when one sees the Nat onslaught on her in parliament. But it is telling on her, according to Anthony Delius.

He told a long funny story about how he and his wife got married. They went to Union Buildings in Pretoria during the war. But nobody could marry them there. So they went to the Registry Office but it was three minutes after closing time. So the Registering Officer got out a ladder, solemnly climbed up to the clock and put it back eight minutes. Anthony D. says that it has always been his hope that they are therefore not married properly.

Liberals and scrambled eggs
(James/ Ralph and Stella Currey, 12 July 1963) Monday was National Holiday (Family Day, the Republic's idea of keeping the Queen's birthday a holiday) and Norah, together with other Black Sash people, went on a retreat of bread, water and silence, as protest at the hypocrisy of it all – the government's policy resulting in the breaking up of families, or at least African families ...

The last week-end was spent liberalising. [The Liberal Party National Congress met in Cape Town.] Great discussions of making the party policy more socialist and whether we should continue to fight parliamentary elections. ...

We had the direct translation system working for the first time in Cape Town. This can carry up to three translations at once. It is particularly valuable in Provincial Congresses where many Africans have a ropey knowledge of English and most Europeans don't know anything of the African languages. The Liberal Party seems to be the only organisation in South Africa which has such a system. It worked very well except for first thing on Sunday morning when somebody forgot to turn on the electricity.

(Clare/ Ruth and Henry Wilson, 12 July 1963) The Congress was quite entertaining. The best bit was when somebody said there should be a party song and suggested a dreadful ditty about 'Give Me Ten Strong Men and I'll Give Ten Thousand More' (most unlikely in the Liberal context); luckily no-one took this very seriously and there were various suggestions about suitable songs like 'We're Marching to Pretoria' or 'Jailhouse Rock'.

(Clare/ Ruth and Henry Wilson, 12 July 1963) Last weekend there was a national meeting of all the Liberals, and it met in Cape Town, so we had a Johannesburg Liberal to stay. He was an awful nuisance, insisting on scrambled eggs when there weren't any eggs, and then when there were eggs, being fussy about exactly how they were cooked; and bringing an unknown chap into drinks, and not saying they were supping elsewhere, so I was busy thinking how to concoct supper for four rather than three. I am sure he's an excellent Liberal but he wasn't well house-trained, and am sure his wife spoils him. [We nicknamed him 'Scrambled eggs Harris'. John Harris was to be the only white South African to be hanged for a political crime.]

American arrested for seeing too many Africans
(James/ Ralph and Stella Currey, 12 July 1963) We went down to Kommetjie last Monday and took with us Mrs Calvin Plimpton who is married to the President of one of these small, expensive American colleges, Amherst in Massachusetts ... Anyhow Ruth Plimpton, whose brother in law is Adlai Stevenson's deputy in the American United Nations contingent, has written a book about an American work camps organisation. We took her down to Cape Point in the morning; Clare and I had never got round to a visit before. A zebra was busy cadging food among the cars.

(James/ Ralph and Stella Currey, 20 September 1963) Some time ago we met Mrs Plimpton at Kommetjie. She ... was arrested before leaving South Africa and had her passport removed for 24 hours. She was told she had seen too many Africans. In a few weeks she is going to be hostess to John F. Kennedy who is opening something at Amherst. We have told Norah to make sure John F.K. knows all about her S.A adventure. What damage these ham-fisted people do themselves!

'I've just been banned!'
(James/ Ralph and Stella Currey, 5 August 1963) It's been a *New African* week-end. The usual paste-up has been complicated by the fact that we are trying a central offset section with photographs and decorations. This is experimental. We have a large review section so we have jazzed it up a bit with pictures from books. If it works out a reasonable cost then we shall be able to add articles on architecture, paintings and sculpture. We seem to have a very white issue for a change. Anthony Delius on Parliament, Mary Benson on the UN, Zac de Beer (Progressive ex-MP).

(James/ Ralph and Stella Currey, 5 August 1963) I went to see Len Lee-Warden, one of the two Directors of Pioneer Press, which prints *The New African*. He greeted me with words 'I've just been banned!' This means, unless the S.B. relent, he may not enter his own printing works. ... He was until 1960, a [white] Native Representative in the House of Assembly. Then of course his position was abolished. But he swears that he has taken no active part since ... It maybe that they want to stop him standing as a candidate as Coloured Representative.

It may be that they think they have got something on him as a result of the tremendous coup (on 11 July 1963) in Johannesburg when they rounded up all those people at Liliesleaf farm [in the Rivonia suburb of Johannesburg]. [Nineteen members of underground charged with sabotage including Sisulu, Goldreich and Wolpe. Mandela, already serving sentence on Robben Island, was brought to trial on capital charge with them at the High Court in Pretoria. Clare Currey gave an account in the *Rivonia Notebook*.]

Cheering escapes from South Africa
(James/ Ralph and Stella Currey, 3 September 1963) There has been great rejoicing over the escape of Wolpe and Goldreich to British Swaziland. [Police described Goldreich as 'arch-conspirator' among those arrested at Rivonia. James Currey Publishers was to publish a book for Unesco by Harold Wolpe.]
(James/ Ralph and Stella Currey, 3 September 1963) And even greater rejoicing over the release of Abrahams and his three companions in Bechuanaland. [Dr Abrahams and three SWAPO members had been kidnapped by the South African Security Forces in British territory and taken to South Africa.] The British, thank goodness, have done the right thing this time. One of the three companions was Andreas Shipanga the person I told you about who was refused service at a bottle liquor store because the assistant thought that he was an African (quite rightly) in spite of his identity card which said he was a Coloured called Andreas Cloete. So he went to get a policeman who insisted that he be served and said, by way of explanation, that he was a 'black bushman'.

The fact that the British have acted properly this time is a legacy of Pat Duncan. It was he who went on and on in *Contact* about the probability that the Xhosa Ganyile was knocked over the head by agents of the South African police and carted off to jail in the Transkei where he could be held secretly because of Proclamation 400 and the State of Emergency. Pat got a piece of blood stained cardboard. The British said that it was chicken's blood. Pat said is it must be analysed and nobody could be found to do it in South Africa. So it was sent to London wrapped round some books and analysed and found to be human blood. Pat went on and on in *Contact* about it. Eventually a habeas corpus case was started and the judge took six weeks to write his judgment and rejected the case. The appeal judges took two days to reverse the verdict. And Ganyile was released. And still the wretched British authorities refused to hold an enquiry. The ridiculous thing was that they could have held an enquiry in the first place and shown that British justice held over the High Commission Territories. Sir John Maud was unfortunately away and his second as High Commissioner was so establishment-minded that he thought that nothing ought to be stirred up when an agitator like Duncan was behind it.

(James/ Ralph and Stella Currey, 5 August 1963) Stan Uys is the Cape Town *Observer* correspondent. He has tremendous reputation as seer over the SA political scene. Though he did not see much but gloom at dinner Saturday. He is extreme left and yet he writes for the conservative *Sunday Times* (Joburg) readership without offending them and without putting a foot wrong. ... He reckons that the Transvaal Nats don't know what is going on in the world outside. Edna Uys went to A.S. Neill's Summerhill. They are both vegetarians ... he dresses most nattily and they drive a German Carmen Ghia.

Tapped telephones
(James/ Ralph and Stella Currey, 21 August 1963) One finds it hard to believe in all this cloak and dagger stuff. But in certain places such as the Liberal Party offices the dial is jammed with a pin so that it will not return to the bottom. Apparently this makes listening through the receiver possible. It may be a fallacy but there is no point in taking risks in places the police believe that they have good reason to watch. Certainly Randolph's phone is tapped. There was evidence of this one night when an Afrikaner friend rang up one of his Nat relations and the tape recorder played back the conversation in Afrikaans.

Shortage of prisons in the 90 day state
(James/ Ralph and Stella Currey, 13 October 1963) We had a wonderful journey from Plettenburg Bay to Hermanus. We went through six passes in the day and travelled four hundred miles. The Swartberg Pass was in the Moroccan Tizn' Test class; not so much in the height as in the precipitousness. We then drove along the dusty Karroo road; we saw one donkey cart and a klipspringer deer and that was all except for a mysterious encampment. We were batting along in the dust, came over a rise and there lay this village which was obviously just springing up. We could only think that it was a prison camp. It might have been something else but certainly convict labour was being used. There was a football match in progress being played by Africans in clouds of dust. The spectators were the prisoners who were behind the fence with warders. A large building was going up which looked very much like a farm jail. They are having to build a lot more prison space to make way for the 90 days people who obviously have to be kept in maximum security.

Albie Sachs in solitary and short of water
(James/ Ralph and Stella Currey, 13 October 1963) Albie Sachs has been kept in solitary confinement with nothing but the bible to read. They hadn't questioned him after a week. He said that he was reasonably treated except that he was short of water. They only gave him one mug with a meal. His lawyer asked for him to be given more. The prison authorities said that the prisoners were not allowed bottles of water in their cells because they could smash them and use them as weapons. But in the end it turned out that the bottles were plastic so he was allowed more water. It is solitary confinement which is the worst aspect of 90 day detention without charge or trial. Some people have been in solitary for over 130 days; they were rearrested at 90 days and can be kept in indeterminably.

'I believe in the lynch principle.'
(James/ Ralph and Stella Currey, 13 October 1963) [Much discussion among white South Africans of the trial of Dr Arthur William Blaxall, an Anglican clergyman who was charged with aiding the PAC and the ANC. He pleaded guilty.] A letter from Randolph was used as evidence in the Blaxall case last week; the unnerving thing was that the letter was so unimportant. Randolph just told Blaxall to contact Marion Friedman, who is one of the Directors of Insight [the company which owns *The New African.*] One couldn't even think why it was necessary.

Grand South African conversation going on in the changing room at the squash club about Blaxall. One chap, English-speaking South African who spent five years in England with Shell, was saying a propos saintly 80 year-old Blaxall 'I believe in the lynch principle.' The other chap disagreed and he just thought that Blaxall was mad and should be locked up. [On 17 October Blaxall was found guilty but did not appeal against the prison sentence. However, on instructions from Vorster, he was released the next day.]

(James / Ralph and Stella Currey, 20 October 1963) The Vignes were raided yesterday morning at either 5.30 (according to Gillian) or 6.30 (according to Randolph). At the same time the Zackons and another Party member were visited. We have not heard whether non-Liberals in Cape Town or Liberals in other towns were visited at the same time. The strange thing was there was Gillian sitting in the garden today calmly – or rather amusingly – telling us about it. It all seems so unreal.

The Methodists elect a Mosotho
[A Mosotho is an individual of the Basotho people who speak Sesotho and often live in Basotho country which spreads out from British ruled Basutoland into the South African Orange Free State on one side and into the new Xhosa-speaking Bantustan on the other.]

(James/ Ralph and Stella Currey, 27 October 1963) The Methodists elected a Mosotho called Mokitimi as next President of the Conference. This is the first time that a major church in South Africa has had an African at its head. Miss Williams was obviously a bit uncertain about it. She made some mutterings about 'Of course the Africans all voted for him while the European vote was split over several candidates.' This ignores, of course, the fact that the Methodists have over 1 million African members while they have only 200,000 whites. It will do them no end of good at a time when the politicians inveigh against the white dominated churches on one hand and Islam makes inroads on the other hand with its non-racial position. Africans tend to think that the Christian God is white.

In the same week the Black Sash has voted to throw open its membership to all South African women. I do not suppose that there will be any great rush but it is a gesture which, as you know, I feel they should have made years ago. Norah Henshilwood voted both this year and last year for a non-racial membership.

Randolph sweats in a police cell
(James/ Ralph and Stella Currey, 17 November 1963) The great drama has been Randolph's arrest. Clare and I were going to a *New African* meeting. We saw Harold Head, recently editor of *Contact*, walking along. He told us how the four opposition Tembuland candidates for the Transkei election had called on the chance of seeing Randolph one by one. But they had been followed by the Special Branch – such is the 'freedom' of the first Transkei Bantustan elections which are tomorrow. They surrounded the house and arrested Randolph. He was in the police station at Caledon Square for forty-eight hours before they charged him. … Randolph behaves with remarkable coolness considering the case might go against him.

Randolph said he thought that he was sweating in his police cell from the heat but he found that the whole of Cape Town had been suffering from the humidity. The weather has been incredibly bad ever since the Wilsons arrived, with few let ups. The high humidity has rather knocked Clare's father for a couple of days.

(James/ Ralph and Stella Currey, 17 November 1963) Gladys Mgudlandu, whose exhibition we arranged at *Contact*, had 500 people at her latest opening and sold 40 pictures in 2 days. The owners of the gallery did not select any of the grotesque ones, only the sweet and nice ones.

(James/ Ralph and Stella Currey, 1 December 1963) Clare does not seem able to get over the fact that it is 1 December, approaching [her first] Christmas and getting hotter and sunnier. Christmas is such a strange thing here. The translation of snow and fir trees is really ridiculous when South Africa is far more like Israel than northern Europe.

Where were you when you heard that Kennedy had been shot?
(James/ Ralph and Stella Currey, 1 December 1963) Kennedy was shattering. We happened to be listening to vile Radio South Africa 9 o'clock news. After about two minutes it was interrupted by a message which had just come in about the shooting half an hour earlier. But it was not certain that he was dead. We listened to the 10 o'clock BBC Overseas News which was full of obituary.

The interest and passion felt among the Africans and coloureds has been most interesting. Randolph said that the African servants of friends of theirs were weeping that evening and saying 'He was our friend. He would have helped us.' Miss Williams was woken up by her servant Maria with the news. Everybody started telephoning one another. Elinor came in and said 'Do you know that Mr Kenneth the Prime Minister of England has been shot?' I must say this pleased me as I would rather have Kennedy's than Lord Home's image connected with England. But it is a serious blow in South African terms. If Wilson gets in and Kennedy had got back I think that there would have been a serious attempt to tackle the question of what to do about South Africa. Kennedy had the sprightliness of mind and the hard touch of idealism to get on with it more effectively. ... But what a year; Gaitskell, Macmillan and Kennedy all going!

The heresy of multi-racialism wins in the Transkei
(James/ Ralph and Stella Currey, 1 December 1963) The Transkei election results have been something of a surprise. The Poto-Sabata united front [backed by the Liberals] has been doing well. They have been standing for the heresy of multi-racialism. The government-backed Chief Matanzima who stands for racialism has been doing less well. So anyway it is something of a triumph for Randolph who has, more than anybody else, enabled some sort of articulation of desires to be made in spite of the government ban on parties. And this why they have banned him, though after the damage had been done.

The issues are far from clear. In Fingoland there has always been collaboration since the mid-Nineteenth Century. The old lot of government stooges (a chief who always subserviently calls Randolph 'Sir') got kicked out and new young members have got in, including some Liberals and one Progressive. In Sabata's own chieftainship there are the most Liberals. There was absolute crookery in Matanzima's own Paramount Chieftainship and there is a move to get the election there declared null and void.

The chiefs who form the automatic majority can still, as up to now, be bullied by the government. On the other hand, the chiefs could be affected by the fact that the populace has voted in the more radical element.

[Randolph later gave an account of what happened after the results were declared in the capital Umtata. Chief Sabata-Dalindyebo, having won the popular vote, left for Tembuland in an enormous crowd of celebrating cars. Pretoria then demanded that the chiefs voted to counter to the popular vote. Paramount Chief Matanzima left Umtata in the opposite direction in a South African police car.]

[In *The New African* Randolph at the beginning of the year ran the headline 'Verweord's fatal mistake' in bringing in the Bantustan and writing that this election is proving it. In fact Verweord had used the British technique of 'divide and rule' to keep white supremacy for a further thirty years.']

Petrol Tin Blues from Somalia
(James/ Ralph and Stella Currey, 22 December 1963) I have been reconstructing a broadcast talk on Somali Poetry for *The New African*. The talk was originally recorded by the Transcription Centre in London funded by the Congress for Cultural Freedom (they back *Encounter*). I have been taking examples out of the new book on *Somali Poetry* by Andrzjewski which is being published by the Clarendon Press in the New Year. This apparently sober and sedate book is full of all sort of entertaining stuff. For instance the latest verse form is the *heelo* or *balwo* and is the equivalent of a pop song blues. Apparently the first one was hammered out on a petrol tin by a Somali lorry driver whose lorry had broken down in 1945. Lorry drivers are particularly respected in Somaliland. They have taken the place of camel caravaners. Do you remember how John Grenfell-Williams at the BBC Africa Service suggested I join the Somaliland Camel Corps for National Service?

(Clare/ Ruth and Henry Wilson, 18 January 1964) Psychologist ... Len Bloom had had an interview on a tape-recorder with Archbishop Joost de Blank before he left. I was asked to get this onto a typewriter, so Len and I had two sessions to get it into shape for the next issue of *The New African*. Joost de Blank evaded a lot of questions but was quite interesting on others.

(James/ Ralph and Stella Currey, 19 January 1964) It took a lot of editing and our flat was turned into a fullscale office for *The New African* for the evening while Len and Clare worked at getting the tape into publishable form ... this was rather a scoop.

Methodist ribaldry & undiplomatic disclosures
(Clare/ Ruth and Henry Wilson, 1 February 1964) Have been doing some work for *The New African* on an electric typewriter which is great fun but a bit nerve-wracking at first.

(Clare/ Ruth and Henry Wilson, 8 February 1964) I've been very busy this week with Lib. stuff, largely finding out addresses. There is going to be a grand Liberal Party party and I have been writing out pompous invitations. Involved visit to Church House while they were electing Archbishop (the Bishop of Grahamstown has been chosen. Libs seem rather sad about this.) Also to various consulates and embassies. I asked the Church of England people about an Roman Catholic bishop, which didn't go down too well – the C of E office filled with three rather stout ladies and a bit forbidding, in great contrast to the Meth bookshop which had an African Rev and some unknown in great bursts of cheerful laughter and ribaldry. I have also penetrated the portals of *Die Burger* the Afrikaans newspaper and had to apologise for speaking English.

(Clare/ Ruth and Henry Wilson, 24 February 1964) Liberal Party party last Friday for press and diplomats ... great swing towards Liberals in interest among pressmen since success of multi-racial platform in Transkei. At the Liberal/diplomatic party ... there were some excruciatingly dull consulate wives (British) but a very amusing Canadian and a nice new Welshman who is coming to dinner. Jas and he clicked immediately because he called somebody in the Foreign Office pompous ... and then tried to be diplomatic and not call him pompous at all. Nice to know that diplomats can be undiplomatic.

And so what's the point of Group Areas?
(Clare/ Ruth and Henry Wilson, 8 February 1964) We trooped out to Wynberg one evening this week to see *Lawrence of Arabia* at a new cinema, which can be non-racial because it is still in an area which hasn't been Group-Areas-ed. So it made the whole of apartheid look pretty silly – there we were, sitting next to Africans and Coloureds and Malays and Indians and

sharing the same lavatories and drinking from the same bar and watching the same film, and who cared? It just goes to show that race divisions become divisions of class – only people with at least 44 cents to spare could have gone to the film anyway and that presupposed fairly bright people with fairly good jobs. And so what's the point…?

Evelyn Waugh-ish film company
(Clare/ Ruth and Henry Wilson, 21 February 1964) … reverting to jobs, I have been to Mrs Farmer's sister's agency and they have produced two temporaries – they rang up two days ago and said could I go and see a film company in Loop Street. So off I dashed, and there I found a very Evelyn Waugh-ish film company with glamorous men around and strange noises emerging from recording studios and people shouting what seemed to me to be absolute nonsense at one another while they were watching a silent film which was obviously meant to have sound as well.

Somebody called Ashley then produced acres and acres of a film script which they wanted stencilled by 11.00 a.m. the next day (it then being 4.20 p.m.) so I said I would take it home and do it here. Which I did but as there was a *New African* meeting which took till 7.00 p.m. I didn't get onto it till then and had to stay up with it till 12.20 a.m. The agency didn't think I could get more than 45/- for all that hard labour, but the film company turned up trumps and produced 70/- , marvellous! The scripts were too comic 'Elephant walking through tree.' Both scripts were for BP advertising films so I must tell Anthony Millar about them when next we see the Millars.

Censorship of The New African by police raids
(Clare/ Ruth and Henry Wilson, 28 February 1964) We gather *The New African* raid [by the Special Branch in January] got into the *Manchester Guardian* … needless to say the cops haven't returned anything that they took away yet, and they say that they only have an hour a day to look at it so that we won't get anything for ages. Trying!

(James/ Ralph and Stella Currey, 11 March 1964) On Monday while I was laid up *The New African* was raided by the police. They removed everything bar a typewriter but, from what was said, they are trying to get us for something we have covered. But it will be a long time before we know. The day afterwards we heard that the Congress for Cultural Freedom is going to give us even more money than we got last year. So that is cheering.

(Clare/ Ralph and Stella Currey, 10 March 1964) Absolutely infuriating about *The New African* just as we had got things in comparative order. We hope the next issue won't be affected, but it is jolly difficult when everything including the list of subscribers has been whipped.

(James/ Ralph and Stella Currey, 9 April 1964) Yesterday morning van Wyk, a Special Branch man, visited Len Lee-Warden of The Pioneer Press which prints *The New African*. I was the first person to see him after he was banned. He was given exemption after that so that he could go into his printing works. This Special Branch man said that the exemption would not be renewed if he did not stop printing *The New African* and other political stuff. So we are without a printer. It was Len Lee-Warden's whole livelihood versus *The New African*. Van Wyk himself used the word 'blackmail' [perhaps it should be 'whitemail'].

(Clare/ Ruth and Henry Wilson, 13 April 1964) And of course what else can the poor man do? It is of course proving terribly difficult to find anyone else to print it, and altho' it is flattering to think that the police go to such trouble for a magazine with a circulation of under 1,000 one does wish they would straightforwardly ban it and get it done that way – but of course they don't want the adverse publicity that banning would provoke, and would much prefer it to get stifled more quietly. As you can imagine the whole business is taking up far too much time and things are getting on top of us.

(James/ Ralph and Stella Currey, 25 April 1964) Well we had to move fast to get a new printer to take us on. And at the present this is becoming practically impossible. I asked Baker at Rustica Press and he said that he would print us for a couple of issues. But then he rang me up privately at home on the Sunday morning and said that he was personally frightfully sorry but that he had consulted some of the directors who are from the board of Hortors, the large group who own Rustica, and that they said that they had one or two large government contracts which they were afraid that they might lose. Really when one looks at *The New African* it is such an inoffensive little magazine. And yet people are funked to print us, not because we have ever been prosecuted, but because the Special Branch just come round and say things.

Anyhow Alan Baldwin, who is a member of the Liberal Party, has a share in a small printing works called Reliance has talked his other colleagues into doing us; he is a printer himself. So we are still afloat. We have other plans so we will not go under yet. It is interesting how the government gets its way by fear. Sensibly it avoids direct action as much as possible and maintains that there is a free press. The major newspapers have a code of self-censorship agreed by the Minister of the Interior. Anyhow getting everything through during the last three weeks has been a bit of an undertaking and one is glad to be free of it for a bit.

(James/ Ralph and Stella Currey, 25 April 1964) We are in Megaliasberg in the Transvaal enjoying having a lazy weekend in for the first time for three or four weeks. All *The New African* crises have meant a pretty exhausting time before going off a week ago today. I was working on *The New African* up until one o'clock on the morning we left. I must say that it is pleasant to be away from that. The police Special Branch still have all our administrative equipment so that, having got the whole thing running smoothly, we are again hamstrung. Luckily the editorial copy was not in the office for the wretched blighters to seize.

Randolph's Trials
(Clare/ Ruth and Henry Wilson, 8 February 1964) You may have seen [in the papers in England] that Randolph's case, due to be held on Thursday, has been postponed yet again till April. We were all sitting there in the magistrate's court, and Randolph in his one respectable and very hot suit, on about the hottest day of the summer – a swelterer. It got put off from 9.30 till 11.00 because one of the cases due to be held the same day involved some Swedish sailors whose ship was about sail at any minute ... Then at 11.00 the trial got put off till April! ... Poor R. had got all keyed up and so had all of us, and now we wait again.

(Clare/ Ruth and Henry Wilson, 28 February 1964) Our English calendars show crocuses and spring trees; we are just beginning to think about autumn. We had two dreadfully hot days on Monday and Tuesday but it's been lovely ever since. Temperature was 96 degrees Fahrenheit in Cape Town on Monday – ugh!

(Clare/ Ruth and Henry Wilson, 21 March 1964) Randolph back from Umtata where the trial has been postponed so that a handwriting expert can compare the two sets of handwriting. We gather he went up there with two Special Branch men and they visited their relatives en route and off route all the way there and all the way back. Gillian tells us some funny stories about it. There is a feeling that cops may be about to ban *The New African*, but there's nothing much that can be done until they do, if they do.

(Clare/ Ruth and Henry Wilson, 13 April 1964/11 May 1964) ... you will probably been as surprised as us to see that Randolph's case [in Umtata about contravening his banning order] has been dismissed for, to all intents and purposes, he was as guilty as anything. Apparently the prosecution fibbed like anything ('So of course did we!' says Randolph) and it didn't hold water at all, and the magistrate dismissed it rather impatiently. But goodness what luck.

(Clare/ Ruth and Henry Wilson, 21 April 1964) I wonder if the English papers have told you that Randolph got off his Cape Town case, the one that started while you were here?!!! You can imagine our feelings in all possible directions! Apparently the State put up a simply hopeless case. And did you see the bit about him in Pendennis in *The Observer* about three weeks ago?

Learning the mindset of escape
(Clare/ Ruth and Henry Wilson, 4 April 1964) The other day Jas met Carl Ohland [a Quaker] on the bus and we find that he's living in Glen Haw, that big block of flats further down the road from us on the corner… So we called on him one evening and he came to supper last night before we trekked out to the airport to meet cousin Roger Wilson.

Carl Ohland got on to his wartime experiences – quite nerve wracking – and Jas and I were both in a high state of tension by the time he left after telling us about crossing the border between Germany and Denmark as a deserter. We long for the next instalment! [He had deserted from the Russian front and decided that he must try to cross the border to Denmark and get to neutral Sweden. At the border all soldiers had to descend from the troop train and queue down a narrow passageway to have their papers checked by two border guards sitting at two desks. He thought that with his papers he had little or no chance of getting through. The soldier behind him pushed him out of the way and he found himself standing between the guards at the two desks. He realised that he had been shoved into no-man's land and walked past the second guard hoping that he would assume he had had his papers seen by the first guard. He was in Denmark. Somehow he got in touch with Danish underground and one night he was rowed out of Copenhagen harbour and across to Sweden. What he told us about handling danger and calmly just taking things as they come was to influence James's mindset during the Cape Escape only three months later].

A heated debate with Muslims
(Clare/ Ruth and Henry Wilson, 28 February 1964) We have heard from George Barron that Roger Wilson is coming out at the beginning of next month en route for Basutoland on behalf of one of the Rowntree trusts, and from Anthony and Anne Wilson that he is fitting in a visit to them in Nyasaland on his way back. He should be there just about a month before we go there ourselves. Our latest plan is to fly to Blantyre from Salisbury, thus avoiding at least three days of wearing travel through Mozambique by car, but as that would make us completely reliant on Anthony and Anne at the Zomba end we are consulting them about it first. In little more than a

month we shall be off to Johannesburg, how exciting.

(Clare/ Ruth and Henry Wilson, 21 March 1964) The Quakers are getting very excited about arrival of Cos Rog, and May Murray Parker is cross he isn't staying longer when he could meet all sorts of people he should meet (It so happens that he is arriving on Friday evening of a long week end – the Monday should be devoted to celebrating the arrival of Van Riebeeck in 1652.)

(James/ Ralph and Stella Currey, 6 April 1964) Roger Wilson, Professor of Education at Bristol, was in Cape Town this weekend. in between United Nations and Quaker appointments abroad. He is the father of the Anthony Wilson who we are to stay with in Nyasaland. He had come for the Rowntree Trust to see about various projects in Bechuanaland and thought that he might fly on to see Friends in Cape Town.

Last night we went with George Barron, one of the most splendid Cape Town Quakers, to hear Roger Wilson address a meeting of young Muslims on the United Nations. It turned out to be a thoroughly fascinating evening. He spoke for about twenty minutes and then laid the meeting open for questioning. This turned out to be a terrific debate. Some of the younger and more militant were full of questions affected by their own their own opinions about Roger being an apologist for Britain, and an apologist for Christians, and an apologist for the whites, and an apologist for the United Nations in the Congo. Morality versus Economic Motives in politics. They knew enough to keep a hot and lively debate going with Roger Wilson. They were muddle-headed in many things and had terrible prejudices. They thought that the United Nations had arranged for Lumumba's murder in the Congo and that it was responsible for everything there. Roger Wilson had spent a year in the Congo as an adviser to U.N. and so knew chapter and verse to disprove. He was on best debating form. He is not a person you would expect to have been President of the Union at Oxford but the way he enjoyed the debate showed his old debating style.

(Clare/ Ruth and Henry Wilson, 12 April 1964) Last weekend was mainly devoted to Roger Wilson… on Sunday went to a Muslim group he was addressing and heard his talk and the very keen and quick and antagonistic discussion afterwards… When addressing the Muslims he got very President of the Unionish and this was interesting to watch, but he was a bit off colour that day (had I poisoned him with the Quiche Lorraine the previous day I wonder?) which was a pity but he was very competent. [Brothers Roger Wilson (1929) and Geoffrey Wilson (1931) had both been Presidents of the Oxford Union!]

Are the noises in the night the police?
(James/ Ralph and Stella Currey, 9 April 1964) It is amazing. The boom is on. Spending on armaments is up 500% in five years. And the whites are a lot more frightened. Now the printers who print *Contact* will not do it any more. Friends of Tim's would not harbour a suitcase of papers for me. Noises in the night a week ago made me go to the window to see if it was the police. (I can never remember this before). One assumes as matter of course that telephones may be listened to. Everybody's fears are worse than reality. If only they stood together.

Bales and bales of Oxfam stuff in Johannesburg
(Clare/ Ruth and Henry Wilson, Pretoria, 16/17 April 1964) I had two very busy days in the middle of last week with Eveline Cadbury at the meeting house which is quite a smart new building much too big for the requirements of Johannesburg Quakers and on a bit of waste ground which to the uninitiated is very lovely but apparently is also very sinister – at least one murder and all sorts of people breaking into the meeting house and peculiar goings on next door. We dealt with bales and bales of Oxfam stuff…and then we left to distribute the parcels we had made up in the morning. This was very interesting.

The surroundings of Jhb not so awful as many had led us to believe – rolling country all golden and beautiful in Transvaal sunlight…Apart from one township named after an early Quaker Jhb councillor, which is very slummy, the ones where we went weren't at all bad; from what we were told a lot can be done by good management relations - telling people that they have to be moved but that they will be getting larger gardens in the new place, etc. The time we went was the church afternoon and there were lots of stately matrons around in their splendiferous church uniforms, brilliant blues and reds, really a very grand sight.

Dread Pretoria for the Rivonia trial
(Clare/ Ruth and Henry Wilson, Pretoria, 16/17 April 1964) The day before, I had got a lift from Johannesburg to Pretoria to come to the Rivonia trial, and this experience made me dread coming back to Pretoria and I feel I loathe the place, although architecturally it is much more interesting than Jhb and also much prettier – jacaranda trees everywhere which must be quite lovely when they are out. I've written to the Curreys about the trial, and expect it is rather an emotional letter, but perhaps it would be a good thing if you asked them if you could see it. I suppose I must go back to the courts today and tomorrow for a bit but don't relish it.

Have never seen James so furious or so upset and hope never to again
I'd been saying as we drove [to Pretoria] yesterday that I didn't want to come back here and then we saw the most awful news in the Sunday paper that made Jas hate the place too, which was that the cops had seized two thousand copies of *The New African* – the latest batch though I hope the previous one has safely got through to you. If so, the cops are after the first story by Can Themba, which I thought out of place and much better as a radio play or dialogue or multi-logue or whatever, and it seems too awful to have this chaos on account of what I at any rate thought not all that important to print. They are after it on the grounds of obscenity, would you believe it! Have never seen J. so furious or so upset and hope never to again. So now he can't wait to leave either. Poor dear, he had worked extra hard at that issue and now it seems all in vain due largely to administrative incompetence when there was no need for it.

(Clare/ Ruth and Henry Wilson, Pretoria, 16/17 April 1964) Am hoping to write about Pretoria trial in the next *New African* if it still appears; if not think I will try it on an English weekly.

Rivonia Notebook
Published under the pseudonym Elizabeth Wilson
The New African, 6 June 1964

The Supreme Court in Pretoria is reminiscent of the Reform Club in London. Both are the preserves of men. Both have marble floors on which high heels make a much louder noise than their size warrants, and in both places it is very difficult to find the ladies' lavatory….Hats aren't essential feminine wear in the Reform Club, but they are in the Supreme Court and if you are not wearing one a policeman taps you on the shoulder and tells you that you should.

The Criminal Court is exactly what a cinema-goer would expect. You are surprised that it is no bigger, that there aren't more people there. You have automatically found your way on to the side for White people and begin to wonder who the others are. The reporters are nearer the judge and dock; the people in the public pen cannot be the press. Are they the relatives of the accused? Special Branch? Young lawyers? Tourists? One woman looks friendly, perhaps an American. [In recent years we met a former Dutch diplomat who told us that they were diplomats. He alone among the diplomatic corps had attended every single day as a witness for the international community, as he saw it.]

Who are the two very well-dressed women just in front who obviously know about the headgear rule since each wears a jaunty hat? (One girl, who has not even the scarf that serves as hat for most White women spectators, sits on the bench with the escort's somewhat grubby handkerchief folded above her beehive). As the case goes on and the benches become harder and you wish desperately that there were something either to lean your elbows on or your back against, you fidget, cross and uncross your legs, with your hands clasped round your knees, change your position several times in five minutes, wonder what the time is, almost envy the man who is being cross-examined because he asks for, and is given, a chair. You find it difficult to concentrate and look once again at the benches of Non-White spectators. There are fewer Africans and Coloureds present than White people. You think you recognise Mrs Mandela and perhaps Mrs Sisulu and wonder how you would feel if it were your husband who was facing the judge, if you knew he faced a sentence of death. Would you be able to bear being there day after day; would you be able to bear *not* being there? And if you weren't allowed to talk to your husband how would you know whether or not he'd want you to witness his trial? Mustn't the brief moments when you see each other in the courtroom be more heart-rending than not seeing each other at all?

There are policemen everywhere. At least two to each exit and several scattered around the courtroom. Each time anyone enters the room he bows to the judge who doesn't notice. The reporters are scribbling at a long table on the right; above sits the judge in scarlet for whom everyone stood up when he entered. Just below sits some official (the clerk of the court perhaps?) who appreciates the prosecuting counsel's efforts to liven up the cross-examination and laughs when Chief Luthuli is referred to as 'the Nobel prizewinner – for peace.' The man in the dock has his profile towards us but sometimes turns towards the questioner and then we can see his face. It is difficult to hear him at first, but then one seems to hit the same wavelength and audibility is no problem. How can a man stand being cross-examined all day, for several days at a time? How does he stay so calm, how can he smile so cheerfully at his friends when there is a recess?

The backs of the eight accused impeded the view of the court. Although spectators are divided into Whites and Non-Whites, the accused are all in the same box, Africans, Whites, and Indian together, higgledy piggledy. Once they have settled down on their bench (always they enter in the same order and sit in the same place) they watch the proceedings and don't look behind them at us. But when they entered they look for their relatives and friends and give huge smiles. Nelson Mandela does look round during the cross-examination and smiles widely towards his wife. Everything seems very slow. The questions come slowly, the man in the dock takes time to answer; sometimes it almost seems like a thoughtful discussion. Documents are produced from a large cardboard box which would seem more at home in the kitchen or a garden shed. There are very few dramatic moments, but occasionally the accused does lose his apparent calm. 'I wish you could be in an African's position,' he tells his examiner 'and see for yourself what persecution is like.' The court is startled, somewhat embarrassed. 'Oh la la,' titters the girl in Army uniform near me. The German woman on the other side is more affected. 'It is terrible, terrible,' she says. 'why *did* they do it?'

Down a cracky road
[In *The New African* of 21 September 1963 had appeared, under the pseudonym Carl Mofoko, a vivid article about the realities of surviving life on a mining compound called 'In a Dim World; the Compound is a Meerkat Burrow'.]

(James/ Ralph and Stella Currey, 11 May 1964) On the Saturday morning after leaving Johannesburg we went to visit a [promising writer] called Jacob Mokholo. His postal address was a P.O. Box number in Pietersburg which is on the main road north [to Beit Bridge, the frontier post between South Africa and Southern Rhodesia.] We decided that it would be interesting and valuable to make contact with him. He sent us instructions about how to get to him. They gave no idea of distance, only of direction. 'Take the road due North from Pietersburg until you get to the junction for the road to Bochum which runs due West. At Bochum Post Office you go South past the Devonia Rolling Mills and turn off for the village of Terbrugge. You ask any African at the store where is the house of Jacob Mokholo. You will find it down a cracky road.'

Well, this all proved to be as nebulous as it seemed on first reading. He also asked us to let him know the week if not the day when we hoped to come. One has been involved in wild goose chases in Cape Town so this venture in the bushveld of the northern Transvaal seemed fraught with the danger of never getting to our target. Well we did.

Outside Terbrugge we were asking for him when a young chap of 18 or 20 tore up on a bicycle. 'Do you know Jacob Mokgolo?' 'Yes' he said breathlessly. 'I am Jacob Mokgolo!' So he cycled off to his home with us following behind in the car. After about three miles we got there. His parents' house was five rondavels grouped round a courtyard made of ant cement and cow dung. Round the courtyard and joining the rondavels was a wall painted with wall designs in ochre. [Venda wall decorations have become renowned.] All very spick and span. His parents were Northern

Sotho [Venda] and spoke no English.

Anyhow we had a long talk under the trees. Three suburban dining chairs were brought out for us and we sat with three little black pigs, very neat and clean, snuffling around in a self-confident way. We encouraged Jacob Mokgolo as much as possible. He has only a few books. A couple of Jane Austens, a Conrad, a George Eliot, a couple of Dickens. As Tim Holmes in Lusaka said 'One could tell he had those books from his writing.' I promised to send him proof copies, out of print copies and Penguins and other books so that he can widen his reading. There is no library for Africans closer than Pretoria.

It was an exciting and worthwhile excursion. I encouraged him to send us anything longer such as a novel or biography for criticism. He is also writing a novel in Northern Sotho which I encouraged him to send me at OUP [as we published new writing in the vernaculars]. He said self-effacingly that at school he had thought that only educated people could write and that he could not understand why his teachers were not all writing books. It took us some eighty extra miles there and back from the main road but it was worth it.

[We had been somewhat naive to have made such a visit; we later learned that on that day or in the night the Special Branch arrived to interrogate the author and his family about us. Indeed Randolph was to see, when the files of BOSS (Bureau of State Security) were opened in the nineties, that the whole of our 'great trek' [to Southern Rhodesia and what were about to become Zambia and Malawi] what we did and whom we met and stayed with had been recorded by *The New African* minder in Pretoria whose job was to also follow up on every author of every article, poem, or short story in the journal. Naively it never occurred to us that we were important enough to be watched so closely.]

HEADING NORTH TO CENTRAL AFRICA

Kruschev, Nikita and Keeler, Christine
(James/ Ralph and Stella Currey, 11 May 1964) We crossed the frontier at Beit Bridge at about three that afternoon. After the dour South African officials the Rhodesian customs were very jolly. They treated the whole operation with cheerful contempt. They had filled in sample Immigration Forms for Kruschev, Nikita and Keiller, Christine. Maybe also for Marx, Groucho and Marx, Karl. As soon as you leave South Africa every official looks much smarter and better turned out. And they all gave you brisk salutes under their wide-awake brims as you crossed the bridge. We shot

up through deserted low forest country with notices for elephant which we did not see. [The main roads were two narrow tar strips and, when you did very occasionally see another vehicle approaching, you had to swing left off the strip and pass leaving the driver's wheel on the tar and the passenger's wheels bouncing along in the potholes at the side of the road. While spinning along endless miles the passenger read to the driver from proof copies of forthcoming OUP books on race relations in Rhodesia by Philip Mason and Richard Gray.]

The Great Zimbabwe Ruins & the politics of race
(James/ Ralph and Stella Currey, 11 May 1964) After dark we reached the rest camp at the Great Zimbabwe Ruins. These are good institutions where for 7/6 [38p] a night per person you can hire a rondavel. There are little cooking huts with old ranges stamped 'Welcome; Dover'. There is a servant to every three or four huts who does your washing up. We had a very affable one. He was most disappointed by the number of infants we had produced. 'I make four. I want make twelve – if I am good.'

(James/ Ralph and Stella Currey, 11 May 1964) Great Zimbabwe is one of the best things I have ever seen in Africa. Aunt Iris was full of wonder and described it as 'out of this world' and she was right. One of the most interesting things about Zimbabwe is the reactions of people to it. The average white southern African does not believe that people indigenous to Africa could have built it. Aunt Iris seems to be in favour of the Phoenicians but others favour the Arabs or the Portuguese.

When one sees it one sees how plainly ridiculous all this is. The buildings themselves are really only remarkable in terms of size. The walls are enormous. And they are all built of stone without mortar or cement. The walls in the 'Acropolis' are natural extensions of the boulders to make this rocky hilltop a good fortification. The people who built the large 'Elliptical Building', which was the temple, did not use measuring rods and had no idea of simple geometry. And yet in terms of political organisation the building is extraordinary because of the sheer volume of stone which has been piled up.

This political organisation has been shown by anthropologists to be greatly developed among a great many African tribes. And since there are a great many mines in this area and trade with the Arabs and Portuguese was highly developed there would be things for the local strong man, who commanded Zimbabwe, to tax. (Unlike areas which depend upon subsistence farming or hunting). In these circumstances the rudimentary buildings do not seem all that remarkable and fully within the capacity of African tribes to build.

One of many mysteries, however, is that no African tribes in southern Africa now build in stone. This can be explained by the decline of the civilisation which built these walls. And when they were no longer politically organised the art of stone building would be forgotten because it was not as suitable as mud for building houses. The dry stone walls would not keep the heat out as effectively as mud. But it is typical of southern Africa that this mystery should have acquired such political overtones. The ordinary white southern African refuses to believe that Africans could have built it. They may not have done so, of course, but the balance of archaeological evidence does seem to be heavily in favour of people indigenous to Africa being responsible.

Dislike of settler Rhodesia
(James/ Ralph and Stella Currey, 11 May 1964) In Salisbury we stayed with Cannon's new choice for the OUP Manager Ken Toogood. He most kindly offered to put us up and was extremely hospitable. Originally from England via Cape Town. Was in ICI (Imperial Chemical Industries). Then in trade magazines. Then Southern Rhodesia Publications Bureau. Should be quite good. Got some drive I think. Though conservative in outlook. Humour is basically immature though entertaining in a slight way to begin with. His wife ran off with a racing driver and they are divorced. He sees his single adopted daughter (three years old) at week-ends. She could only stay in the house because Clare was there. One can see that he would get on well with Cannon.

Treatment of Africans: the usual munt-cursing brand which is rawer than that of the same kind among ordinary English-speaking South Africans. After getting back from Nyasaland we stayed with him again and he took us to the Show Jumping Championships where everybody was being very double-barrelled on beautiful horses. Every time the ice cream seller went round in front of us Toogood yelled at him to get out of his view.

[In 1960 David Philip had gone up from Cape Town to open a sales office in Salisbury, Southern Rhodesia and to also cover Northern Rhodesia and Nyasaland in the Central African Federation. In 1959 James had been sent out to OUP Cape Town to take over David Philip's job under Leo Marquard. In 1962 James had been asked to take over this new office in Salisbury from David Philip. It was of immense relief when Leo Marquard decided that that he wanted James to stay in Cape Town to continue work on editing and production with David Philip. Cannon then appointed Toogood. The

Southern Rhodesians had run and exploited the Central African Federation bringing the copper profits south. In 1966 the white settlers were to declare a Unilateral Declaration of Independence (UDI), and after 1980 it became Zimbabwe under Robert Mugabe. This trip confirmed James and Clare's dislike of the settler colony.]

Malawi's Independence Office
(Clare/ Ruth and Henry Wilson, Lusaka, 11 May 1964) I think our last letter [lost?] was from Zomba the capital of Nyasaland and the Anthony and Anne Wilson ménage. Master Kenneth is quite a joke and stomps around demanding 'more'. [Anthony was for seven years head of Community Development in Nyasaland which was training people about local government as independence approached. They supported the 'Miss Independence' contest as a means of giving confidence to women. Chris, a Quaker, is Deputy-Headmistress of Lilongwe Girls' High School which is surrounded by a seven-foot high fence to keep the girls in. Soon after independence a member of Legco asked whether the fence was high enough to keep out the police, who are camped next door… a secondary school education improves the girls' marriageability.] We had a most interesting time in Nyasaland which included bumping into a cabinet minister on a ferry, a most charming and entertaining man. [John Msonthi, Trade and Industry who says 'Who knows? The Doctor may have a Cabinet reshuffle tomorrow!' But he is not really unsafe as Dr Banda has already drawn upon almost all the men of cabinet calibre. But the atmosphere is very much that of all gifts flow from the Doctor.]

Everyone in Nyasaland was in great curiosity about the Prime Minister, Dr Banda, having left the country secretly in an aeroplane and not telling anyone where he'd go to. We saw an aeroplane coming back from a most unusual direction and put two and two together to assume that he had been visiting Mozambique [which was still under the colonial rule of the Portuguese who worked in close collaboration with South Africa]; when we got to Salisbury we found that everyone there knew where he'd been to…. [Nyasaland was due to become independent as Malawi on 6 July 1964. Clare's photograph of 'The Independence Office' appeared on the front of *The New African* which had a seven page illustrated article by James on the independence of Malawi, from which the quotes in square brackets in this paragraph have been taken.]

Northern Rhodesia becoming Zambia
(Clare/ Ruth and Henry Wilson, Lusaka, 11 May 1964) We flew from

Blantyre to Salisbury and were met by Ken Toogood ... set off early on Sunday for Northern Rhodesia, visiting Kariba on the way – the dam which holds back the Zambesi. [Northern Rhodesia was in October 1964 to become independent as Zambia.]

(Clare/ Ruth and Henry Wilson, Lusaka, 12 May 1964) Incidentally I suppose it is too late now, but you can say what you like in letters to Northern Rhodesia and probably Southern Rhodesia too. Particularly if all they are referring to is South African internal politics.

Where the Cabinet Ministers went to School
(Clare/ Ruth and Henry Wilson, Lusaka, 11 May 1964) In Lusaka Tim and Sally Holmes have largeish house in school grounds at Munali Secondary School and there is palatial swimming pool not far away which we patronise – it now being the school holidays.

(James/ Ralph and Stella Currey, 3 June 1964) Lusaka was interesting. A main street romantically called the Cairo Road but looking just about as attractive as the main street in Romford. Munali Secondary School where Tim teaches and where they live, is quite large and impressive. Eleven of the fourteen members of the new Northern Rhodesian/about to be Zambian Cabinet were educated there.

Tim and I went on a most interesting pub crawl to see a cross-section of Lusaka society. From the middle-class newly rich government officials mixing in a bar freely with middle-class white commercial travellers and shop owners. Via the clerks, black and white, into the spit and sawdust in the Nag's Head with a juke box throbbing out African tunes. Then the Tombola Bar where a Congolese served drinks in a beer Hall. Then the Africa Bar where three electric guitarists, black, were copies of the Beatles – no long hair, jeans (but tight), the uniform machine gun action with their guitars spraying noise at the audience. Tim's supposition was that the audience were mostly new immigrants to the town and that the guitars cut out the need for talking so that they did not feel lonely. Then we finished off more sedately among the plashing fountains of the Ridgeway Hotel, the best in Lusaka. There were as many groups of well-dressed Africans as there were Europeans; mostly administrative grade of civil servant and successful businessmen. In fact little difference in price for drinks between the Ridgeway and the most sordid bar.

An exciting cathedral in Lusaka built in the last few years. Winning design chosen by Basil Spence and the result is reminiscent of Coventry cathedral. Lots of coloured glass in windows which introduces vivid colour which is splendid in the harsh sun. Everybody very optimistic about Northern Rhodesia becoming Zambia (October) though quite a lot of white civil servants are going because Africanisation removes a career from under them and merely offers temporary contracts. Afrikaans names up outside all the farms for sale; all being bought by English-speaking people who seem greatly confident. The copper riches should give the country a good chance to do rather better than most of these states.

Will the Rivonia accused be hanged?
(James/ Ralph and Stella Currey, 11 June 1964) This news about Phipson book being accepted by OUP came at the end of the day when there had been the inevitable verdict of guilty at the Rivonia Trial. Tomorrow will be the verdict. [Will they be hanged?] I was on the telephone to Sheila Clare the Liberal Party Secretary when the news came onto the Telenews, the big news-in-lights strip on the top of the tallest Cape Town building which I can see from my tenth floor office. I read the Rivonia Trial guilty news out to her. It said that one of the accused BERNSTEIN WAS FOUND NOT GUILTY AND DISCHARGED. This news-strip moves very slowly so that you have to wait a long time for each word. Sheila was saying meanwhile 'How wonderful! How unexpected! I know his sister.' Meanwhile I was reading slowly on. 'AND IMMEDIATELY REARRESTED AND RECHARGED.'

(Clare/ Ruth and Henry Wilson, Cape Town, 26 June 1964) We are amazed by the reactions of the world to the Rivonia trial. What country of those accusing SA of imposing very heavy sentences on Mandela and co would tolerate sabotage or treason themselves? In our view they are extremely lucky not to have the death sentence. This is just the kind of attitude that discredits the U.N. here, and one that seems so thoughtless and foolish..... My article 'Rivonia Notebook' is in the current issue of *The New African* which will we hope reach you in due course (The issue not designed by J. because of our being away, and therefore a bit of a mess production-wise. Cannot think what they will do without James when he leaves; nor for that matter what he will do.)

(Clare/ Ruth and Henry Wilson, Cape Town, 20 June 1964) We gather Gillian V. is out of hospital but not back at work yet. In an anti-asthma campaign the Vignes have had to get rid of the cat and of dear Willie, who was sent back to the people from whom he came, via an aeroplane to Johannesburg. Poor Randolph misses him dreadfully!

The sociology of cancer in Cape Town
(Clare/ Ruth and Henry Wilson, Cape Town, 20 June 1964) We still don't know when J. is going to South West Africa or Basutoland. It rather looks as though I may have a week or ten days off at the end of next month because the Dr Grieve part of the book on *Cancer in Cape Town* will be more or less finished – I go to University of Cape Town at the beginning of August to go on with the sociological side of the book but there will probably be a lapse of time between one ending and the other beginning. So we might manage to go somewhere then – preferably South-West Africa because of the warmth. I'm sure Basutoland is feet deep in snow and frost at the moment. The new part of the job should be more interesting and I expect that I'll get more out of it because it will be in more comprehensible language.

Just in time for James to talk to the first Transkei Minister of Education
(Clare/ Ruth and Henry Wilson, Cape Town, 4 July 1964) On Tuesday James flew up to Queenstown for an educational conference [with Mnyakama who was OUP's first African rep]; thanks to the OUP car at the other end spending most of it time breaking down he didn't see much of the conference but did apparently manage to get to see the Transkei Minister of Education which was probably more valuable.

(James to Clare, King William's Town, July 1964) It's already happened. Mynakama's car gave up at some place fifteen miles outside King on the Queenstown Road. The lights went suddenly dim and the pulling power packed up. We decided we had better get back to King and in turning round the engine stalled. A passing truck loaded with wood stopped and hundreds of black running figures came through the darkness and pushed us back on the road. Then we started it again. Gouts of exhaust and then, when the lights were turned on, the engine died. Then we got a lift with three Afrikaner boys back into King.

Anyhow I am tomorrow having to go the East London to hire a car. I shall ring Cannon. Real crabby I am – exhausted with Cannon's idiotic money-saving attitude towards cars. I wasted two or three working days and now, if we are not careful, I shall be miserably late for this conference which was considered important enough to fly me up for.

The usual South Africanisms. R. Mynakama was at the airport all right. He has been flu-ridden and thus did not get to his post-box – of course there is no telegram delivery for Africans. He was the only *Nie Blanke* and was in a little pen all to himself.

One of the Afrikaner boys who gave us lift offered me a cigarette in the car. Very nice of him. Would have been nicer if he had offered one to

Mynakama as well.

When we got to the hotel Mynakama came in to see if I was fixed up all right.

I asked 'Have you got a room for tonight?'

The owner looked a bit disconcerted. He was wearing a blue blazer with a badge. 'Just for you?'

'Yes. Just me.'

'I was going to say we had no room for your ...' Here he hesitated slightly and looked at 60 year old Mynakama before saying '... your boy.'

[The Transkei Bantustan had just been established. The new OUP schools rep Mynakama mentioned to James, on collecting him after breakfast on the last morning, that he had grown up with Mdledle the new Minister of Education. James asked him when he was going to visit him. He had not made arrangements. So James said 'Ring him up and try and get an appointment this afternoon in Umtata.' 3 o'clock! But could they get there in time across the back roads of the Transkei without the hire car breaking down? According to Caroline Davies in her book *Creating Postcolonial Literature* 2013 the Transkei was central to the take off of Oxford University Press's sales in South Africa because the Press was favoured against the Afrikaner publishers who had previously almost monopolised the government Bantu Education markets in the Republic.]

Grapefruit rolling down the road
(Clare/ Ruth and Henry Wilson, Cape Town, 4 July 1964) We are just recovering after having had Gillian Vigne for the night and from having dispatched her, per air, to Port Elizabeth where her in-laws live and where she and the children are going to spend a month. Randolph got exemption from his ban to drive the children up yesterday together with Gillian's Mama who has been helping ever since the asthma crisis, so that meant that Gillian had a night here on her own; it seemed easier for her to come and stay with us rather than the other way round, so after much fuss and commotion (all of it highly amusing) we got her here together with a strange assortment of luggage, most of it grapefruit which she had inadvertently ordered for the family for the week, forgetting that everybody was leaving. She wisely thought she would try to take as many as she could with her to Port Elizabeth and was proposing to take them in their orange sack but at the last moment James persuaded her to pack them loose in his suitcase – this last minute packing was done in Kloof Nek Road and she and I were in the car waiting to go to the airport. One grapefruit escaped and started

rolling down the road but J. just managed to retrieve it, and ultimately we got to the airport and got her all weighed and dealt with and much to our surprise she got the whole lot included within her 44 pounds weight limit. Great drama!

[This was last letter from Clare in Cape Town on 4 July 1964, the day of Special Branch raids right across the country. On 9 July 1964 was the *Cape Escape* by Randolph Vigne which is reprinted in the next part of this book.]

PART THREE

James Currey *Cape Escape 1964*

*With contributions by Jean Ridge, Gillian Vigne, Clare Currey,
Norman Bromberger & Randolph Vigne*

The Thorstream, pictured above, was due to sail for Montreal from Cape Town Docks at 5 o'clock on the winter afternoon of 9 July 1964. There was only one cabin free. The Holland Afrika Line were the agents and at 3 o'clock that afternoon had, suspiciously late, sold a single ticket to James Currey for the three week voyage to Canada. He had signed the emigration papers for the Holland Afrika agent in the office. How could Randolph escape for Canada under the name of James Currey and how could James Currey remain in South Africa?

Towards 5 o'clock in Cape Town docks Jean Ridge, Randolph Vigne and James Currey walked up the gangplank near the stern of the Thorstream. There was no check of passports and all three went to the cabin which had been taken in the name of James Currey. After a short time Jean Ridge, to our amazement, established that my passport would not need to be shown. We headed off to leave the ship along the deck and towards the gangplank when we saw it was being watched by the very Holland Afrika agent who two hours had earlier sold me my ticket. He would surely recognise me?

The ever resourceful Jean said 'Leave this to me'. I ducked into the crew's cabins but thought that I would look as though was I was stowing away. I emerged to find that the attractive Jean Ridge had succeeded in seducing the Holland Afrika man away from the gangplank. When he saw me on deck looking anxious he asked Jean whether everything was all right. It broke Jean's powers of seduction and he turned to walk back along quay to the gangplank.

I had seen that the ship was riding about 6 feet higher than the quay and six feet away from the quay. I swung my legs over the railing and jumped. I banged a shin on wooden edge of the quay and found I was dropping towards the water. I was certain I would be pulled out of the water in dripping winter suit and all would be revealed. I saved myself with the fingers of one hand and pulled myself frenetically up onto the quay. Passengers were screaming but apparently the Holland Afrika agent did not turn round to see what was happening. Jean Ridge drove me off like mad round the cooling sheds.

Randolph Vigne stayed in his cabin for two days until the Thorstream was out of South African waters and past Walfish Bay. A former army Major, who was a director of the Natal company which was shipping the sugar to Canada, introduced himself to 'James Currey'. He told how he was on the bridge with the pilot and the master and they had all seen the jump of his young visitor. The pilot failed to be able to stop the master from continue casting off. The pilot said 'We'll get him.' The Major asked 'What happened to that friend of yours? Was he drunk? Did you have a party?' From there until Canada Randolph was certain he would be arrested on arrival in Canada. Fortunately the Norwegian, British and Canadian consuls made sure that he was discretely taken ashore in Montreal to protect James Currey as a British citizen.

Above: Here a South African freighter is moored in Berth B in the Duncan Dock in Cape Town. That is the quay where the Thorstream was moored on 9 July 1964.

In the background can be seen the Sanlam Building on the Foreshore where was the office of the immigration official who should have checked the papers which James Currey had urgently signed in the Holland Afrika office in the last two hours before sailing. I was the one passenger embarking in Cape Town. Peter Hjul the Chair of the Cape Liberals was editor of Shipping and Fishing News and therefore had constant professional dealing with immigration office and afterwards told us what had happened.

James Currey had signed to depart South Africa and to enter Canada; the travel agent in the Holland Afrika office had immediately in a routine manner sent these documents by messenger to the immigration officer in the Sanlam Building for him to check personally. Randolph and I had the amazing good fortune that the immigration official had scarpered off early to go away with his family on a national holiday week-end. He would surely have spotted that I as a Liberal activist was leaving South Africa in a suspicious rush. By the time he saw the papers on his desk on Tuesday the Thorstream with Randolph aboard was out of South African waters and James and Clare were in London. When the Thorstream came back to Cape Town from Canada the Special Branch swarmed in frustration over the ship.

*Randolph Vigne
in the early 1960s*

*Clare and James Currey
in 1963 or 1964*

On 9 July 1964 I enabled Randolph Vigne, clandestine editor of The New African, *to escape from Cape Town to Canada. I was urged by Clare Currey, after they themselves had escaped to England on 11 July 1964, to write down his account, and the first part of this narrative was written by the end of July 1964. I used it during 2013 to interrogate the memories of the other people most deeply affected; Norman Bromberger, Randolph and Gillian Vigne, Clare Currey and, most heroically, the photographer Jean Ridge.*

Gillian Vigne had recently had so dangerous an asthma attack that it had led to cardiac arrest. She said in 2010 that 'I spent most of June 1964 in Chris Barnard's vast heart valve ward at Groote Schuur Hospital emerging rather weak so that Randolph drove the children to visit his parents in Port Elizabeth.' Adrian Leftwich was to have taken them but just before the departure date he said he could not do it after all. As a banned person Randolph Vigne was not allowed to leave the Cape Town magistracy so he appealed to Major Rousseau of the Special Branch, 'a decent chap in his way', who got him the permission by telegram. Randolph remembers that he drove out to the Port Elizabeth airport to get *The Sunday Times* of 5 July 1964 which had just been flown down from Johannesburg. There he read with shock that Adrian Leftwich had been arrested in what became known as 'the Fourth of July raids'. Gillian Vigne says of Randolph that day 'I always remember his face as he read the Sunday papers.'

Monday 6 July 1964
Randolph says that on Monday 6 July 'I remember waking Gillian very early to say good-bye as I was leaving for Cape Town about 7.30 a.m.' In the car Randolph told the news to Norman Bromberger, a lecturer at the Rhodes University branch at Port Elizabeth and a Liberal Party and ARM member, who was driving with him to the Cape to visit his mother; Norman said recently that 'I was a little surprised at the intensity of Randolph's concern about Adrian's arrest.' Despite this concern Randolph reported his return at Caledon Square police station where his telegram of permission was rubber-stamped on the back with the date 6 July 1964, although on the front it stated that he should be back on 5 July 1964. Norman Bromberger recalls him 'booking into a hotel under an assumed name in central Cape Town. Long Street?' At some point Randolph went to Jean Ridge's studio in Long Street.

Clare and I intended to go to a film that Monday evening. Supper was nearly ready when Jean Ridge arrived at our flat at 101 Kloof Nek Road. She asked us for blankets for Randolph Vigne, who was staying for the night in her studio. Randolph had asked her to go into his home Clifton House to fetch some things and to see if the police had paid a visit. She was already late for her appointment and had a friend with her in the car with whom she was going on to Sea Point to have dinner.

Jean Ridge told us how worried Randolph was. There was a change of attitude and he now felt that to get out of South Africa might be essential. 'Our boy is *really* worried. He's talking of bolting for it.' I went to see Randolph who was pacing up and down in Jean's pretty bed-room at her photographic studio in Long Street. He had a dark worsted suit on. He was worried about who was arriving. He was worried about Jean going to his house lest she be picked up, questioned. He was worried that the Special Branch would then be round like a shot to search Jean's studio. Randolph said he had not wanted to involve me.

We discussed the alternatives. Bechuanaland? He could do a bolt for the border, but there would be road blocks, would there not? And if he got to the border without being checked could he really get across? Probably. But the distance there was so great. It would be last choice if he really had to. I offered Randolph our VW beetle in exchange for his. He pointed out the danger that the police might question Clare or me. I offered to lend him money. The other alternative was the docks. Stowaway on a Scandinavian boat? Or promise a passage payment to a Scandinavian captain? Or buy a passage? What about the Union Castle mailboat to Southampton leaving on Thursday at 4 o'clock? If there was a spare first-class berth might somebody we knew in the Transit Class take it and put JRV under the bed? Wouldn't the SB be watching the gangplank? And wouldn't the stewards find him? What if he took a ticket, hid and then appeared after 'sea-sickness' four or five days out? But people would recognise him. What if he stowed away? But they were surely expert at detecting stowaways. What if he was put ashore at Walvis Bay, which was still sovereign South African territory? I said to Randolph at one point, 'Of course there are lots of things I am not able to ask you.' Clare and I could only judge that he was deadly serious and determined to leave the country as soon as possible.

Who might help Randolph get on a ship? Randolph specifically mentioned 'Scandinavian ships' which reflects his and Gillian's friendship with the Norwegian consul. On the drive from Port Elizabeth he had asked Norman Bromberger if he might buy a First-Class ticket on Union Castle; however Norman did not feel that he personally could try it. The best chance seemed to be 'the Bowater plan'. Mrs Ethel Bowater had lived in Martin Melck House, a magnificent Dutch merchant's house in Strand Street. She had made it into a most desirable lodging house for young people in the centre of Cape Town (and indeed for older gentlemen such as the Managing Director of Shell). Gillian and Randolph Vigne first met there and had their wedding reception there. Her son Bill Bowater, Commander RN retired, had told Randolph how much he disliked apartheid, that he was only working in South Africa because of his mother and that he would not mind leaving the country at any time if it could be useful; he was later illegally to marry a Cape Town girl Rita across the colour line and move to England. He had a job selling the new IBM golfball electric typewriters which, thanks to him, we had recently started using to cut down typesetting costs for *The New African*. Bill Bowater became the great hope as the person who might buy a ticket on a ship either to travel himself with Randolph hidden or to leave Randolph on board in his place while he took another way out of the country. He had a British passport and thus could travel without a visa and could buy a ticket at short notice.

Tuesday 7 July 1964
Randolph remembered in 2013 that in the morning after his return he headed 'for the flat of a friend in Sea Point who had experienced the dangers of Nazi Germany and given him a spare key "in case you ever need to use it". No reply and the key didn't open the door. I rang the next-door bell and was dismayed that it was somebody I slightly knew who answered the door. I was told that my friend had given up the flat and gone to Europe.' He then tried another address and the maid told him that the person was out for the day. Randolph had been doing much work for the renowned Dutch publisher A.A. Balkema who had transformed typographical standards at the Cape. The Balkemas were in Europe in July 1964 and Randolph was looking after the business – and their 17-year-old son Annatjis – in their absence. Though Randolph had been in breach of his ban much of the time, the Special Branch apparently had no knowledge of this job and were never to go to Balkema's office when searching for him. It seems probable that on Tuesday morning that Randolph went, as though things were normal, into Balkema's office At lunch time Bill Hoffenberg was alone in the Liberal Party office in Parliament Street when the telephone rang and a voice said 'Eddie has been arrested' and hung up. 'When I put the phone down I realised that with Adrian Leftwich and Eddie Daniels arrested, Randolph was likely to be next.' He headed straight for the Balkema office which was only a few hundred yards away across the gardens in Victoria Street. He went down to the basement office and wrote down on a pad 'Eddie has been arrested.' Bill later wrote 'Randolph blanched, said goodbye to me and left the premises.' Eddie Daniels had indeed been arrested by the security police at 1.30 a.m.

the previous night.

Randolph decided to go to the King's Hotel in Sea Point, which he knew well as a younger brother of his father used to stay there when in Cape Town. It is probable that it was Jean Ridge who telephoned me at OUP on Tuesday afternoon to tell me that she had rung up the King's Hotel to book in 'Mr Evans' and that I should go to the hotel, check in and sign the register under Evans with a Johannesburg address so that I could give the key to JRV who would go up the back stairs to stay in the 'Evans' room. I may well have driven Randolph out there; it was certainly sensible for him to leave his car in Bree Street. Norman had borrowed his brother's car so that he could come in from lower Wynberg on Tuesday evening to disperse or dispose of evidence scattered round Cape Town and the southern suburbs. It seems likely that Randolph spent Tuesday night as well as Wednesday night at the King's Hotel.

Thursday 9 July 1964
I drove over Kloof Nek to the King's Hotel, Sea Point where JRV was staying. I came in through the back of the hotel. He was in his room with the door wide open. When he was ready to leave I went to Reception to pay as though I was Evans and had stayed for a couple of nights. There was a difficulty because the African night porter had not got the bill and the receipt. He rang up the manager to add to my fright. But the manager's wife said that I should pay and that the receipt would be posted to the non-existent Evans on Louis Botha Avenue, Johannesburg who had signed the register.

We drove along the lower Victoria Road in Clifton so as to avoid passing Randolph's house on the upper road. The sun was coming through over the sea on a misty winter morning. Randolph was in his overcoat. At 101 Kloof Nek Road Clare and I moved the dining table behind the desk so that he was out of sight from the road for breakfast. Randolph again made it very clear how anxious he was to go. We went over the alternatives once more. We discussed who should be brought in to help. He suggested Norman Bromberger as a sound bet. And the Bowater plan was most favoured. 'What if we do not find Bowater?' asked Randolph. 'There would be me of course.' I regretted saying it a little. Clare agreed that I was a second string if necessary. At that moment I really rather hoped that she would say 'no' and that I would have an excuse to duck out. But she said firmly to me 'We are friends of both Gillian and Randolph.'

Clare dropped us off at Jean's studio and then drove off to her job at Groote Schuur hospital. During the morning Randolph, Jean and Norman made the following moves. They immediately started to try and contact

Bill Bowater. Jean, at Randolph's suggestion, went to see Jon Aase the Norwegian Consul. Gillian and Randolph knew him well because he was a close friend of the Brazilian Consul, Lael Soares, under whom Gillian Vigne was a Vice-Consul. Norman Bromberger had to be vouched for to the Norwegian Consul by Peter Hjul, formerly the Cape Liberal Party Chairman. The Consul told them that a Norwegian cargo boat would leave Cape Town that evening at 5 o'clock. One of the twelve passenger berths had just become free. Passengers had to be on board by 3 o'clock. The boat was sailing for Canada. Norman visited the docks on several occasions to see whether anybody looking like a Special Branch man was keeping an eye on the gates. There was a man at the Heerengracht gate who looked suspicious. At other gates there appeared to be nobody but the Customs men.

Attempts to contact Bill Bowater failed. Messages were left for him to phone. It seemed to be that he was working out at Paarl, some sixty miles from Cape Town. At 12.30 Jean rang me up at OUP. She spoke firmly and calmly and said that I should take a taxi up to her studio. There were no taxis. I ran and walked alternatively through the midday sun. I leapt up the stairs to the top of Jean's building and was told what had happened so far. As Bill Bowater had not been contacted Randolph asked me to step in. He said he was sure that we should have to leave the country afterwards and that he would pay for our fares. I said I thought that that was out of the question. I put off saying 'yes' while we tried to think of how to make a last attempt to get hold of Bill Bowater. Randolph, as on previous occasions, suggested Ohlsson's Breweries to get the number of The Fireman's Arms where Bowater often went at lunchtime.

Randolph rang Clare at the hospital where she was working. She happened to be by the phone. Randolph said 'You know those chairs in your flat which need mending? Well, I've found somebody. But you must come home. Meet me where you left me this morning.'

At some time after 1.00 Clare came upstairs to Jean's studio. Randolph says 'I remember your saying to Clare: "Shall I do it?" or words to that effect and her very positive reply. How I blessed you both! Still do.' I said we must get some money and my passport and a suitcase for Randolph. His own suitcase had J.R Vigne stamped across it. We drove up Kloof Nek Road. I said to Clare, 'You must realise the consequences of this for us. Randolph thinks we should have to get out. I don't think so.' At the flat we pulled down a heavy leather suitcase with Capt. R.N. Currey stamped across it. We started filling it with my unwanted or old clothes. They would be too small for Randolph but it would look suspicious if there was nothing in it. We got some books for him. *Buddenbrooks*: good and long. Jane Austen's

Northanger Abbey and *Persuasion* in a single Oxford volume: a bit lighter. And Clare found the *Oxford Book of Canadian Verse*. We went down to Barclays Bank in Adderley Street and Clare got out the maximum she was allowed. She then saw the cashier and got out more to a total of R500 (about £250 in those days). Randolph remembers 'I did withdraw what was in my current account at Barclay's, Long Street, meeting Hans Fransen in Strand Street who told me at length about his visa problems, while I was dying to get away rather than be in full view while a search was on for the people Leftwich had betrayed.' Norman Bromberger also remembers 'a get-together in the Gardens when Hoffenberg popped out from behind some bushes to say goodbye to Randolph.' Norman has found that his 'scrap of diary' does say that he saw Bill Hoffenberg at Groote Schuur on the morning of Wednesday 8 July which reveals that he had been acting as a go-between in handing over Randolph's papers.

Clare and I returned about 2 o'clock to Jean's studio. There still had been no reply from Bowater. So we moved into our next phase. Clare went back to the hospital by bus leaving me our red VW Beetle. Jean was out. The telephone rang. It wasn't Bowater. It was one of Jean's clients saying with advertising huff 'If I can't have Miss Ridge's colour shots today I can't use them'. If he only knew what we were doing. The time was all too short for self-important account executives.

We synchronised watches – this much one has learnt from adventure stories – and made plans for the next stage. The telephone rang again. Jean was now back and answered. It was Bowater. 'Thank you so much for ringing, Mr Bowater. It's all right now. We won't need your services this time. Perhaps another time.' Randolph wanted to repack Capt. R.N. Currey's suitcase so I had to get that from our car.

Jean and I were to go to see the Norwegian Consul first. Norman was to go to the Holland-Afrika shipping line office and hold the reservation. Jean and I walked into the Consul's office, fourteenth floor, African Life Centre. The Venetian blinds were pale blue, as one felt they should be. I found out afterwards that the Consul was surprised by my being 'the victim'. He said that he had been expecting an 'elderly gentleman'. That was because Jean and Norman had told him of Commander Bowater, RN retired.

Jon Aase was extremely charming and told us the possibilities and the dangers. 'There is never any check on the gangplank. I know the Mate. He is reliable. But I cannot vouch for the Captain. The immigration man will have you summoned from your cabin to the lounge where he will sit with the Captain or an officer.' He talked in calming tones. 'I can only ask you one thing. If the police ask why you came here then you can just tell them I gave you information about Norwegian ships. If you are successful then you must come to see me tomorrow morning and ask for help. Then I shall send a telegram to the Foreign Office in Oslo asking them to get our Montreal Consul to do his best to get Vigne landed safely. I cannot promise that this will happen. But I think that the case will be given a sympathetic hearing. I'm sorry I cannot be more definite than that.' This of course was a crucially important promise. It made the risks less great since Randolph, his passport having been withdrawn even before he was banned, would be trying to land in Canada without papers.

Jon Aase asked us, 'Do you know which boat it is?' We didn't. So he pointed from his high window to the small ship lying in Duncan Dock B berth at right angles to the Union Castle mail boat in A berth. 'Where is it going to?' I asked. 'I think Montreal. But you can find that out at the shipping agents.' Later he asked me 'Have you a story ready?' 'I am going to work for the Oxford University Press in Toronto.' 'Have you got their address?' 'No. But I will find it.' Just before we left he said 'By the way. When you come to visit me don't take the lift to the fourteenth floor. You don't know who might be watching the lifts. Get out a couple of floors up or down and use the stairs.' I was soon to find this more difficult to carry out than I expected. He was security conscious all right. When he said 'Randolph' he glanced at the phone.

Norman was waiting outside the Holland-Afrika Lijn shipping office, which was just round the corner. We began negotiations for the ticket. It was suspiciously late. In fact it was already about the time when I should be aboard. A Dutchman was dealing with me. Somehow the process seemed more complicated than buying an air ticket. But I suppose that it seemed that way because of worry. Although I was reasonably relaxed, Norman and I hung over the desk watching paper after paper being filled with details of my voyage which I wasn't going to take. I filled in a South African Emigration form and a Canadian Immigration form. The details of my passport were included. I signed myself into a false declaration.

There was some bother over paying for the passage. It was in Canadian dollars which had to be translated, at the price of the day, into South African rands. The pleasant Dutchman got into a muddle and telephoned a bank and came back with the news that a machine was working it out. The Dutchman had been un-inquisitive. His boss showed more concern over my lateness. He asked questions. They may have been suspicious questions, but they were reasonable ones for a shipping agent to ask. What money had I got? I had the twenty rands allowed in South African currency. I was then being met by the firm's representative in Montreal. Money was being transferred by my bank. I was glad that I had been able to give a garbled version of the OUP address so that there was one less suspicious detail. '40 Wynford Drive, Don Mills, Toronto' sounded like a genuine address – which it very nearly was.

At last the ticket was ready. I followed Norman who had gone to put sixpence in the parking meter, only to find that the red VW beetle had got a parking ticket. Jean and I had arranged to rendez-vous on the Foreshore near the skyscraper Sanlam building. Jean and Randolph were already sitting there waiting in her grey Opel. They were my visitors coming to see me off. We agreed to meet in Cabin 5. They were to go in the Dock Road entrance and we at the Heerengracht entrance. There was no trouble for us. Randolph said afterwards that he was very worried about passing the gate because Bill Hoffenberg had told him about Schneider. The police had found dynamite in Schneider's garage in Sea Point, he had been arrested and had then given the police the slip at the police station. It was said that they were watching everything; airports, docks, roads. Randolph remembers at one point Jean stopping the car, saying 'Open wide!' and popping a tranquilliser into his mouth.

When we got into the docks and were approaching the South Arm of the Duncan Dock we saw Jean and Randolph in the grey Opel some fifty or a hundred yards in front. We parked among the large number of cars near the Union Castle mailboat. This was the ship Randolph had thought of trying to get aboard. He had rung up from the King's Hotel, but the whole ship had been taken by the MOTHS and MOTHWAS. (The 'Memorable Order of Tin Hats' is the South African war veterans' association; MOTHWAS is the women's association. The ship was called 'Neptune's Shellhole' for that voyage and was taking both men and women on a tour of the battlefields and war graves of Europe.)

A Cape porter took Capt. R.N. Currey's bag. He thought we were going to the mailboat but we redirected him. The *Thorstream* was a small ship, pale blue with Scandinavian freshness. On the prow a copper Thor figurehead cast thunderbolts shaped like dumbbells down on the sea. Thor stood in a recess against a scarlet background. Norman and I discussed Thor and talked about Canada.

Forty or fifty yards ahead of us were Randolph and Jean: Randolph with hands in the pockets of his worsted suit, Jean was talking hard and looking extremely soignée. As the Consul had said, there was no check on the gangplank, which was towards the stern of the ship, and Jean and Randolph walked up and then down on to the deck. As Norman and I came on board everybody was busy preparing to sail; hatches were being battened down by young Scandinavians and people were hanging around the gangplank to watch the departure.

We all met in Cabin 5. Another stage was completed. The next thing was to wait for the immigration official. To begin with we were worried lest he had already been. Jean found out from a steward that he hadn't. We then started alternatively to work on one another's nerves and to relieve the tension with laughter. We tried to hide the South African currency as it was illegal to take more than twenty rands (£10) out of the country. We looked into cupboards. We looked at a ventilator grill. 'What if it all gets sucked in?' said somebody to a nervous roar of laughter. We looked at the light holder and decided that if we put it there it would still be visible.

We decided that Randolph should wait in the bathroom lest a steward appear and ask us to go to see the immigration official. Randolph stood in the bathroom doorway ready to close it. At one point he said 'I've looked out of the porthole three times and each time a police launch has gone past.' We began trying to polish up the weak details. 'What I cannot understand', said Jean, 'is why the Oxford Press should be sending you on a slow boat when you are going on business.' 'That's the speed the Oxford Press moves,' I said to everybody's grateful amusement. We then muddled around with various unlikely answers to the immigration man such as my need for a rest. But wasn't I sorry to be leaving my wife? In the end several ideas had been thrown up and I was left to choose. Jean went out to try and find out about the immigration man. He still hadn't come. We talked about the apparent casualness and the lack of police. I asked Jean if she couldn't find the purser or somebody in a more important position than the steward she had spoken to so that we might be a bit more certain what was happening about the immigration man. This was the last part of the ordeal and I was longing to go through with it. It seemed a high danger spot. It never occurred to us that I would not have to see him at all. But Jean came back with the news from the chief steward that this might well happen. In fact, he had said that it was so late that the immigration officer might not even come on board at all. We restrained ourselves from rejoicing too early.

Jean and I decided that we ought all to say goodbye to Randolph and then wait at the top of the gangplank so that we could get off easily if the immigration man did not come. So we said goodbye. Randolph asked if this was goodbye or whether we should nip back later. In fact we decided that this had better be the last goodbye. I said 'Send me a Christmas card when I am in jail.' He said as we left 'Please tell Balkema what has happened.'

Jean and I met Norman outside the cabin. He said 'There's a policeman near the gangplank but he doesn't appear interested.' He said that he was just going to see Randolph and say goodbye. Jean and I moved to the top of the gangplank. A girl staggered up the gangplank on to the ship. Dark, in scarlet and black, she was very much the worse for a party. She was clutching a brass model mosque. The aged little South African in charge of the gang of Cape workers who were to remove the gangplank said 'One of the crew gave her that. Real nice! Got a light inside you see! But the customs won't let her take it ashore so she's got to take it back.' The girl giggled on to the deck, high heels scuffed and askew. We asked him if the immigration man had been. No, he hadn't. Would he be coming? 'He might and he might not. But it's getting late.' It was after 5.00 and the boat was now to sail at 5.30. After waiting a bit longer I drew Jean aside and said 'Let's wait on the quay. Then if the immigration officer comes we can nip up the gangplank.' So we stood chatting on the quay. Jean said 'I wonder what our little bugger's been up to.'

We watched out for white officers' caps. One appeared confidently striding along the quay on top of a South African sea-going face. He did not look like a customs or immigration man. He looked more weather-beaten. A man in a sports jacket appeared near me with a bundle of papers in his hand. He had a certain casualness and lack of rush which suggested that his job was already done. I looked over his shoulder and saw 'Mate's Manifest' stamped on the papers. Two white hats appeared at the end of the pre-cooling sheds. Could these be customs men? They approached the ship and then started inspecting the ropes and the plimsoll line. As they got nearer we anxiously saw that their features were Scandinavian rather than South African. It was after 5.00. It really seemed too good to be true.

Then bouncing bumptiously along the quay came another white cap. Jean and I looked at one another. Was it possible that he wasn't the immigration man? He was very short. White shirt. White shorts. Long white socks. He bounced up the gangplank. 'Up we go,' said Jean matter of factly. The girlfriend in black and scarlet was staggering in a giggle down the gangplank. 'Don't wait; straight past her,' urged Jean. I found out from the old South African at the head of the gangplank that indeed it was the customs man. We pounded after him. He bounced up an outside metal ladder. We followed to the first deck level and then went to Randolph's cabin. Jean said 'You wait here. I'll go and find out whether he wants to see you and when he leaves I shall knock three times'. Here I was back with Randolph. He was shocked to see me.

The three taps came soon. As I was rushing out Randolph said 'James, just one thing, please tell Bowra'. He reckoned that Maurice Bowra, Warden of our Oxford college Wadham, would be willing to contact the Foreign Office if there were difficulties about him getting into Britain without papers. Jean and I moved along the deck towards the gangplank near the stern. Suddenly we realised that the Holland-Afrika shipping office man was standing on the quay by the gangplank. He was our miscalculation. He was the person who knew that I had, only three hours before, bought a ticket and signed myself out of South Africa. He was the flaw we had not foreseen. Jean said 'You wait in here.' I nipped into a passage to the officers' cabins in the centre of the ship. She and Norman went to the gangplank. I thought it would be ridiculous if an officer saw me acting like a stowaway so I came out on to the deck and saw Jean on the quay talking animatedly to the shipping office man and steadily seducing him away from the gangplank. I rushed rather too frantically towards the passengers' cabins. Apparently at this moment the Holland-Afrika man saw me and said 'Everything all right?' Then I saw Jean's powers of seduction had failed and that he was walking back to the gangplank at the stern. I had no hope of getting off the ship by the gang plank without his seeing me. Jean was saying to Norman, 'Well, that's two of our boys for Canada.'

I had looked earlier to see whether the ship was within jumping distance of the shore and had decided that it was. I slipped over the teak rail and stood on the flange outside where the metal of the boat was riveted to the solid metal side of the ship. And I leapt. My feet slipped. I knew these shoes were slippery. My shin crashed against the quay. The water looked filthy as I fell. And I thought 'This is the finish. I've messed it up. They'll drag me out dripping from the dock in my charcoal grey suit and it'll all be over.' Then with a jolt I found myself hanging by my right hand from the solid wad of timber which was fixed as a cushion to the stone quay.

Jean Ridge in 2012 recalled her reactions 'When I saw you jump overboard twixt boat and quay, missing the target and landing I knew not where. Horror and impotence! You had disappeared down the side of the ship to the murky depths below. Gone! Neither time nor place for me to call for help. No rope to throw! I thought "This is it! Our game is up and how were you to extricate yourself from certain catastrophe." But you made it! With Herculean effort, crashing your shins en route, you clawed your way up the side of the quay and gratefully and together we beat a hasty and inelegant retreat from this lunatic act. Walking and running, not breathing, we ran to the car, fortunately without interception.' Norman Bromberger in 2013 said 'I remember with utmost vividness your slipping and disappearing totally from view, and then the quite miraculous sight of your clawing fingers on the quayside edge and then your scrambling reappearance. What at the time seemed so miraculous was nobody seemed to have registered what had happened, of if they had didn't do anything about it.'

The short screams of two women passengers seemed certain to be followed by shouts and yells of 'Stop!' Jean helped me up and was starting to run. I said 'Don't run!' We walked as though it was entirely natural to take a short cut off the ship. And then our nerves broke and we ran round the end of the pre-cooling sheds. Apparently nobody but the two passengers had seen me. As we moved away we saw Norman's reassuring bulk calmly approaching. He told us that he did not think that the railway policeman had even turned round. We asked him to drive the red VW Beetle up to our flat. I had already given him the keys lest anything might happen.

Jean accelerated away and drove us at enormous speed right down the South Arm behind the pre-cooling sheds. I was bent double with pain clutching my shin which I felt even might be broken. I moaned 'I am no good at this sort of thing!' Jean said sharply 'Yes, you are!' She slowed to a crawl as we got closer to the Green Point customs gate and told me to put my hand behind her seat, draw myself up, relax and look natural. The customs man looked in on my side of the car. I said there was nothing to declare. Jean leant across and smiling brightly said, 'Is that all right, officer?' in Afrikaans.

Outside the dock gates we drove through Cape Town's rush hour traffic to Jean's studio in Long Street. As we crossed Wale Street into Loop Street another car, whose right of way it was, stopped. A fashionably dressed plump man and model-looking girl were in the car. Jean and the man did elaborate 'After you!' signs. Jean finally went first with an extra elaborate bow over the steering wheel. 'Who's that?' I said. 'My ex-husband', Jean replied.

We drove up to our flat under Table Mountain which overlooked Table Bay and the docks. Jean dropped me to wait for Clare and Norman. She wanted to go up Signal Hill to see whether the boat was clear. Clare arrived on a bus almost immediately. She had rung up the OUP at 4.45 to ask whether I was there and had been told that I had not come back. She thought I had been arrested. She had made plans that if the police were already at the flat she would keep out of their hands until she knew whether Randolph had got away. When she got off the bus a stop earlier than her usual one to allow time, and saw a figure standing outside 101 Kloof Nek Road she thought it was a policeman. Then she saw the policeman was wearing a pale blue tie. It was only me.

Jean Ridge remembers in 2012 'From the heights of Signal Hill I nervously waited to see the little boat with its illicit passenger leave Cape Town harbour for what we hoped would be the safety of a foreign land. We had helped a friend and in his escape from the Security Police, the details of which we knew nothing, we had been entirely complicit. Our own future in the land very quickly began to look bleak!'

Norman arrived in our car. Jean came back with encouraging news from Signal Hill. As far as we could see from the balcony of the flat the *Thorstream* was now in the mouth of the docks. Outside the dock gates a little boat started heading back with the Pilot. So we all drank to the future of Randolph. We rang up Bill Hoffenberg to say 'We are having a celebration party. Wish you were here!'

Later in the evening, when my leg was stiffening up, we remembered that the car ought to be put away. Clare took it down to Cotswold Avenue so that it should be out of the way of the smearers and daubers; several Liberal Party members had recently had their cars attacked by people who had probably been tipped off by the Special Branch. As Clare came back she saw a tall figure near the house and thought 'It's them – the police'. But it turned out to be Terence Beard, another Liberal Party lecturer from Rhodes University. He made jokes which showed he had heard the news. Jean had apparently told him. She obviously felt she had to unwind. But we were a little shocked. We felt the fewer people who knew the better. However in the atmosphere of euphoria it was a relief to be able to talk about what had happened.

Friday 10 July 1964
At about ten o'clock I was rung at the OUP by Peter Rosling the Political Officer at the British Consulate near the OUP office in Thibault Square. 'I've got one or two things for *The New African*. Could you nip over and have a cup of tea with me?' 'I am just going out to the bank in African Life Centre. I'll nip up and see you'. 'Nip' did not exactly describe my movements which were seriously hobbled by my cut and bruised leg. I seemed to have forgotten that Jon Aase had said that if we succeeded that I ought to come to his office and ask for help.

When I got to Peter Rosling's office he gave me a couple of articles about Malawi. 'I'll come to the point. These are really a blind.' 'Well, I was thinking about coming out to see you last night.' 'Jon Aase told us. He is in with the Consul Dick Ballantyne at the moment. Don't tell me anything. We'll discuss it in there.' When we had sat down in the Consul's office Jon Aase said 'So he got off all right?' After I had explained how, they discussed the question of my passport. They were pleased and relieved to find that it had not been stamped. They said they had been expecting to have to give me a new one. There was now a better chance that the arrival at Montreal could be hushed up. The British were willing to tell the Canadians what had happened and ask them to keep everything quiet at that end. The situation was immeasurably improved.

As soon as I had finished my account Ballantyne said 'And what are you going to do about it?' I wanted to say 'Nothing'. I said that I thought that with the help of the Norwegians the affair could be hushed up. Ballantyne said that the British would co-operate and get help from David Miller of the Canadian Embassy who knew Randolph. He diplomatically made one thing clear: 'We have no interest in Vigne. We are only concerned with your safety as a British subject.'

Ballantyne then said 'I reckon you have eighteen days to get out of South Africa.' That was the length of the *Thorstream*'s voyage to Canada. And it would be even better if I could get out sooner. He reckoned that there were far too many chances that the story would come out. He said we ought to be aware of what might happen before one decided to stay. At worst I could be linked with the impending sabotage trial. 'The police will think you were willing to do all this to enable Randolph Vigne to escape from the country. Therefore there is a good chance that you know what he did and are willing to try and cover it up. They could charge you and try you. I am not saying they would convict you. But they could keep you for a long time and make it unpleasant.

'The best that could happen would be that they would deport you. That would save everybody a lot of trouble. But it is far from certain that they would. Goldreich in the Rivonia trial is a British subject. What is most likely is that they would get you in some way for aiding and abetting the escape of somebody wanted by the police. You might be able to get round that. No warrant has been issued. But they could hold you for some time. In any case there is a good chance, since you are known to be an associate of Vigne's, that they would take you in for 90 days.'

On leaving the British Consul's office my attitude was 'Thank you for your advice but I'll sit it out until the end of my contract in five months with OUP, South Africa.' Nevertheless my work that morning was hampered by worry.

At lunchtime I went to meet Terence Beard, Jean Ridge and Bill Hoffenberg. We sat in a car with steamed up windows by the crashing winter waves at Three Anchor Bay. I told them that I had been advised by the consular people to go. Jean said 'I woke up at 6 o'clock this morning and I thought "That Currey boy has got to get out".' Bill had no idea that I was so close to leaving. He said that this altered his whole attitude and he thought that it would be stupid to stay. The risks were not worth it for a few months more; it was better to go rather than be useless to the Oxford Press because of nerves and being in and out of court or jail. He said 'Quite frankly James, they've got far more on you than any of the rest of us. It would be safer for us all if you went.'

It was decided that we ought not to tell Gillian Vigne of Randolph's whereabouts and that if anything was done to her, doctor's evidence of allergic asthma would be presented to the police. 'Gillie damn nearly died!' said Bill. He also said that none of the conspirators should meet or communicate if possible. I was overcome at the unanimity of their opinion that we should return home and was nearly crying. I said 'Anyone would think I didn't want to go back to England.'

Bill drove me out to find Clare at Groote Schuur hospital, where he was a member of the Barnard heart transplant team and did the tissue typing to avoid rejection. He said he thought that the OUP London office would take it well. 'The British have a great sympathy I have found and they admire people who do something.' At the hospital I managed to find Clare's office. When I saw her I broke into tears. I simply could not tell her what had happened. She thought that, at the very least, the police were after me. At last I was able to say that everybody thought we ought to go. Clare said calmly 'Well if that is the case then we must go.' She went and told Dr Muir Grieve, for whom she was working, that my mother was seriously ill and that we had to go; she thought he understood. She had almost completed the editing of his work on the pathbreaking study on *Cancer in Cape Town*.

We went back into town to the British consulate and saw Ballantyne. We discussed with him and Rosling whether we ought to tell Fred Cannon, the Manager of Oxford University Press, South Africa. Bill Hoffenberg had thought we ought not. Ballantyne was certain that we should and was willing to follow up on the offer he had made to me in the morning, that he would go and see him to say that he thought I must go. 'He won't want the name of OUP in the papers.' He made an appointment with Cannon for 4.15. We said we should go upstairs and tell the Norwegian Consul what we were doing. As we left Clare said 'I am so sorry that we are causing you all this trouble.' Ballantyne replied, 'Don't be sorry.'

Jon Aase was most friendly and hoped that we did not feel that he had encouraged us to do something which was dangerous. We told him how there was really no choice. He showed us a copy of *The Argus* evening paper with a story headed 'Where is Vigne?' It turned out that this headline was the hunch of an *Argus* reporter who had rung up Jill Jessop at the Liberal Party. She had thought she had the answer when she said that Vigne was no longer a member of the party because he was banned. But the paper still posed the problem she was trying to avoid. The story had broken far sooner than we had hoped. We conspirators had intended 'to keep Randolph alive in Cape Town' as long as possible by saying that we had seen him 'only this morning' and so forth. We were also determined to give false scents to head people off. What we did not know was that his home Clifton House had been raided by the police on the very Thursday night he had escaped. *[July 1964 transcript ends]*

So that Friday afternoon at 4.15 Clare and I crossed to Thibault House with the British Consul and went up to the Oxford University Press offices on the tenth floor. I told Cannon the story very briefly. When I had finished Cannon was apoplectic – red face and staring eyes. He launched out 'Do you mean to say? …' Then with the British Consul being there he stopped. 'Well, no recriminations now!' He saw Ballantyne's logic that it was better for me to get out before I was caught and the name of Oxford University Press was all over the papers. He asked what he would say about my sudden departure. I said 'I am having to go back to England because my mother is dangerously ill.' We agreed that it was simple and plausible. I had told the Consul that I thought that it would be essential to put the case to Cannon as though it was for his decision, even though we had already made up our minds. Indeed, with a holiday week-end coming up, I had that very afternoon with no authorisation booked with Oxford University Press's travel agent the earliest flight possible out of South Africa on Saturday. Cannon quickly came to the conclusion that he thought I must go.

Afterwards, as Clare and I were driving up Kloof Nek Road in our red VW Beetle, we saw Jean Ridge driving down the hill towards the city; she waved frantically at us to stop. Journalist friends had told her that there were rumours of nationwide raids by the Special Branch that night. There had been widespread raids the previous Saturday night 4 July 1964 when Leftwich had got arrested. She had arranged for us to spend the night in a safe flat on the Foreshore; Jean told us that it covertly belonged to a Liberal Party member but that she was confident that it was not on any police list. She pointed out that if we were raided at our own flat in the early hours of the next morning we might well be delayed just when we needed to get away to Cape Town airport to catch our plane to Johannesburg.

We continued on up to our flat to pack necessaries. Then we drove out along the de Waal Drive motorway, past the Groote Schuur Hospital, to leafy Scott Road in the southern suburb of Claremont; David and Marie Philip lived in a coachman's cottage on what had been a substantial family estate. David Philip was the Editorial Manager of OUP and we had been colleagues – both devoted to typography – for the five years I had been in South Africa. We told David that I was in trouble with the police and that Clare and I had to leave the country next day. David asked whether it was civil, criminal or political and we assured him that it was political. He asked no further questions but calmly discussed what needed to be done after our departure.

We drove back into Cape Town to the safe flat in Radio City in a small square of enclosed ten-storey buildings on the Foreshore approached under an arch from the street. I had watched from my office in OUP these buildings grow on the tenth floor of the building opposite. We left the VW Beetle in the waste ground car park decided upon by David Philip so that he could pick it up next day and hide it in their garage at Scott Road. The service flat was overheated in mid-winter, we could not find out how to open windows, and we both remember it as a sweaty and sleepless night. Up to that point everything had moved at such a pace that I had not much time to worry. It was during that night that I became desperate to get out of the country.

Saturday 11 July 1964
Another advantage of Jean's clever borrowing of this safe flat was that, early next morning, we just had to walk round the corner to the airline terminal in an ordinary shop on the Heerengracht on the Foreshore leading down to the Duncan Dock; it was just opposite the skyscraper SANLAM building. As the airline coach pulled away we saw a *Cape Times* billboard with handwritten headline 'SEARCH FOR VIGNE CONTINUES'.

We had no money. All we had were our airline tickets and passports. We could only take twenty rands out of the country. The banks had closed for the holiday week-end at 3.00 on Friday afternoon and we had not had time to go through the lengthy currency control hassle of buying foreign exchange. Perhaps we had enough small change to buy a copy; or perhaps we picked up a free copy of the *Cape Times* on the aircraft and we still have the copy in which the main headline read:

CONFESSION BY SABOTEUR, POLICE CLAIM
More Arrests – Search For Vigne Continues

Alongside was a story quoting 'Leo Marquard, South African historian and publisher, whose home was raided by the Security Police last Saturday, yesterday accused the Minister of Justice, Mr Vorster of "scare tactics" against "Communists and leftists...and liberalists".' David Philip and I had deeply admired Leo Marquard when, up to 1962, he was the OUP

Editorial Manager for whom we worked. Cannon, who was his conservative United Party opposite, would have been relieved that name of the Oxford University Press was left out of this story.

In 1964 Cape Town's D.F. Malan airport was small and entirely for South African Airways domestic services. We checked in for Johannesburg where we were booked on the Alitalia flight for Rome. Clare sat on a round banquette in the centre of the compact entrance hall to watch for men in suits who might be Special Branch. I disappeared into a cubicle in the lavatory in order to keep out of sight. Announcements on the loudspeakers were first in Afrikaans and then in English. As I sat I heard in an Afrikaans announcement the name 'Kerry', which was the pronunciation Afrikaners often gave to 'Currey'. Then clearly in the announcement in English 'Will passenger Kerry please go to South African Airways flight desk.' On the principle that it was best to act as though one had nothing to hide I emerged from the gents and said to Clare 'This sounds like it!' I went over to the desk and found that there was indeed a passenger called Kerry on the flight list who was already making himself known. After I had told Clare I returned to the lavatory cubicle.

The flight to Johannesburg in a turboprop Vickers Viscount took some two and a half hours. There is a lot of South Africa after the plane crosses the Cape mountains. We both riffled through the piles of magazines. Among them were the shiny pages of the *Illustrated London News,* which was about all I could concentrate on. In the middle of one of the pages was a photograph of a young Englishman standing trial in Budapest for having helped a Hungarian escape. The words of the British Consul Ballantyne came to mind 'If you are arrested, we shall do our best to get you deported.' I said nothing to Clare. I hoped she would not see it. She said later that she too had seen the picture and that her thoughts had been identical. She hoped I had not seen it.

In mid-morning, as we were landing at Jan Smuts Airport in Johannesburg, we could see the tailfins of a small number of airliners across on the international side of the long terminal building. There was no Alitalia tailfin. At the check-in desk we found that there was a delay in the arrival of the flight from Rome and Léopoldville, the capital of the newly independent Congo. I filled in the second form for departure from South Africa within forty-eight hours. We showed our blessed British passports and went into the international departure lounge. I disappeared into the gents again. We had no rands even to buy coffee. Realising that it would be a Saturday the British Consul in Cape Town had given us the home number of the duty officer at the British consulate in Johannesburg; his name was James Currie.

In case she had to make this emergency phone call Clare had carefully kept a 'tickey', which was the South African round silver threepenny bit used in telephone booths, which were known as 'tickey boxes'.

The touchdown of the Alitalia plane was at last announced in early afternoon. Eventually our flight was called and the passengers started out across the tarmac on a fine but cloudy winter's day. The passenger steps were towards the tail of the aircraft. As we got closer I saw a tall thin Afrikaner with piercing blue eyes, who had been standing near the steps, start to walk towards us with purpose. Clare thought 'Police. This is it!' (Clare remembers him as being in a khaki uniform with a peaked cap. I remember him as having a battered trilby hat and baggy tweed jacket.) He walked past us. In fact he was supervising the Africans who were handling the hoses refuelling the jet aircraft.

Several hours late the plane took off in the late afternoon. As it rose up above the clouds into the setting sun we could only allow ourselves to feel that another stage had been reached. What if there was a mechanical problem with the plane so that it had to turn back to Johannesburg? We were certainly glad of the belated airline food; lunch reached us at tea-time. When we were out of South Africa and over half of the way to Léo we let our hopes rise. As the plane began the descent to Léopoldville (now Kinshasa) in the Congo we dared to hope we were free. Even when I had been in Léo in 1962 the United Nations control was not altogether secure. In the very *Cape Times* we were carrying there was a front page entry under the Vigne story which reported that 'Moise Tshombe had yesterday been sworn in as the Congo's Prime Minister.... The communiqué also said that the curfew imposed in Léopoldville seven weeks ago after a rash of bombings would be lifted.' Independent Congo at that time had the reputation in South Africa of being the most hazardous country in the whole continent. At least, as we were sent to wait in the terminal building, we were walking on safer ground for us than South Africa. At some stage we were told that the flight was going to arrive too late in Rome for us to be able to catch the last flight to London and that Alitalia would put us up for the night. On arrival Clare remembers large banners for 'Vatican II' at the airport and looking out of the bus at a hot late Saturday night Rome. At the hotel we were given what seemed to be the honeymoon suite with an enormous double bed with dangly bits in the best Italian bad taste. The room, up under the eaves, was very hot and Clare was awoken during the night by the first of my prison nightmares. These were to recur, though with decreasing frequency, for years; they replaced my previous set of nightmares which were about taking Finals at Oxford.

Sunday 12 July 1964

The Alitalia desk at the hotel did not seem able to find us seats on a flight to arrive in London until after mid-day. Clare pointed out to Alitalia that we had to send a message to our family about the delay. We were told, somewhat reluctantly, that we could send one cable at Alitalia's expense. At that moment our parents had every reason to assume that we were both in Cape Town. We decided to send our one cable to Clare's parents Ruth and Henry Wilson in Cambridge and say that our flight was delayed and that we would be arriving in Heathrow at such and such a time, love Clare and James. Just as though they were expecting us.

Here we were unexpectedly in Rome on a summer Sunday with time to have a walk. I had damaged my right leg in the leap from the ship when my shin hit the wooden edge of the quay. I do not remember limping around Cape Town and Johannesburg airports but by Sunday morning I had developed a limp Groucho Marks would have admired. We had absolutely no cash – or at least did not remember until later that we had a single dollar bill. We could not sit at a cafe table and watch the world go by. Eventually we found a wall under some trees to perch on.

We could only hope, as we arrived at London airport, that the one cable had reached Clare's parents. Perhaps they were away. We did have English bank accounts though even at Heathrow, in those days before bank cards, cashing a cheque on a Sunday might be impossible. But when we went out through arrivals on Sunday afternoon, all four parents were there to meet us. Clare's parents had rung Ralph and Stella Currey in Colchester and they all agreed to go to Heathrow to find out why we had left South Africa so precipitately. They had assumed that we were in trouble. I was slightly apprehensive about my father's reactions. His mother was South African and he had always been loyal to his South African and Rhodesian cousins and argued that the situation was different for them as their whole lives were tied up in those countries. However my father's unquestioned loyalty was to his immediate family. I have recently been told by Nick Elam, whose father had been my father's headmaster at Colchester Royal Grammar School, that coincidentally he had been reading all these consular exchanges with Cape Town about our hasty departure while on the South African desk at the Foreign Office just before going at the end of July 1964 to go to work at the British Embassy in South Africa. He was thus able to give advance warning to my father that Clare and I would be arriving in England at any time.

Clare's parents borrowed a friend's flat for us near Regent's Park so that I could put in my unexpected appearance at Oxford University Press first thing on Monday morning. They certainly had had no warning.

Monday 13 July 1964

It was the beginning of the working week and before hours I was on the doorstep of Amen House near the Stationer's Hall and within the shadow of St Paul's. On Friday afternoon, at the end of the last working week, we had been in Fred Cannon's office in Cape Town with the British Consul. It being the gentlemanly Oxford University Press, I was not too frightened that I would be sacked.

The Publisher of the London business (managing director in a limited liability company) was John Brown (not yet Sir John). He was one of the 'Indians'; just as the Indian Civil Service was considered superior to the Colonial Service, so the expatriates who had run the Indian branches of the OUP considered themselves superior to those of us who worked in the other colonies. I sat before John Brown's desk in his magnificent eighteenth-century room and told him of what I had had to do at very short notice for a friend in need. It was fortunate that Randolph Vigne had not told me before he left that he was wanted for sabotage. It was easier to explain that the person I had enabled to escape was a publisher and a banned person. John Brown was not sympathetic. I do not remember what he said. It later became clear, via other people, that he felt that I had imperilled the South African business and my colleagues. I did not seem to have been sacked.

Philip Chester, the Deputy Publisher, was another India hand. He had published my father's anthology *Poems from India* during the war. He always had a smile that welcomed you. He was the person responsible for the day to day administration of the branch offices across the world. The sun never set on his publishing empire. He had a calm reaction and said 'Accidents happen. You might have been run over by a bus! … It may be a bit of time before we can find a job for you here.'

David Neale, the Manager of the Overseas Education Department, had been my boss while I was training. He dragged on his cigarette and said gruffly: 'You could not have done otherwise! Can't think what job we've got. Better take three weeks leave while we find something.' To Rex Collings, the publisher of the new Three Crowns series of writing from the third world and of academic books on Africa, I was a hero.

The next few weeks of summer were concentrated on re-ordering our personal lives and my professional life. Our early return was a shock for a former Cape Town colleague Ken White and his wife, who were renting Clare's Hertfordshire village cottage. I had promised David Philip, my Cape Town Manager, that I would immediately write down a detailed report of the editorial production details of all the books going through the Oxford

University Press in Cape Town. I gave details of each book on a separate sheet and was relieved to get this sizeable packet of some fifty sheets of quarto paper into the airmail.

One of the last things that Randolph had said to me in his cabin in the *Thorstream* was that I should contact Bowra. Sir Maurice Bowra was the renowned Warden of Wadham College in the University of Oxford. Randolph and I had both been undergraduates at that college, though we were there some eight years apart. Randolph was remembered as a lively young South African who ran the 120-yards high hurdles; he had been too young for military service and, in the period after the war when servicemen were trying anxiously to complete their interrupted degrees, he was keen to bring some *Brideshead* into his Oxford life. My tutor A.F. Thompson told me that during a party Randolph had once for a bet leapt out of a first-floor window down into the quad. Bowra had sent me Christmas cards in South Africa with cheerful remarks like 'Keep your escape routes clear!' He was proud of the anti-apartheid activities of his Wadham men. I typed a letter to him, hoping that Bowra would be in Oxford during the vacation and not out of reach on the continent. I explained briefly how I had got Randolph onto a ship for Canada and that he might need Sir Maurice's help with the Foreign Office to get into Britain without papers. Fortunately Bowra was there and immediately invited me to go and tell him the story over lunch in the Warden's lodgings. He was a brilliant conversationalist, but on this occasion he wanted to hear every detail and listened intently. It was the first time that I had witnessed him silent except for the occasional question. It was most useful support because Sir Maurice was a Delegate to the Oxford University Press; this meant that he was the equivalent of one of my directors.

However I had accidentally left a carbon copy of my letter to Bowra in the packet of some fifty sheets that I had airmailed to David Philip. Cannon went off with a bang. It gave him the chance to get his own back on me with the Publisher. He said that the Special Branch would be round and that it put the lives of their staff in danger and the business in jeopardy. Later that autumn, Randolph was to ask Bowra whether my situation at the Oxford University Press was all right: Bowra said, 'The Publisher was confused. I told him not to be confused!'

Randolph: from Cape Town to Montreal

In July and August 1964 we were still on 'radio silence' about Randolph until we knew after about three weeks that he was safely ashore in Canada. When we met members of the South African exile community in London we just had to tell them that my mother was ill and that we had come over in the emergency. A friend arranged for us to borrow a flat in Mecklenburgh Square. We bumped into Merle Babrow (later Lipton), an old Cape Town friend who was in a London University postgraduate flat nearby. After the news about Randolph was public she exclaimed to me that I was a marvellous liar.

Randolph took a look at Canada to see if he might settle there and did not arrive in London for some six weeks after his escape from Cape Town. During that time we heard nothing and said nothing. Suddenly on 16 August 1964 Clare and I were summoned to the St John's Wood house of Maurice Brown, who was a producer for the BBC Third Programme and a relation of Randolph's. I remember being struck by the stylish brown wallpaper in this handsome terrace house. On a warm evening people from the press were coming and going. One of the reporters was from the *Guardian* and his story resulted the next day in a publishing job for Randolph. A replacement copy of the Oxford edition of *Northanger Abbey* and *Persuasion* was given to us. It was inscribed 'James Currey with unending gratitude from "James Currey".'

Randolph told us his matching story. This is as Clare and I in 2012 remember his description. Day 1; euphoria but he lay low in his cabin, missing dinner. Day 2; he was tackled after breakfast by Major Fortune a director of the company in Natal whose sugar the *Thorstream* was carrying. He was on a free passage and as the ship had been preparing to sail he was up on the bridge with the Pilot, the Master, and the Chief Engineer, who was in effect the Mate. Major Fortune had the English middle class style of many Natal settlers. He said 'Well, Currey? Was your friend drunk?' Randolph had no idea what he meant as he had been below in his cabin. This was the first that Randolph had heard about my leap. Major Fortune said everybody on the bridge saw it. The Pilot had demanded the boat should not leave. But the Master said that they were already days late and continued with orders for casting off. The Pilot said 'We'll get him!' Major Fortune clearly assumed that we had had a drunken farewell party. Randolph realised that he should have sniggered and played up to white South African middle class assumptions about a young white South African man in a suit taking the short cut over the edge, like Randolph's own exit from his Wadham party. But, ramrod shocked by the news as he was, he could only think to say 'Oh, yes! He's a young man from my office. He's a bit vague. He must have been thinking about something else.'

Two other women passengers also told Randolph of my leap. Jean and

I must have heard their screams. They said I had gashed my head and that I ran with a lady to catch a bus. Randolph said later that he pictured that I had been delayed by his request to contact Bowra and that by the time I got on deck the gangplank had been removed. One way or another the news was alarming. The *Thorstream* had a long way to go north in South African territorial waters. Even when it passed the north-west point of South Africa there was still Namibia. South-West Africa, as it was then, was held by South Africa under a United Nations mandate under a defunct League of Nations mandate, and South Africa repeatedly refused to hand it over to the UN. Even worse, its only deep-water port, Walvis Bay, was South African territory. Randolph imagined a speedboat carrying out Special Branch men from Walvis Bay. It was to be a blessed relief when another ship of the same Norwegian line steamed out to exchange papers with the *Thorstream* so that they did not have to go into port. He had been told that the ship would put in to the Cape Verde Islands which were Portuguese. The PIDE, the Portuguese Special Branch, worked closely with the South African Special Branch and was even less scrupulous. In 1962 the poet and non-racial sports campaigner Dennis Brutus, although he had a British passport, had been kidnapped by the PIDE as he crossed from Swaziland to Mozambique and illegally handed over at Ventersdorp to the South African Special Branch who next day had gunned him down as he tried to escape in central Johannesburg. At least the South African papers had reported his near death so that it was more difficult for the Special Branch to dispose of him without people knowing. In fact only month later in August 1964 Neville Rubin, whose name stood alone on *The New African* as editor, was to be imprisoned while leaving Swaziland for Mozambique. When he and Muriel had left Cape Town in January 1963 to go to SOAS in London to teach law he still had a valid South African passport. But that would have prevented his entering most independent countries in Africa to pursue his research. So SOAS had applied to the Foreign Secretary to use his discretion to issue him with a British passport. It still took a week for the British diplomatic authorities, with protests in the British press, to get him released. Randolph's first night's relaxed voyaging was over.

On the stately voyage the other fifteen or so passengers had nothing better to do than to find out about one another. Here was Randolph Vigne travelling as James Currey. He did his best to put together his memories of my life and of that of my father, whose Indian suitcase had been brought aboard. He made the decision to tell everybody that he was 'on the wagon' to try to reduce the chance of suspicious slips in his account. An attractive divorcee was clearly rather intrigued by the sparseness of his story.

After a week or ten days at sea they were sailing into the dreaded Cape Verde Islands to moor in the harbour. Randolph stayed in his cabin but then realised that would look strange. He came up on deck to see an official hat coming up the ladder; it must be the policeman coming on board to arrest him. His fears were not realised, but new fears filled his mind as they sailed off through the Atlantic towards the mouth of the St Lawrence. It was to take two and a half days up the St Lawrence Seaway to reach Montreal. What would he do if the Canadians refused him entry and he was sent back to South Africa? Every daylight and a lot of night hours Randolph watched to see where the shipping channel ran close to the shore noting where he might swim for it.

Randolph set out to cultivate the Mate/Chief Engineer, whom Jon Aase described as reliable. He kept as clear as possible of the conservative Master, who had a reserved relationship with the Mate. Major Fortune approached Randolph on the last day as they were still sailing up the St Lawrence and said; 'Well Currey! As the youngest passenger I think that you ought to propose the health of the Master and crew at the last dinner.' Randolph said that he gave an unctuous speech, scarcely mentioning the Mate but praising the brilliance of the Master whom he feared might have a crucial role at docking the next morning. Randolph had to get through the last night. The *Thorstream* docked at dawn. There was a knock at the door. Randolph opened it in dread. The passengers had to gather in the lounge for immigration and Randolph anxiously prepared to admit he had no passport. A dark suited member of the Canadian foreign service said 'Mr Currey? Please follow me.' Up to the deck and off the ship. Randolph said 'He seemed to think I was a VIP and not a hot potato.' The official, deputy director of immigration, booked Randolph in at the Queen Elizabeth Hotel and was asked for his name: 'Finlay', he said – using his own. How very unlike South Africa, Randolph thought.

There followed a day of formalities to re-establish his identity. All went smoothly with the immigration procedure, until Randolph could go back to relax in his hotel room. The friendly divorcee was also staying in the same hotel and invited Randolph round to her room for a drink with her brother and a few passengers from the ship. Randolph was hoping for a telephone call from his sister Phoebe in New York and asked the switchboard to transfer the call to the divorcee's room. A little later the telephone rang, the divorcee picked it up and said 'There's no Mr Vigne here!' and was about to put the phone down when Randolph grabbed the receiver from her and said, 'Hello. Is that you Phoebe? Randolph here!' One of the passengers said

'But isn't your name Currey?' and Randolph said 'No, it's Finlay, here'. The divorcee seemed ever more entranced by this mysterious stranger with his aliases.

Randolph visited cousins in Ottawa, who were advised by the Canadian Foreign Office that he should stay there until his departure. He was asked to call at the Foreign Office and met an official, one Hicks, who showed him the airmail London *Times* with the story of the burning of Clifton House. Hicks was unsympathetic and clearly knew of his ARM membership. He flew to London under arrangements made by Finlay, who was as friendly and helpful as ever. However he got Randolph's flight details wrong and when Randolph landed at Heathrow, passportless, the immigration people knew nothing about him. The then proprietor of the *Spectator,* Sir Ian Gilmour M.P., vouched for him, in the absence of the Editor Iain Macleod M.P. who had published Randolph's articles about the Transkei. The first contact he made was with Clare and me. Special Branch reports later claimed that Randolph had visited his sister Phoebe at her New York address, which they got almost right, and had gone on to report to the CIA. Randolph says: 'Mr Hicks would have been furious.'

Sabotage
It was shattering for Clare and me to hear in Britain the news of the bomb on Johannesburg station on 24 July 1964 which had injured passengers, one mortally. How did it fit in with what had been happening in South Africa?

In April 1964 I had been visiting primary schools in Soweto and then in the Pretoria townships for the Oxford University Press. Clare went to the Rivonia trial every day in the Courts of Justice and wrote an article for *The New African* under the name Elizabeth Wilson capturing the atmosphere in the court as the trial dragged on. The case reflected the fact that during the fifties the radical political movements of South Africa had failed to get change using Gandhi's methods of non-violent protest. The tactic had worked against the occupation of India because the British decided it was not worth the cash and dead bodies to stay on. In South Africa the British and Afrikaner settlers were ruthless in their use of state violence to remain in South Africa. The victims of Sharpeville and Langa in 1960 had been making peaceful protests. The NCL (National Committee for Liberation) and several other groups came round in the early sixties to the realisation that they had to see if violence could bring change. In June 1964 after the Rivonia verdict was announced there was a banner headline across the top of the front of the Johannesburg *Sunday Times* quoting the chief of police boasting that all resistance in South Africa was crushed. That night on the

Rand and near Cape Town electricity pylons were toppled. There was still resistance. But from whom? They did not seem to know of the African Resistance Movement (the NCL had been renamed the ARM). The Saturday night raids of 4 July 1964, which led to protests by Leo Marquard, were so widespread because the police had no idea what organisation was involved. The police were impressed by their professionalism. Their disciplined aim was to hit targets such as electricity pylons or railway signal cables in order to cause disruption but without injury to people. After Leftwich's chance arrest and betrayal of the others, unfortunately John Harris, as a final message to the Government and its supporters, broke the ARM rules when he left the bomb on Johannesburg station, and his warning telephone call to newspapers to clear the concourse was not acted upon quickly enough by the police.

We only learned after we reached England that Randolph, Neville and Norman had been involved in sabotage. Unknowingly Clare and I had been footsoldiers. Randolph would borrow our flat on Sundays when we were going to be out for the whole day; he made sure that we never saw who else came to these clandestine meetings. We knew that as a banned person he was not allowed to meet more than one person at a time and assumed that the meetings in our flat were so he could get together with several people; we knew nothing of the ARM and its objectives. I now had to face up for the first time to the question of what was my attitude to sabotage. I rationalised that it was their country. It was up to them to judge what was necessary. I admired their bravery. I was relieved that I had never been asked by any of them to join the ARM. For Clare the discovery was much more difficult. She had grown up in a Quaker family with the traditional commitment to non-violence. Her father had been a conscientious objector during the First World War.

Vigne was vilified in the press and in books as the 'ringleader' who had cunningly made a planned getaway and had left behind his associates to be caught and jailed in South Africa. If his escape had been planned it would not have worked. It was put together hour by hour, step by step. Our luck held in so many ways. Randolph had returned to the Cape Town Magistracy from Port Elizabeth but had not gone back to Clifton House where he would have been detained. I had been four fingers from disaster when I saved myself by one hand from falling into the dock. The Holland-Afrika agent had his back to me and nobody – railway policeman or anybody else – gave chase. Jean Ridge responded to every emergency as a new challenge to her ingenuity. Nothing was planned.

It was of immense luck that it was a holiday week-end (now replaced by Mandela's Day). Peter Hjul, formerly Chairman of the Cape Liberals but banned in 1963, was permitted to continue as Editor of *Fishing News International*. He learnt through his contacts that my immigration papers out of South Africa would have been sent by messenger from the Holland-Afrika office to the immigration offices many floors up in the SANLAM skyscraper with a view of all the docks including the *Thorstream* in the Duncan Dock. The purchase in the last hours of a ticket with the stated reason of a business trip to Canada would have looked suspicious. Even in those days before computers the number of European people involved in active radical politics in South Africa was lamentably small and 'C' for Currey is quite early in the alphabet. It would not have been difficult especially with police making arrests all over South Africa, to decide that it was worth intercepting the ship. The immigration officer had skived off early to take his family away for the holiday weekend. He only got back the following week when the *Thorstream* had left SA territorial waters off South-West Africa. He was sacked. From Security Police files in the National Archives in Pretoria we now know that I was suspected of being a conduit between the ARM in South Africa and its members in Britain and Africa, because of my trips outside South Africa as they thought for the OUP; in fact my travels on leave outside South Africa were at my own initiative and at our own expense. In any case they undoubtedly knew that I was constantly in touch with Randolph Vigne and probably assumed that it was for more than for design and production work on *The New African*. Though they had got it wrong, they had got me in their sights. Consul Ballantyne had been right: the more I insisted that I knew nothing about ARM the more pressure they would have put on me.

Though the Special Branch missed the getaway, they knew of it later and swarmed over the *Thorstream* when it docked in Table Bay after its return from Canada. Norman Bromberger, who was a member of ARM, was flown down to Cape Town in detention. His account in 2013 captures the twisting realities of interrogation: 'I did not mention Jean Ridge. I substituted your wife Clare as the woman on the quay in my account of the escape day's events which they would be able to check with uninvolved outsiders – such as the man at the shipping office, and people on the boat or quayside. And they did do some checking – e.g. the hotel booking under an assumed name in Cape Town – Long Street? The Branch took me there after I had made a statement. The point about putting that sort of checkable statement was to lend creditability at no cost to anybody. As to why there was any need to make statement at all, I guess you understand the pressure put on one and the apparent pointlessness of holding out as they bring news of statements they've got from others. As regards the escape, someone from my "cell" in Port Elizabeth told them that I had been present at the escape and though I denied it for some time I realised that I would need to give them something plausible eventually, and worked out that if Jean were protected nobody apart from myself would be implicated (given that the brief appearances of Hjul and Hoffenberg could be suppressed).'

Gillian & the Consuls
It is clear from this account that the Vignes, the Curreys and the Rubins all benefited from the help of foreign consular officials. It had been the convention in South Africa that diplomats only kept in contact with the parliamentary government and opposition. Coincidentally it was under the Canadian foreign service of the conservative administration of John Diefenbaker which ended in April 1963 that their diplomats led the way in keeping in touch with the extraparliamentary opposition in South Africa; they reasoned that under the racially exclusive franchise they needed to understand the political positions of parties that set out to represent the whole of the South African population. Once the Canadians started this policy they were followed by some of the diplomats in some of the other legations. But opinion was divided among the diplomats.

Jon Aase, the Norwegian Consul in Cape Town, was sacked by his superior in Pretoria who was of the old school and pro-South African Government. Jon Aase appealed to Oslo, was reinstated and his boss was withdrawn instead. The next summer Jon Aase and I met at the Houses of Parliament in Westminster and were able to put our memories together. Coincidentally Gillian Vigne experienced a similar episode in her job as Brazilian Vice-Consul. She said in 2011 '… my boss Lael Soares called me in to tell me that the Counsellor at the Embassy in Pretoria had flown down specially to tell him to sack me as an undesirable person. To his enormous credit, Lael refused.'

Gillian Vigne said in 2011 'I stayed on in Port Elizabeth until Clifton House was fire bombed on 29 July 1964. The next day Randolph's father drove me and the children [Piers aged 7 and Lucy aged 4] back to Cape Town … The children and I stayed with Ethel Bowater at Taunton House, and I went back to work after my mother rushed down from Pietermaritzburg to keep me company. The Special Branch came to see me – I remember coming out of my bedroom at the back on hearing a kerfuffle, and seeing Ethel blocking the way with arms typically akimbo; "This is my house and you cannot come on to private property!" she boomed at them. The next day of course they returned with a warrant to speak to me; they sat in my rather dark bedroom and I replied desultorily and genuinely ignorantly to their questions.

Randolph had parked his VW Beetle in Bree Street in Cape Town which runs parallel to Long Street. Jean Ridge wrote in 2012: 'I was given the key but did not go near the car until days after the boat had sailed. I found a revolver in the glove box! I intuitively thought it should be removed and did so and thereby was left holding an unwanted baby. I went to Johannesburg to be with David Craighead. The revolver accompanied me! David offered to secure it in his office safe at the African Life Insurance Company of which he was manager. He was also chairman of the Defence and Aid Fund and as such his office was raided by the SB and the gun discovered. David obviously had no licence to show and was hauled before the courts, most generously on my account! Defended by Ruth Hayman, he paid a hefty fine but luckily the dots were not connected that the licence had been held by an escaped member of the ARM, or his wife. Once again we had a lucky break!' Randolph explained that the little automatic was 'for Gillian's reassurance when I had been in the Transkei.'

Randolph's father saw the head of the Special Branch, Colonel McIntyre ('English-speaking and therefore not fully in the loop' says Randolph) who told him that Randolph had abandoned his car on the border when he escaped into Basutoland. Randolph's father and Gillian later recovered the car from Bree Street where it had been all along. Gillian also remembers 'Bill Hoffenberg taking me out for a long drive one day, pumping me gently to know how much I knew and therefore what risk I was, I totally aware of what he was doing but going through the motions to reassure him! .... Margaret Hoffenberg was a wonderful friend during that time, and drove me to see if anything could be salvaged from the fire, but my big desk with my lifetime papers, diaries, photos (and the lavish Queen's appointment of me as Brazilian Vice Consul!) were totally burnt. And of course Randolph's little study with MS on Chinnery etc. R had put down 21 bottles of special port for Piers when he was born; it had gone but not burnt which means they had searched the house (and stolen the port!) before petrol bombing it.

'So I went on working. Then Jean Ridge sweetly rang me one day in mid-August and said "I've just had a cable saying that the pineapples arrived safely", which I fully understood though meaningless. Thereafter one began making plans to sail to England ... The children were stateless because as South Africans they should have been on their father's passport. So the British Consul instead put them on my British passport. In September Margaret Hoff drove us down to the docks to embark, and the British

Consul accompanied me and stuck to me like glue to my cabin until he felt all was well and he finally had to go ashore. My mother voyaged with us which was lovely.

The day before we had taken the children up in the rickety old cable car as a last look at CT, and as the ship pulled out there was the traditional sad/happy custom of throwing streamers to those on shore.' Jean Ridge was among the waving crowds on the quay. She could not escape. Jean says 'Following Randolph's illicit get-away ...the import of what James, Norman and I had done hit me like a stone. We had been culpable in aiding and abetting the escape of a person who became notoriously wanted for questioning by the Apartheid Security Police. I examined my position and sought advice from my lawyer, Tom Walters, whose liberal politics and friendship encouraged me to recount the events of 8/9 July. Tom advised me to leave the country. I was in no position at the time to consider this option and decided to brazen things out and remained in Cape Town. Time passed nervously until information came my way that the SB had believed that the woman on the quay in the docks drama had been James's wife Clare. Suspicion was averted and from then on I relaxed and resumed normal life.' Norman Bromberger's subterfuge under interrogation had worked. Stowed in the hold of Gillian's Union Castle mailboat was the Currey's red VW Beetle; this car, which had almost become a character in its own right, was the one which we had offered to Randolph for him to try and escape to Bechuanaland; David Philip and Miss Olwen Williams at OUP had got the belongings at our flat packed up and the car shipped to Southampton. Many people had loyally helped one another without question.

It would take a thirteen-day voyage to Southampton before Gillian could be told in September what had happened. At that moment she had no idea of the drama which had taken place yards away from the Union Castle mailboat on the south arm of the Duncan Dock.

Gillian can find out what happened to Randolph at last
(Clare in UK/to RS in the US, 30 August 1964) Randolph is safely in this country, as you may have seen – great relief for him, since he had all sorts of false alarms on the journey to Canada, about which we must tell you. He came here last weekend and was absolutely whacked and spent much of the time asleep. The telly got hold of him as soon as be arrived but no-one we know saw him on it, and there were paragraphs in the *Times* and *Guardian*. He's job hunting now [offer at Stillit Books as result of *Guardian* story].

Waiting till Gillian and the children arrive before house hunting. They come (on the same boat as our car) at the end of this week. We were sent some pictures of their departure from with streamers from the Union Castle boat leaving Cape Town, Gillian looking very cheerful, and the newspaper account sounding rather jaundiced that her only answers to newspaper questions were 'No comment'. [This was accurate. She did not know what on earth had happened to Randolph until she reached London.]

The Cape Escape Team

Norman Bromberger was Lecturer in Economics at Rhodes University, Port Elizabeth campus. As a member he had done organizational work for the Liberal Party in Grahamstown 1961-2. He was a member of NCL/ARM and was taken in for interrogation in July 1964. He was released but banned in 1965. He later worked with Francis Wilson at SALDRU (South African Labour and Development Research Unit) at the University of Cape Town and then in research at the University of KwaZulu Natal Pietermaritzburg.

James and Clare Currey had been married only eighteen months at the time of the Cape Escape. At the Oxford University Press in Cape Town James Currey started on a lifetime of publishing books on Africa. After the Cape Escape he ran Three Crowns for OUP in London. In 1967 he went to work at Heinemann and, with Chinua Achebe as adviser on the first 100 titles, published a total of 270 titles in the African Writers Series. He had first come across many of his authors through their work in *The New African*. In 1985 Clare and James Currey established their own imprint which, in close liaison with publishers in Africa and the United States, became an outstanding list in African Studies. James Currey has received awards from African Studies Associations in Canada, the United States and the United Kingdom.

Bill Hoffenberg was the endocrinologist who advised Christiaan Barnard on tissue typing for the world's first heart transplant. He was chairman of the Defence and Aid Fund in South Africa until it was banned in 1966. He was banned in 1967 and went into exile in 1968; as he and Margaret walked out to their plane at Cape Town airport the assembled members of staff of Groote Schuur hospital and UCT Medical Students revealed their white gowns in support. He was appointed Professor of Medicine at Birmingham in 1972 and President of the Royal Society of Physicians in 1983, was knighted in 1984 and became President of Wolfson College, Oxford in 1985. He died in 2007.

Jean Ridge was well-known as a professional photographer in Cape Town. She went on to be founding director of Grassroots Educare Trust for preschoolers in the Cape's townships. Later, when she had emigrated to England she worked with Sir Robert Birley to form the Lomans Trust to raise money for black secondary education in South Africa which was initially filtered through the SA Institute of Race Relations and then directly to selected schools.

Randolph Vigne played an important role in the radicalization of the South African Liberal Party in the period before and after Sharpeville in 1960 and worked closely with the Pan-Africanist Congress. He wrote much for Patrick Duncan's newspaper *Contact*. In 1962 he founded *The New African* as a political, literary and artistic review with Neville Rubin, Tim Holmes and James Currey. He was excited by the positive response he found to the Liberal Party in the Transkei and assisted in forming the Transkei Democratic Party with Chief Sabata. In 1963 he was tried under the emergency regulations imposed at the birth of the Bantustan. He was banned in 1963. In 1960 he was a founder member of the underground NCL which in 1964 became the African Resistance Movement (ARM).

In London in 1965 he re-established *The New African* which survived from 1962 to 1969 for a total of 53 issues. He was for 22 years secretary of the Namibia Support Committee and he worked closely with the International Defence and Aid Fund. In 2010 he was awarded The Order of Luthuli. He has written several books including *Liberals against Apartheid*, and his biography of *Thomas Pringle* came out in 2012 from James Currey Publishers.

Writers from southern Africa (left to right); Albie Sachs, Doris Lessing, Alex la Guma and Richard Rive with James organising the photographer from behind. James had got to know them while in Cape Town and here they are all about to have books published by Heinemann in London in 1972.

Clare and James Currey in their Islington basement office surrounded by some of the academic books on Africa and the Caribbean which they published in the first ten years of the imprint they had started together in 1985.

INDEX

Aase, Jon 112, 161-63, 169, 171, 181, 185
Abrahams, Ibraham, 85, 87
Abrahams, Dr Kenneth Godfrey, 130
Achebe, Chinua, 2, 112, 115, 189
Africa South, 90
African National Congress (ANC), 34, 38, 45, 56, 60, 80, 82, 83, 101, 132
African Resistance Movement (ARM), 3, 157, 182, 183, 184, 186, 189, 190
African Writers Series (Heinemann), 2, 61, 189
Allen & Unwin (publisher), 106
Alport, Cuthbert, 37
Andrew, *see* Currey, Andrew
Andrzejewski, B.W., 135
Anglican *see* Church of England
Anglo-American (multinational), 102
Angola, 69, 114
August family, 60-61, 104

Baaskap, *see* White racism
Babrow, Merle, 179
Baden-Powell, Robert, 5
Bailey, Jim, 79
Balkema, A.A., 6, 29, 30, 159, 165
Ballantyne, Dick, 169-74, 184
Ballinger, Margaret, 7, 37
Banda, Hastings, 57, 149
banning, 45, 82, 122-4, 138-9, 189
Barbour, Jock, 26
Barron, George, 140, 141
Basson, Jack, 97
Basutoland (Lesotho), 13, 36, 58, 59, 60, 61, 62, 75, 93, 103, 111, 133, 152, 186

BBC (British Broadcasting Corporation), 35, 36, 64, 79, 81, 109, 134, 135, 179
Beard, Terence, 96, 120, 169, 170
Bechuanaland (Botswana), 58, 83, 130, 141, 158, 187
Bell, John, 65
Benjamin, Victor, 105
Benson, Mary, 129
Bernstein, Lionel 'Rusty', 151
Bertram, Dieter, 54
Beynon, Gwydion, 41
Birley, Robert, 189
Bjil, Art, 109
Black, Kitty, 27
Black Sash, 48, 53, 55, 80, 119, 128, 133
Blackwell, Basil, 74
Blaxall, Dr Arthur William, 132
Bloom, Harry, 36
Bloom, Len, 135
Blumberg, Myrna, 50
Bookshops, 25, 28, 41, 94-5, 106, 136
Botswana, *see* Bechuanaland
Bowater, Ethel & Bill, 158, 159, 161, 162, 185
Bowra, Maurice, 20, 32, 166, 178, 180
Brand, Dollar, (Abdullah Ibrahim), 56, 102
Brecht, Bertolt, 17-19
Britain, 1, 4, 37, 74, 103, 124, 141, 182
British Petroleum (BP), 11, 15, 42, 93, 137
Bromberger, Norman, 157. 158, 160, 161, 162, 164, 167-9, 184, 187, 188
Brown, John, 177
Brown, Maurice, 179

Brown, Peter, 7, 38, 111-12
Brutus, Dennis, 2, 99, 110, 180
Bunting, Brian, 34
Bureau of State Security (BOSS), 146
Butler, Guy, 30

Canada, 3, 178-9, 184, 187
Cadbury, Eveline, 142
Cannon, Freddie, 5, 16, 20, 50, 73, 94, 97, 102, 103, 112, 113, 120, 148, 152, 171, 172, 174, 177, 178
Cape Argus, 11, 19, 51, 65, 66, 80, 83, 99, 111, 171
Cape Times, 6, 11, 14, 16, 19, 24, 34, 51, 65, 68, 80, 83, 87, 111, 121, 173, 175
Cape Malays, 65, 67, 70, 76, 136
Cape Verde, 180, 181
Cato Manor, 36, 44, 56, 126
Caute, David, 81
Censorship, 2, 5, 61, 74, 111, 125, 137-39
Centlivres, A. Van de Sandt, 55
Chapman, Winston, 96
Chester, Philip, 177
Chiefs, 3, 56, 63, 111, 135
Church of England (Anglicans), 42, 60, 132, 136
CIA, 112, 121, 182
Cillie, Piet, 99
Citizen Group, 78
Clare, Sheila, 151
Clark, John Pepper, 115
Clouts, Sydney, 63
Coetzer, Deputy Minister, 126
Clarendon Press, 65, 74, 83, 135
Colborne family, 13
Colchester, 5, 21, 27, 88, 101, 111, 113
Colchester Royal Grammar School (CRGS), 104
Collier, Mrs, 55
Collings, Rex, 4, 90, 115, 177
Collingwood, August, *see* August family
Coloured People's Congress, 34, 80
Coloured People's Convention, 80
Commonwealth (British), 36, 37, 74, 77, 78

Communist Party (South Africa), 34, 79, 82, 83, 94, 122
Congo, 62-3, 103, 113, 114, 115, 141, 175
Congress Alliance, 1, 34
Congress for Cultural Freedom, 109, 112, 121, 137
Congress of Democrats, 34, 80, 189
Connolly, Cyril, 20
Contact, 1, 2, 3, 7, 32-33, 36, 48, 51, 53, 56, 60, 67, 70, 74, 80, 82, 84, 87, 94, 95, 99, 104, 105, 110, 111, 124-5, 130, 133, 134, 142, 190
Contrast, 65, 113
Cowen, D.W., 61, 68, 73, 77, 81, 83, 90, 92, 106
Craighead, David, 186
Cross, John, 111
Cruise O'Brien, Conor, 99
Cruttenden, Alan, 106-07
CTC Bazaars, 67
Cuba, 99, 116
Currey, Andrew, 63, 64, 95, 105, 106, 109, 113
Currey, Clare, 2, 3, 113, 117ff, 130, 143, 157, 189
Currey, John & Edith, 5, 13
Currey, Stella & Ralph, (R.N.), 5, 13, 20, 21, 22, 27, 63, 64, 84, 88, 106, 113, 117ff, 161, 162, 164, 176
Currey families, 26-27, 64, 113
Curtis Brown, 27

Daniels, Eddie, 80, 159
Daniels, Joe, 94
Davin, Dan, 65
De Beer, Zac, 129
de Blank, Joost (Archbishop), 27, 54, 55, 135
de Gaulle, Charles, 115
de Villiers Graaf, David, 54, 84
de Wet Nel, Michel D. C., 43. 49, 123
Defence & Aid Fund, 186, 189, 190
Defiance Campaign, 1, 28
Delius, Tony ('Adderley'), 30, 37, 54, 63, 82, 83, 90, 96, 99, 121, 127-29

Dent (education inspector), 127
Die Burger, 13, 14, 19, 37, 51, 70, 80, 97, 99, 100, 136
Diemont, Marius, 53
Diefenbaker, John, 185
District Six (Cape Town), 34, 70, 76, 77, 80, 102
Drum, 14-15, 32, 35, 66, 75, 79, 88
Dugard, J., 41
Duminy, Jacobus Petrus, 19, 73, 112
Duncan, Patrick, 1, 13, 28, 33, 36, 37, 43, 48, 51, 53, 61, 62, 65, 68, 74, 79, 84, 85, 98, 100, 104, 105, 110, 111, 124, 130, 131, 190
Durban, 88, 90, 92, 101; *see also* Cato Manor
Durrant, Geoff, 40

Elam, Nick, 176
Elections, 3, 23, 28, 43, 91, 95-96, 111, 128, 133-35
Encounter, 112, 135
Erasmus, François Christiaan (Minister of Justice), 43, 47-8, 53, 54, 56, 68, 83, 92
Ernest, 101

Faber (publisher), 5, 13, 20, 59
Farquarson, Robin, 105
Fortune, Major, 179, 181
Fourie, Sakkie, 97
Fransen, Hans, 70, 162
Freedom Charter, 46
French presence in Africa, 61, 98, 113, 114, 115
Friedman, Marion, 132
Fugard, Athol, 107

Gagarin, Yuri, 79
Gaitskell, Hugh, 134
Gallo, Ernest and Jerome, 101
Gandhi, Manilal, 62
Gandhi, Mohandas, 182
Ganyile, 103, 130
Gardner, Helen, 19
Gcabashe, Tulani, 110

Ghana, 114, 115
Gibson, Rufus, 49
Gilmour, Ian, 182
Golden City Post, 32, 35, 66, 68, 79, 126
Goldreich, Arthur, 130, 170
Gordimer, Nadine, 65, 88, 95
Government Gazette, 60, 95
Gregory, Theodore, 102
Grenfell-Williams, John, 13
Greyling, Cas, 124
Grieve, Dr Muir, 171
Grimond, Jo, 74
Grocott's Daily Mail, 40
Group Areas Act, 22, 68, 69, 72-3, 77, 136
The Guardian, 106, 137, 179, 187
Guinea-Conakry, 115, 116

Hamish Hamilton (publisher), 20
Harare, *see* Salisbury
Harris, John, 129, 183
Hart, Tom, 88,
Hayman, Ruth, 186
Head, Bessie, 2
Head, Harold, 133
Heinemann (publisher), 189
Henshilwood, Norah, 119, 133
Hermanus, 11, 13, 21, 33, 68, 69, 104, 131
Hendrickse, Kenneth, 67, 78
Hicks, 182
Higgs, Cecil, 33, 54, 88, 99, 109
Hitler, Adolf, 81, 86, 96, 109
Hjul, Peter, 7, 43, 53, 56, 58, 62, 70, 71, 72, 74, 80, 86, 122, 123, 161, 184
Hoffenberg, Bill & Margaret, 159, 162, 164, 169, 170, 185, 186, 189
Holmes, Tim, 1, 2, 7, 38, 52, 53, 56, 62, 68, 71, 74, 80, 81, 84, 85, 87, 98, 9, 109, 111, 113, 142, 146, 150, 190
Home, (Lord, Alexander Frederick Douglas-Home), 134
Hopkinson, Tom, 14, 79, 94
Howell, Henry, 88
Huddleston, Trevor, 80
Hulton (publisher), 15

Human & Rousseau (publisher), 36
Hundleby, (school principal), 42
Hutchinson, Val, 83, 97, 109

Immorality Act, 57, 101, 121
Indian Congress, 34.
Ibrahim, Abdullah, *see* Dollar Brand
Insight Publications, 122

James Currey Publishers, 4, 130, 190
Jenkins, Arthur, 59, 75
Jessop, Jill, 171-2
Johannesburg, 2, 3, 34, 85, 90, 94, 95, 97, 116, 120, 123, 128, 129, 130, 141, 142
John Murray (publisher), 20
Jonathan Cape (publisher), 20
Jonker (censor), 125

Katanga, 103
Kennedy, Cecil, 63
Kennedy, John F., 65, 129, 134
Kerr, Bill, 72
Kgosana, Philip, 1, 43, 44, 56
Khaketla, B.M., 60, 61
Khalifa party, 65
Khumalo (ANC), 60
Kime, Tom, 27
King William's Town (KWT), 38, 152
Kirwood, Mary, 32-4, 38, 40, 71, 101
Klopper, Henning, 84
Krige, Francois, 88
Krushchev, 106, 146
Kunene, Daniel, 61
Kwela, 34, 97

la Cock, Dirk, 54
La Guma, Alex, 79
Langa (township), 2, 39, 43, 44, 47, 53, 71, 83, 109, 120, 182
Lawrence, Harry Gordon, 84
Lee-Warden, Len, 129, 138
Leftwich, Adrian, 157, 159, 162, 172, 183
Legco, Malawi, 149
Legum, Colin, 127
Leibrandt (Chief Magistrate), 126

Lessing, Doris, 65
Lesotho *see* Basutoland,
Lewin, Hugh, 126
Liberal Party, 1, 3, 7, 17, 28, 37-38, 50-58 passim, 61, 62, 65, 66, 68, 70, 72, 74, 76-82, 86, 88, 91-2, 94, 95, 100, 102, 109, 112, 122, 123, 124, 126, 128, 131, 134, 135, 136, 138, 151, 161, 169, 171, 184, 189, 190
Liliesleaf farm, 130
Linder, Iver & Iris, 11, 28, 33, 42, 96, 104, 147
London College of Printing, 4
London Magazine, 89
Longman (publisher), 50, 71, 72, 88
Louis (African medical student), 38-39
Lourenço Marques (Maputo), 105
Louw, Joe, 32, 34, 35, 56
Lumumba, 141
Luthuli, Albert, 34, 37, 65, 100, 109, 111, 112, 144

Macbride (Father), 80
MacInnes, Colin, 100, 112
McIntyre, Colonel, 186
Mackenzie, Kenneth, 37, 50
Macleod, Iain, 4, 23, 182
Macmillan, Harold, 1, 4, 23, 36-7, 48, 77, 103, 134
Mafeking, 4, 5
Mafeje, Archie, 5
Mahomo, Nelson ('Nana'), 32
Majija, Hammington, 80
Malan, D.F., 49
Malawi *see* Nyasaland
Malays, *see* Cape Malays
Mandela, Nelson & Winnie, 79, 87, 130, 144, 151
Maputo *see* Lourenço Marques
Marais, David, 14, 75,
Margaret, Princess, 75
Marquard, Leo and Nell, 5, 6, 14, 16, 21-25, 29, 30, 32, 36, 41, 42, 43, 50, 51, 54, 57, 58, 70, 73, 77, 88, 94, 95, 97, 99, 100, 102, 103, 108, 112, 122, 127, 148, 173, 174, 183,
Martin, Alice, 97

Martin, Hal, 13,
Martin, J.P. & Nancy Martin, 5
Martin, Stella, 5, 12
Maskew Miller (publisher), 1, 20, 29, 49
Matanzima, Kaiser (Paramount Chief), 91, 111, 120, 125, 134, 135
Matthews, Joe, 60
Matthews, Z.K., 42, 60
Maud, Sir John, 104, 130
Mbari Club, 115
Mboya, Tom, 99
McGraw-Hill (publisher), 22
Meidner, Hans, 72, 92
'Memorable Order of Tin Hats' (MOTHS, MOTHWAS), 164
Methodists, 5, 13, 38, 133, 136
Methuen (publisher), 108
Mgudulana, Gladys, 99, 133
Mill, John Stuart, 92
Millar, Joy & Anthony, 6, 11, 15-21 passim, 24, 26, 30, 37, 42, 55, 72, 83, 88, 93, 137
Miller, David, 170
Milne, Douglas, 120
Mitchell, Julian, 81
Mnyakama, R., 152-53
Modisane, Bloke, 112
Mofoko, Carl (pseudonym), 145
Mofolo, Thomas, 61
Mokgolo, Jacob, 145, 146
Mokitimi, Seth, 133
Morgan, Sally, 33, 34, 39, 45, 50-57 passim, 71, 89, 109, 150
Morris, James, 5
Mower, Jack, US Consul, 112
Mozambique, 13, 105, 140, 149, 180
Mphaphlele, Ezekiel, 105, 112
Msonthi, John, 149
Mugabe, Robert, 149
Muslims, 25, 102, 133, 140-41

Namibia, see South West Africa
Namibia Support Committee, 190
Natal, 5, 7, 13, 16, 23, 44, 57, 72, 78, 86, 91, 92, 95, 111, 121, 179

National Committee for Liberation (NCL), 182, 183, 189, 190
National Liberation Front of Angola (FNLA), 114
National Party, 7, 14, 16, 36-38, 41, 50, 96, 121, 124, 131
National Union of South African Students (NUSAS), 6, 7, 41-3
Nazis, 57, 85, 92, 125
Ndibongo, Mongi, 101
Ndlumbini, Shibi, 71
Neale, David, 30, 177
Nehru, 77
Nelsons (publisher), 94
New African, 2, 3, 7, 89, 99, 100-101, 104, 106, 109, 110, 111, 112, 114, 120, 121, 124, 132, 135-9, 143, 146, 149, 151, 159, 169, 182, 184, 189, 190
New Age, 68, 94
New Statesman, 2, 65, 89, 90
Nigeria, 114-15
Ngũgĩ wa Thiong'o, 2
Nkatlo, Joe, 62, 79, 110
Nkosi, Lewis, 2, 88, 89
Nkrumah, Kwame, 115
Nododile, Cromwell, 66
Nolan, Sidney, 100
Nolte, Ferdy & Helene, 70, 86
Non-racial, 57, 95, 102, 133, 136, 180
Non-violence (violence), 1, 2, 62, 124, 182. 183
Norman see Bromberger, Norman
Northern Rhodesia Literature Bureau, 120
Norton, Victor Sidney, 87
Nuttall, Jolyon, 89
Nyanga (township), 43, 44
Nyasaland (Malawi). 120, 124, 140, 149, 169

Observer, 18, 74, 80, 89, 105, 127, 140
Ohland, Carl, 140
OK Bazaars, 66-8
Okigbo, Christopher, 115
Olosula, Segun, 115
Oppenheimer, Harry, 103

Orange Free State, 6, 133
Ovamboland, 69, 77
Oxfam, 142
Oxford University Press (OUP), 3-6, 11-20, 23, 25, 30, 41, 50, 51, 59, 65, 70, 84, 90, 97, 107, 108, 112, 113, 126, 127, 152-3, 163-65, 168, 170-78, 182, 184, 189; offices in Africa 98-9

Paarl, 32, 161
Pahl (Inspector of schools), 38, 40
Pan Africanist Congress (PAC), 1, 32, 43, 56, 65, 80, 83, 120, 190
Parker, Mary Murray, 141
Parliament, 3, 7, 16
Parnwell, Eric, 3, 98
passes, 44-46, 91, 119
Paton, Alan, 6, 7, 17, 32, 58, 65, 90, 92, 97, 99, 123, 126
Penguin Books, 4, 94, 104, 146
Petersen, Molly, 48
Pethybridge, Roger, 106
Philip, David & Marie, 3, 5, 6, 11, 12, 16, 18, 23, 108, 148, 172-3, 177, 178, 187
Phipson family, 5, 13, 63
Picture Post, 14-15
PIDE (Portuguese Special Branch), 180
Pierneef, Jacobus Hendrik (Henk), 27
Plimpton, Calvin, 129
Plimpton, Adlai & Ruth, 129
Pogrund, Benjie, 104
Pondoland, 89, 103
Poqo (Azanian People's Liberation Army). 120, 124
Port Elizabeth Evening Post, 68
Portugal in Africa, 36, 105, 114, 149, 180
Poto-Sabata front, 134
Press, Solly, 107
Progress Publishers, 94
Progressive Party, 7, 57, 74, 80, 81, 84, 92, 96, 97, 121, 127, 129, 135

Quakers, 52, 56, 141, 142, 183

Rand Daily Mail, 104
Randolph, *see* Vigne, Randolph
Ravilious, Eric, 81
Reitz, Denys, 21
Rhodes, Cecil, 5, 26-27, 33
Rhodes University, 33, 120, 157, 169
Rhodesia (Zambia & Zimbabwe), 4, 12, 18, 30, 37, 63, 73, 79, 103, 120, 124, 146-51
Rietstein, Amy, 45, 189
Ridge, Jean, 157, 158, 160-62, 164-73, 179, 183-7, 189
Rivonia Trial, 2, 130, 142, 143-5, 151, 170, 182
Roberto, Holden, 114
Roberts, Colin, 3
Robinson, Robert, 64
Rodda, Peter, 32
Rog, Cos, *see* Wilson, Roger, 141
Rollnick, Julian, 6
Roma University, 59, 75
Roman Catholic church, 59, 71, 136
Rosling, Peter, 169, 171
Ross, Neil, 68, 79, 83, 91, 93, 97
Rousseau, Major (Special Branch), 157
Rubin, Leslie, 7, 28, 100
Rubin, Neville & Muriel, 2, 7, 99, 112, 113, 180, 185, 190
Russia, 39, 79, 94, 99, 100, 101, 106, 114, 115, 116

Sabata Dalindyebo, Paramount Chief, 91, 111, 134, 190
Sabotage, 3, 111, 124, 130, 151, 173, 177, 182-3
Sachs, Albie, 34, 37, 45, 52, 80, 132
Salisbury (Harare), 4, 42, 43, 73, 98, 106, 120, 140, 148
Samson, 71
Sancroft-Baker, Ralph, 28
Sandys, Duncan, 77
Sauerman, S.I., 53
Schneider, 164
Segal, Ronald, 102
Sharpeville, 1, 2, 42-4, 49, 84, 182
Shipanga, Andreas, 69, 130

Shooter & Shuter (publisher), 126
Sicgau, Chief Botha, 103
Sisulu, Albertina & Walter, 130, 144
Sithole, Ndabaningi, 5, 13, 81, 99
Smith Le Roux, Le Roux, 36
Smuts, Jan, 7, 103
SOAS (School of Oriental and African Studies), 180
Soares, Lael, 161, 185
Sophiatown, 22
South Africa Act, 112
South Africa Foundation, 111
South African Broadcasting Corporation (SABC), 35, 36, 62, 78, 80, 88, 99, 103
South African Institute of Race Relations (SAIRR), 6, 50, 73, 189
South West Africa (Namibia), 69, 77, 152, 180, 184
Soweto, 182
Soyinka, Wole, 2, 4, 114, 115
SPCK, 95
Special Branch (SB), 2, 3, 49, 50, 51, 53, 56, 62, 66, 67, 68, 82-4, 87, 120, 123, 126, 129, 133, 138-9, 146, 154, 157, 158, 172, 174, 180, 182, 184, 185-7
Spectator, The, 18, 37, 102, 182
State of Emergency, 43, 45-7, 52, 54, 68, 80, 87, 103, 125-6, 130, 190
Stay at Home, 45, 52, 56
Stellenbosch, 5, 15, 19, 32, 36, 107
Stevenson, Adlai, 65, 129
Stillit Books, 187
Stott, Eulalie, 80, 97
Strydom, J.G., 49
Sunday Times (Johannesburg), 2, 20, 64, 66, 79, 80, 105, 121, 131, 182
Sunday Times (London), 18, 57, 80
Suppression of Communism Act, 34, 79, 111, 122
Suzman, Helen, 97, 127
Swanzy, Hank (Henry), 81
Swanzy, Rick, 109
Swaziland, 13, 58, 84, 85, 87, 88, 94, 95, 130
Sypkens, Sylvia, 101

Tabata, 91
Tambo, Oliver, 79
te Water, Charles & June, 27-8, 70
Terblanche, I.P. (police colonel), 43, 47, 53, 56
Themba, Can, 143
Thompson, A.F., 178
Thompson, Paul, 76
Thorstream, The, 3, 164, 169, 170, 178-81, 184
Times, The (London), 18, 19, 76, 182, 187
Times Literary Supplement (TLS), 95, 109, 127
Three Crowns series, 4, 90, 94, 115, 177, 189
Toogood, Ken, 148
Touré, Sékou, 115
Transkei, 3, 38, 89, 90, 91, 103, 111, 119, 120, 126, 130, 133, 134, 136, 152, 182, 190
Transvaal, 1, 22, 36, 63, 64, 83, 85, 95, 131
Treason Trial, 79
Tshombe, Moise, 103, 175

United Nations, 103, 106, 113, 114, 129, 141
United Party (UP), 7, 16, 17, 28, 54, 65, 76, 96, 97
University of Cape Town (UCT), 19, 61, 81, 112, 152, 189
University of KwaZulu Natal, 189
Uys, Edna, 131
Uys, Stanley, 66, 74, 80, 105

van den Berghe, Major, 87
van Heynigen, Christina, 40
van Riebeeck, 49, 112, 141
van Ryneveld, Clive, 16, 7
van Ryneveld, Marie, *see* Philip, Marie
von Stauffenberg, Claus, 109
van Wyk (Special branch police), 138
Vatcher, 65
Verwoerd, Hendrik, 36, 37, 49, 77, 78, 83, 84, 92, 96, 123, 135
Via Afrika (publisher), 41

Vigne, Lucy & Piers 105, 125, 185, 186
Vigne, Pamela, Phoebe & Thea, 76, 182
Vigne, Randolph & Gillian, 1-3, 7, 20-21, 27, 29, 31, 33-4, 36-39, 43-4, 46, 48-50, 53, 56-9, 62, 65, 69, 74, 76, 84, 86, 89-91, 94-101, 104, 105, 110-12, 121-5, 131-5, 139. 140, 146, 151, 153ff, 190
Vinnicombe family, 5, 13, 63
Vorster, J.V., 92, 123, 126, 132

Walsh, Peter, 59, 60, 93
Walvis Bay, 158, 180
Walters, Tom, 66, 87, 187
Wesleyan Methodist, 5, 13
West, Rebecca, 57
White, Ken, 97, 107, 177
White, Patrick, 64
White racism, 5, 22, 152
Williams, Miss Olwen, 14, 17, 18, 24, 25, 42, 43, 88, 108, 133, 134, 187

Wilson (PR chief), 102
Wilson, Anthony & Anne, 140, 141, 149
Wilson, Elizabeth (Clare Currey), 143, 182
Wilson, Francis, 189
Wilson, Geoffrey, 141
Wilson, Monica, 5
Wilson, Roger, 140, 141
Wilson, Ruth and Henry, 117, 119, 133, 176
Wolpe, Harold, 130
Wright, Alec, 18
Wright, Ian, 106

Yale University Press, 105

Zackon, Barney, 72, 83, 109, 110
Zambia *see* Rhodesia, Northern
Zimbabwe *see* Rhodesia, Southern
Zulu, Gideon, 17, 24, 47

Also from The Merlin Press

London Recruits
The Secret War Against Apartheid

Compiled and edited by Ken Keable
With an introduction by Ronnie Kasrils and a foreword by Z. Pallo Jordan

The history of the Anti-Apartheid movement brings up images of boycotts and public campaigns in the UK. But another story went on behind the scenes, in secret, one that has been never told before. This is the story of the foreign recruits and their activities in South Africa, how they acted in defiance of the Apartheid government and its police on the instructions of the African National Congress. It tells of:

ANC Banners that unfurled;
ANC speeches that sounded through public places;
Buckets that exploded and showered ANC leaflets;
Transportation of weapons, communications, logistics;
Helping ANC fighters to enter South Africa;
and more …

Many recruits were Young Communists, others were Trotskyists or independent socialists; from the UK, Ireland, the Netherlands, and the USA, and they all took amazing risks. Some paid a heavy price for their support. This is their untold story. Royalties from this book will go to The Nelson Mandela Children's Fund.

Soon to be the subject of a film due for release in 2021

ISBN. 978-0-85036-655-6

364 pages, 216 x 138 mm. paperback

Slumboy from the Golden City
Paul Joseph

With a foreword by Lord Joel Joffe

Paul Joseph's memoir starts with his childhood in the slums of Johannesburg in the 1930s. His political awakening and activism began as a 15-year-old Indian in a racially segregated school. It continued with his commitment to the fight against an oppressive regime. Paul participated in virtually all the political campaigns including the passive resistance of the 1940s. In 1956 he was one of the 156 people accused of high treason by the Apartheid government alongside Nelson Mandela, Walter Sisulu, Ahmed Kathrada, Lilian Ngoyi, Ruth First and Helen Joseph. Paul was held in detention following the Sharpeville Massacre, the banning of the ANC and the imposition of the state of emergency. He was amongst the first recruits into the armed wing of the ANC UmKhonto We Sizwe (spear of the nation) or MK as it was known. He was placed under house arrest and put into solitary confinement.
With an eye for detail and extensive knowledge of South Africans across the racial and class divides, Paul documents one of the most significant struggles for liberation in the 20th century.
'Uncle Paul and Aunt Adelaide Joseph are second parents to me and in that way their story is inseparable from mine.' Zenani Mandela
'Paul Joseph's courageous role in South Africa's anti-apartheid struggle is inspirational. His life in that struggle for justice is both moving and uplifting. An incredible man!' Baroness Helena Kennedy, QC
'Paul Joseph's story is of a life of struggle for human liberation and a courageous struggle for life under apartheid. Electrifying!'
Professor Gus John

ISBN. 978-0-85036-750-8

pages, 234 x 156 mm. paperback

www.merlinpress.co.uk